THE COURAGE TO QUESTION

WOMEN'S STUDIES AND STUDENT LEARNING

Edited by Caryn McTighe Musil

ASSOCIATION OF AMERICAN COLLEGES AND
NATIONAL WOMEN'S STUDIES ASSOCIATION, 1992

THIS WORK WAS SUPPORTED BY
THE FUND FOR THE IMPROVEMENT
OF POSTSECONDARY EDUCATION,
U.S. DEPARTMENT OF EDUCATION

GENERAL EDITOR: CARYN McTIGHE MUSIL

COVER: Quilt from the collection of
Marjorie A. Laidman (detail).
Courtesy of
Hearts and Hands Films,
San Francisco, California

Published by
Association of American Colleges
1818 R Street, NW
Washington, D.C. 20009

ISBN 0-911696-55-5
Library of Congress Catalog No. 92-71982

THE COURAGE TO QUESTION

WOMEN'S STUDIES
AND STUDENT LEARNING

Edited by Caryn McTighe Musil

ASSOCIATION OF AMERICAN COLLEGES
AND NATIONAL WOMEN'S STUDIES ASSOCIATION

CONTENTS

PROJECT PARTICIPANTS
1992

Project Director
CARYN McTIGHE MUSIL
Senior Fellow
Association of American Colleges

Project Associate
SUZANNE HYERS
Association of American Colleges

Project Coordinators, Participating Colleges and Universities
ANITA CLAIR FELLMAN, Old Dominion University
LAURIE A. FINKE, Lewis and Clark College
ROSANNA HERTZ, Wellesley College
MARY JO NEITZ, University of Missouri–Columbia
MICHELE PALUDI, City University of New York–Hunter College
SUSAN REVERBY, Wellesley College
LINDA R. SILVER, Oberlin College
JOAN TRONTO, City University of New York–Hunter College
GAY VICTORIA, University of Colorado
JEAN WARD, Lewis and Clark College
MARCIA WESTKOTT, University of Colorado
BARBARA A. WINSTEAD, Old Dominion University

National Assessment Team
CAROLYNE W. ARNOLD, University of Massachusetts–Boston
LEE KNEFELKAMP, Teachers College, Columbia University
JILL MATTUCK TARULE, Lesley College
JOAN SHAPIRO, Temple University
MARY KAY THOMPSON TETREAULT,
California State University–Fullerton

External Evaluator
PATRICIA HUTCHINGS, American Association for Higher Education

ACKNOWLEDGMENTS

In keeping with its leadership in the assessment movement, the Fund for the Improvement of Postsecondary Education (FIPSE) of the U.S. Department of Education funded our three-year grant and this volume, *The Courage to Question*. FIPSE did so in a period when backlash against women's studies had just reemerged with a new vehemence. This project could not have come into being without the quietly insistent and shrewdly wise counsel of our first FIPSE program officer, Constance Cook, now executive assistant to the president at the University of Michigan.

A special debt also is owed to the Association of American Colleges. Paula P. Brownlee, president of AAC, and AAC's executive vice president, Carol G. Schneider, agreed a year ago to collaborate on the publication of *The Courage to Question*, repeating the earlier cooperation between the National Women's Studies Association (NWSA) and AAC that had produced *Liberal Learning and the Women's Studies Major* and AAC's *Reports from the Fields*. AAC has graciously provided office space for me and my project associate, Suzanne Hyers, and welcomed us as sojourners. Gary Egan, director of finance and administration, and his staff have been especially helpful with financial arrangements and Lenora J. Wilson, associate director of administration, with setting up our office.

We asked AAC to cosponsor *The Courage to Question* in part because of the high quality of its publications. Our volume has benefitted immeasurably because of AAC's Publications Office. We are particularly indebted to the support, editing, and productive cooperation of its director, Sherry Levy-Reiner, and to the editing, planning, and good humor of Kristen A. Lippert-Martin, editorial associate, who saw our project through from start to finish. We are grateful as well for additional editorial support from David M. Stearman and Lisa L. Magnino.

NWSA housed the grant during its first two years, and the project ran more smoothly because of administrative support from Sharon Neufeld, NWSA's office manager the first year, and particularly Melinda Berriman, its office manager the second year. Loretta Younger, NWSA's current office manager, has assisted this year with the financial administration of the grant.

It has been a personal as well as a professional joy to have the opportunity to work once more with Suzanne Hyers, NWSA's former national conference coordinator, who graciously agreed to be the project associate and lend us her legendary administrative skills. No problem is ever unsolvable when Suzanne is around, and she makes it fun to come into work. She also is a superb editor.

While there are single names attached to articles in this volume, the fi-

ACKNOWLEDGEMENTS

nal product has been enhanced by the collective effort and conversations of many people. Each of the seven participating women's studies programs has included specific acknowledgments within their chapters. All of us benefit-. ted from the invigorating dialogue shared among the various people who have moved in and out of the project over a three-year period. The project was especially enriched by the practical expertise and conceptual challenges of the National Assessment Team—Carolyne A. Arnold, Lee Knefelkamp, Joan Shapiro, Jill Mattuck Tarule, and Mary Kay Thompson Tetreault—and the project's external evaluator, Pat Hutchings.

Finally, we thank the thousands of students whose comments and opinions are the heart of this research. You will hear some of their voices woven into the text. They have given us courage to ask difficult questions, confirmation that our commitment to feminist education makes a difference, and hope that the world can one day be made anew.

Caryn McTighe Musil,
Project Director,
and Senior Fellow,
Association of American Colleges

■

INTRODUCTION

Students say:	"It changed my life."
Critics say:	"It's propaganda."
Students say:	"It expanded my mind in every direction."
Critics say:	"It's unintellectual, touchy-feely stuff."
Students say:	"It gave me a voice."
Critics say:	"It silences everyone who disagrees."

These contradictory and intense responses to women's studies courses have typified the debate about this fast-growing discipline since the late 1960s, when women's studies courses began to emerge spontaneously on campuses around the country in response to the women's movement. The criticism about women's studies was rarely generated by students who took classes but by people responding to what they thought was going on in women's studies classes. Women's studies programs, especially in their first decade, often were established despite an atmosphere of hostility, suspicion, or indifference to their enterprise. Women's studies faculty members, on the other hand, were sustained both by their own intellectual and political commitment to the discipline and by the intellectual and personal transformations they consistently witnessed in their students. "It gave me courage," explained one student. To understand more about how that learning process occurs, we undertook a project that has resulted in *The Courage to Question: Women's Studies and Student Learning*.

If women's studies develops in students the courage to speak their minds, can women's studies faculty members display a similar courage in asking tough questions of our programs? Having done that, do we have the courage to go public with what we find? Even though in many respects women's studies has come into its own as it moves into its third decade, the political context once again is reminiscent of the acrimonious attacks of the early 1970s.

The power and production of feminist scholarship as an intellectual enterprise usually is ignored by conservative critics, who dismiss and trivialize women's studies as "oppression studies" or "a grievance industry." With inflammatory attacks against women's studies, ethnic studies, and other aca-

Women's studies has affected almost every
discipline, secured a foothold within academia,
and continued to attract students in ever-
increasing numbers

---

demic efforts that advocate a more diverse curriculum, small but influential
organizations such as the National Association of Scholars or the less significant Accuracy in Academia have generated a frenzy of emotionally laden,
wildly distorted representations of women's studies.[1] Such critics suggest that
by including women and a gender analysis in the study of human culture and
history, women's studies—rather than the curriculum that made women invisible in the first place—is guilty of threatening other people's academic
freedom. In such a politicized and polarized climate, equity and excellence
have been posited as diametrically opposed; critical thinking has been labeled as "anti-American"; and the study of two-thirds of the human race has
been characterized as "special interests." In the midst of such misinformed
and dangerous polemics, The Courage to Question seeks to bring light where
there has been only heat, clarity where there has been deliberate obfuscation
of the facts.

The national assault on women's studies has a special urgency precisely
because women's studies has affected almost every discipline, secured an institutional foothold within academia, and continued to attract students in
ever-increasing numbers. The first women's studies program was formally approved at San Diego State University in 1970. When the National Women's
Studies Association (NWSA) was formed in 1977, there were already 276
programs. Ten years later, the total topped 500; and in the most recent
NWSA national survey published in 1990, 621 women's studies programs
were listed.[2] Within those programs, 425 offer a minor, certificate, or area of
concentration; 235 offer a major. In the 1984 American Council on Education survey, Campus Trends, Elaine El-Khawas noted that women's studies
courses could be found at 68.1 percent of universities, 48.9 percent of four-
year colleges, and 26.5 percent of two-year colleges. At the graduate level,
the number of institutions offering women's studies work has expanded
rapidly from 23 in 1986, to 55 in 1988, to 102 in 1990.

The increased institutionalization of women's studies has been accelerat-
ed by the explosion in feminist scholarship. In 1984 alone there were reput-
edly more than four thousand books published on women. There are more
than thirty journals in women's studies and dozens of feminist presses, and
most university presses publish so many titles in women's studies that they
have special sections in their promotional materials. More than 170 professional associations for academic disciplines have instituted a women's caucus
or women's division, thus guaranteeing a forum within mainstream disciplinary conferences for new feminist scholarship.

Women's studies also has been involved in hundreds of curriculum transformation projects around the country since 1980, when the first project at Wheaton College began. Wheaton's project has been imitated and modified on many campuses, clustered in regional approaches such as the Western States Project out of the Southwest Institute on Research on Women, and adopted as a statewide strategy as represented by the New Jersey Project funded through the New Jersey Department of Education. Typically designed to incorporate the new scholarship on women throughout the curriculum, though often particularly in general-education courses, curriculum transformation not only has brought the new scholarship to a far broader student constituency but also engaged a wide range of faculty members in the scholarship, pedagogy, and curriculum development so central to women's studies. The most recent national project, "Mainstreaming Minority Women's Studies," sponsored by the National Council for Research on Women and funded by the Ford Foundation, attests to ways that ethnic studies and women's studies have begun to combine their powerful analyses about the social construction of knowledge. The national call for academic institutions to rethink their curriculum to reflect the knowledge produced by a diverse human culture over time was represented most recently in the title of the Association of American Colleges' 1992 national conference, "Recentering," and many of the curricular innovations generated by AAC's project, "Engaging Cultural Legacies," funded by the National Endowment for the Humanities.

In 1989, as executive director of the National Women's Studies Association, I was planning an invitational conference, "Women's Studies: The Third Decade," for women's studies directors to celebrate the achievements of two decades of women's studies programs and to determine the agenda for the 1990s. It was within this context of celebration and attack that our project, "The Courage to Question," was born. The first workshop funded by the grant was attached to the "Third Decade" conference and underscored the purpose of the grant: to assess student learning in women's studies classes in order to make more informed decisions about program development in the 1990s.

While women's studies was under attack, students were painting a different portrait about their experiences in women's studies classes. For two decades, women's studies faculty members knew something was causing students to become intellectually and personally engaged in ideas and issues raised in women's studies courses. Certainly, women's studies set out to do something that had never been done before. Although inspired by black

Assessing the impact of feminist scholarship on
the way we view the world would be "like trying
to describe the Renaissance—ten years after it
began"

studies programs before them, women's studies stood out as an academic
anomaly by virtue of its focus on material about women and gender that previously had been excluded from study, its explanatory critique of the construction of knowledge and unequal arrangements of power, and its determination to offer a pedagogy of student empowerment commensurate with
feminist theory. Most professors who have taught women's studies could ex-
pound anecdotally for hours on the students whose minds and lives were
changed by women's studies—students who felt personally and intellectually
affirmed in women's studies as they did nowhere else on campus.

However, we had no systematic explanations for these transformations;
no fuller, sustained explanations of exactly what was happening or how. We
had many studies on the transformation of the curriculum both inside and
outside of women's studies, information about how faculty members shifted
intellectual paradigms, and some research about students' attitudinal
changes. But we had no national study that probed the learning process itself, that turned to the students to hear in their own voices a description of
what was happening to them as thinkers, as inquirers, as people. "The
Courage to Question" sought to do just that.

We sought to do that for our own benefit in terms of improving our programs. But we sought to do it for the benefit of a larger national public as well.
Our study comes in the wake of a number of national reports elucidating
crises in education and suggesting avenues for reform. The University of
Colorado chapter discusses these reports in more detail. Some reports expressed concerns about a fragmented curriculum without coherence; a faculty
more concerned with its research publications than its teaching; and a passive
student population, uninvolved in academic questions and reluctant to embrace values. In women's studies, we saw a dramatically different student profile. Women and gender as a centralizing concept for student inquiry provided
overall coherence for students, whatever their discipline; within women's
studies itself, teaching was as central to our mission as our research. Students
we observed in our classes were passionately engaged in the subject matter,
spurred to voice by the dynamics of feminist pedagogy. Our two decades of experience suggested that women's studies offers students a dynamic, interactive
environment that encourages critical thinking, empowers students as learners,
enriches their sense of civilization's heritage, connects their knowledge from
other courses, and challenges them to become actively engaged in shaping
their world. We hope our three-year research project, then, will be an important contribution to the conversation as we in higher education jointly seek
solutions for crises on our campuses and in our classrooms.

In addition to ways our research might enhance our understanding of how to improve the quality of undergraduate learning as a whole, we also hoped the project would benefit women's studies itself. Many realized we needed a vehicle that would allow us to pause and reflect about what we had created over the span of two decades. Even though women's studies programs increased dramatically over that period, growth was uneven, and the majority of programs were underfunded and understaffed.[3] It was all some faculties could do simply to maintain their programs. Others worked overloads to develop new courses, plan cocurricular activities, and increase institutional support. Many complained of having too little control over which courses were offered, when, and by whom. Few had time to take stock either of where we were conceptually and pedagogically or where we needed to go next. A grant from the U.S. Department of Education's Fund for the Improvement of Postsecondary Education (FIPSE), along with some important internal institutional support given to several of the programs in our project, provided us with that much needed opportunity.

Gerda Lerner, pioneer feminist historian, has said that assessing the impact of feminist scholarship on the way we view the world would be "like trying to describe the Renaissance—ten years after it began." While it may be premature to attempt to measure the transformative effect of feminist scholarship, it is appropriate and timely to begin to listen attentively to what students tell us about how women's studies is affecting what and how they learn.

THE DESIGN OF THE GRANT

To ensure a textured sample, ten women's studies programs representing a wide variety of institutions were invited to participate in "The Courage to Question." They included both public and private; large and small; urban, suburban, and rural; coeducational and single sex; and research universities and liberal arts colleges spread geographically from one coast to the other. The sites also were selected so the project as a whole represented a diverse student population that included variables such as sex, race, ethnic background, class, and age. Two persons from each program were to be part of each institutional team; most typically they were the women's studies director and a women's studies faculty member. Everyone was expected to consult widely and regularly with the students and faculty at their home institutions. The ten women's studies programs invited to participate included:

☐ University of Colorado
☐ Oberlin College

- [ ] University of California–Los Angeles
- [ ] Wellesley College
- [ ] University of Wisconsin
- [ ] City University of New York–Hunter College
- [ ] Bennett College
- [ ] University of Missouri–Columbia
- [ ] Old Dominion University
- [ ] Lewis and Clark College

Of the ten, nine referred to their programs as "women's studies." The tenth, Lewis and Clark, calls its program "gender studies." In gathering national data for NWSA's 1990 women's studies directory, a similar ratio of 9:1 held; the overwhelming number continue to name their programs "women's studies." Lewis and Clark makes a strong case for the institutional appropriateness of its linguistic choice. Since its founding in the nineteenth century, Lewis and Clark always has been committed to a single curriculum for men and women; in this latter part of the twentieth century, the gender studies faculty members specifically are aiming to involve male as well as female students in the program. At the same time, Lewis and Clark makes it clear that feminist inquiry and theory are at the center of their program. Its title thus represents a strategy, a curricular theoretical framework, and historical continuity with their institution.

To provide the necessary assessment expertise, a national assessment team was created to work closely with the women's studies programs and function as an advisory board to the project director. The five members of the National Assessment Team and the external evaluator for the project are nationally and in some cases internationally recognized experts in assessment; they also have a familiarity with feminist scholarship and women's studies. Their range of expertise was deliberately diverse, both in terms of their methodologies and their focus. Some were most facile with quantitative analysis, others with qualitative. Collectively they had done research in feminist pedagogy, curriculum transformation, faculty development, student development, and institutional evaluations. Their task was to give the sites an overall perspective on the assessment movement, train the women's studies faculty in a variety of assessment methods, assist in developing assessment plans for each institution, and make site visits as needed. Each member was assigned a program, designated its principal source of expertise on assessment, and evaluated a preliminary report made at the end of the second year.

In the first year of the grant, the programs were asked to define the learning goals of their respective women's studies programs in four key areas: knowledge base, learning skills, feminist pedagogy, and personal growth. By mid-year, after several months of campus-based consultations with faculty members and students, each program submitted its program goals; these became the basis for the questions most campuses eventually posed about student learning in women's studies at their campus. Having established their program's learning goals, faculty members were introduced to the various assessment methods, established at least three focused areas of inquiry, and created by the end of the first year what we came to call "An Institutional Research Design Assessment Plan."

The second year's work was campus-focused. Each program began to create specific questions for its surveys and assessment instruments, gather data, and write a preliminary report of findings by the year's end. A project workshop at the end of the year gave participants the opportunity to read one another's reports, consider modifications, and exchange information about programmatic changes that were taking place on their campuses as a result of their discoveries.

During the third year, some programs collected additional information and analyzed data, and each site revised its preliminary report to serve as a case study for *The Courage to Question: Women's Studies and Student Learning*, the most comprehensive of three publications evolving from the FIPSE grant. *The Courage to Question* contains the heart of the research discoveries about how and what students learn in women's studies courses. A synopsis of key findings about student learning can be found in the *Executive Summary of The Courage to Question*, which is funded by the Association of American Colleges and designed to make the information easily accessible to a wider population.

Because how we went about assessing student learning became almost as revealing a process as what we actually discovered, we have produced a third publication from the FIPSE grant, *Students at the Center: Feminist Assessment*. As most people agree, methodology and content cannot be severed neatly from one another. *The Courage to Question* chapters, then, describe assessment designs and methodologies and include the most relevant questionnaires at the end of each chapter. Foregrounded in *The Courage to Question*, however, are the results. *Students at the Center* foregrounds assessment: what we came to call "feminist principles of assessment"; innovative assessment designs; how our project fits into the spectrum of assessment approaches nationally; and practical advice about how to do a productive assessment project on a campus. *Students at the Center* contains a more expansive sample of questionnaires, scoring sheets, and interview questions. It also includes a directory of consultants and a selected bibliography on assessment. We hope *Students at the Center* will serve as a catalyst for assessment projects in women's studies but also in many other disciplines as well.

QUESTIONS GENERATED
ABOUT STUDENT LEARNING

Over time, the project created a series of institutionally specific questions around which each women's studies program designed its assessment plan. To prepare, each participant in the initial grant workshop generated a series of what we called "passionate questions" about women's studies and student learning.[4] Our lists were very long. At that point, we did not seek to create a common set of questions or reduce the diverse voices and concerns. Participants then went back to their individual campuses, where they initiated a series of extended conversations and consultations with faculty members and students. On the basis of those extended dialogues, we met again as a group midway through the first year and created a set of eight key questions that we agreed all of our programs had in common.

The eight questions covered developmental, disciplinary, and pedagogical issues. Does women's studies cultivate personal empowerment and social responsibility? How successfully does women's studies support students as they express their feminism on campus? Is the authority of experience legitimized and are students urged to comprehend the experience of others? Does women's studies foster connected learning (see page 77)? Are students introduced to the constructed and situated character of disciplinary knowledge? Are students encouraged to reconstruct knowledge from multidisciplinary and cross-cultural perspectives? How do programs navigate tensions between creating safe but challenging classroom space? Finally, how do we shift and make explicit the power relations both in the classroom and the institution? All these questions were understood to be posed within the larger framework in which gender, race, class, sexuality, and other categories of analytic differences intersect.

These eight questions were not created as controlling questions for the project, nor were participants compelled to include them in their particular institutional assessment design. Nonetheless, these questions acted as a common background for the project against which other questions were posed. They also led some campuses to explore issues in common with other programs; as a result, we have a collection of case studies that are both particular and general, unique and widely applicable.

CONTEXTS FOR CASE STUDIES

The more we met as a national group, the clearer it became that institutional context was very important. Feminist theory argues persuasively that positionality and particularity influence what we know. Our exchanges bore that out. As a group, we were also wary of aggregate statistics and generalizations that too often erase significant insights or particular groups of people. We were convinced that universalizing students would distort their distinct realities and therefore be less useful in efforts to improve undergraduate education. We decided not only to write a series of case studies, therefore, but to offer an institutional and student profile in each report so readers would have a more accurate context for understanding the research results. Almost every report begins, then, by orienting the reader to a specific academic institution and student population. The concluding chapter of *The Courage to Question* does offer a national picture of student learning but one that is rooted firmly in the particular student experiences generated in the research findings of participating campuses.

The University of Colorado set its assessment project in the larger social context of the decade-long educational reform movement. The Colorado program then went directly to students with the questions: "From your standpoint, what do we in women's studies actually do? What actually happens to you as a learner in women's studies courses? What do you learn and how do you learn it?" The students articulated from their own experiences three components of women's studies courses—course content, course structure, and classroom dynamics—which Colorado explored in more depth for the next two years. Primarily through an ethnographic methodology, Colorado's study compares women's studies and non-women's studies courses to define what accounts for the active engagement and sense of empowerment and difference students claimed typified their learning experiences in women's studies. By examining what they refer to as personalized learning and the influence of student culture on that learning, they suggest future areas of research.

By contrast, Lewis and Clark linked its questions directly to specific program goals for its Gender Studies Program. Wanting to pose some questions about the construction of gender studies as a discipline, the project coordinators asked, "How effectively do our students learn and apply gender analysis?" In answering this question, they sought to define a knowledge base or what they referred to as "knowledge plots" in women's studies, investigating whether there might be some developmental logic to learning one plot before another. They also compared gender studies and non-gender studies classes and sought to explore some of the distinctions between courses where gender is the central focus of inquiry and others where gender balancing is considered when a course is constructed but is not necessarily foregrounded. The second question had to do with gender studies' impact in the classroom and on the institutional climate as a whole. Finally, coordinators asked of both alumnae/a and current students, "What impact, if any, has gender studies had on your personal growth?"

As at Lewis and Clark, the participants at Old Dominion University (ODU) were interested in trying to define some key concepts in women's studies and asked, "How well do students learn the knowledge base of women's studies?" They followed up questions about the knowledge base with questions about learning skills: "Do students become connected knowers, individuals who use self-knowledge and empathy to learn?" Paralleling that concern about *how* students learn as opposed to *what* students learn, ODU participants also asked, "Do students acquire the ability to examine and evaluate assumptions underlying culturally accepted fact and theory?" Because ODU students were insistent that the most defining experience for them as learners was related to finding and using their voice, a third question became part of ODU's assessment study: "Was your voice heard and respected in the classroom?" In examining how a sense of community, or what ODU called "we-ness," affected students' personal growth, they investigated whether women's studies affected friendship patterns in and out of class. Adding a fifth category to the grant's original four about knowledge base, critical skills, pedagogy, and personal growth, ODU asked a question that reminded us that faculty members were learners, too. They asked, "How did women's studies affect the teaching and scholarly lives of women faculty members associated with the program?"

Unlike program participants at the coeducational institutions, those at Wellesley College wanted to ask what makes women's studies at a women's liberal arts college different. To answer that question as they compared women's studies and non-women's studies courses throughout their study, they focused on three questions. The first involved students' growth: "Did the courses change or affect students' personal lives, their intellectual lives, and their political beliefs?" Their second question was pedagogical and went directly to the most frequently repeated accusation by those unsympathetic with women's studies: "Did students feel pressure to give politically correct answers and identify only with feminist ideas? If so, where was the pressure coming from?" Finally, their third question, which led to some fascinating insights about the debate generated by women's studies courses: "Was the pedagogy different? If so, how?"

Reflecting both the political commitment of its women's studies program and the richly diverse student population, project leaders at Hunter College wanted to know if the women's studies program fostered an awareness of multiculturalism and, if so, where one might begin to learn how to do that. What appears at first glance to be a relatively simple second question—"Does women's studies foster critical thinking?"—became more complex as Hunter's project participants suggested that to think critically students first needed to have confidence and a sense of self through which to voice their critical judgments. Echoing a concern of project participants at Old Dominion about connected learning, Hunter's participants' third question was, "Do students learn how to integrate knowledge they acquire in women's studies?"

Project representatives at Oberlin College wanted to explore whether students in their program were gaining a sense of the multiplicity of women's lives understood to be complicated by such markers as class, race, and sexuality. They explored that question by asking, "Does student learning entail self-empowerment?" This allowed them to take a closer look at the process through which students came to an understanding of the history of their own group by understanding the histories of other groups. Empowerment of the individual was defined in Oberlin's women's studies program goals, as it was in the other six programs, as inseparable from a sense of social responsibility to others. Their second question was pedagogical: "To what extent does collaborative learning occur, and how effective is it?" Threading the notion of difference throughout their three questions, the Oberlin participants wanted to gain more information about how collaborative learning becomes a vehicle for helping students mediate differences as they work with diverse groups in their classes. Finally, the Oberlin participants asked students directly whether specific women's studies courses "fostered a relational understanding of race, ethnicity, class, gender, and sexuality."

Sharing similar concerns about personal transformations, pedagogy, and difference, participants from the University of Missouri–Columbia wanted to find out what kinds of personal transformations occur in students who take women's studies courses. Because a commitment to teaching united women's studies faculty members in their program, the Missouri survey also asked, "Do students think women's studies courses are taught differently than other courses and if so, how?" Their third question echoed those of Hunter and Oberlin Colleges: "Do students in women's studies gain a new understanding about the connection between gender, race, class, and sexual preference?"

While there was, then, no externally imposed uniformity in the questions each campus examined, these seven sites do speak back and forth to one another when their case studies are read as a group. The concluding chapter of The Courage to Question draws together some of the cumulative findings from the seven discrete reports and reflects upon the configurations and potential national implications that emerge when the seven are seen in relation to one another.

INSTITUTIONAL CHALLENGES
TO PARTICIPATING IN THE PROJECT

Although ten institutions originally had been invited to participate, by the third year there were seven programs remaining with the project. After the initial grant workshop in October 1990, the University of Wisconsin withdrew because the project participants felt the commitment of time and staff outweighed other pressing priorities. There also had been a change in personnel within their program. While a team from Bennett College participated in part of the October workshop, team members were unable to attend the winter workshop or complete any of the initial descriptions of women's studies program goals. By the end of the academic year, both project representatives had left Bennett and no one was designated to replace them. The team from the University of California–Los Angeles had been active throughout the first year and completed the description of program goals and established questions to pose for the second year's research. Just before the second year began, however, the program's research assistant, who had taken responsibility for producing documents for the FIPSE project, left the university; UCLA consequently withdrew from the project.

While the three programs had institutionally specific reasons guiding their choices, their reasons for withdrawing reveal something about the challenges of administering women's studies programs nationally. The institutional culture at larger research universities does not tend to value assessment research as highly as other kinds of academic research projects. Such institutions also give fewer rewards for the kind of curricular, programmatic, and attention to teaching so important to women's studies programs and so central to this specific FIPSE grant. Although research universities often have access to graduate student research assistants to help in such instances, those students usually are attached to a project for only a year at a time. By contrast, for smaller institutions like Bennett, the loss of one or two key women's studies faculty members can have a significant impact on a program.

The kind of institutional support for the participating programs varied almost as widely as it does among women's studies programs nationally. Some received internal grants for faculty development workshops, others had research assistants at the graduate or undergraduate level attached to the project, and still others were allocated some institutional money for photocopying, typing, and postage; none were given release time, and some programs stayed with the grant by virtue of their own energy, commitment, and overtime investment, again reflecting the national profile of many women's studies programs.

Not enough time, not enough staff, and not enough money were persistent comments from most program participants. While they were excited about the project, they wondered how they were going to fit it in with their other women's studies responsibilities. *Students at the Center* explores in more detail how we sought to resolve some of these dilemmas. With long experience administering programs without sufficient support, the women's studies faculty members and administrators in the project drew on that history to create assessment instruments that were embedded in what they already do; weave data analysis into student research projects; create methods that could also have a life beyond the grant such as alumnae/a questionnaires and interviews; and make use of the project to further women's studies programmatic goals. Still, their commitment to the project meant some people spent midwinter vacations writing drafts of their reports or summers analyzing data rather than finishing a book or an article. It is just that sort of dedication that is most responsible for the creation, stability, and growth of women's studies programs nationally, but it is just that sort of overload that threatens to exhaust faculty members unnecessarily and impose constraints on the institutional impact of the program.

To create an academic program dependent on such volunteer efforts by its faculty members is like creating a hospital emergency room staffed with doctors and nurses who already have spent a full day on the ward and in the operating room. It is imperative that institutions find ways to support women's studies programs, invest in improving teaching and curriculum, and value the kind of research that helps all of us understand how students learn.

One Hunter College student explained,
"[women's studies courses] open with questions…
that's really the biggest difference…
you question all the time, all the time"

These institutional tensions are not unique to women's studies, but they
characterize the experience of most women's studies faculty. To solve the
problems of understaffing and underfunding in the 1990s—when most institutions will have to do the same or more with fewer resources—will be a
challenge indeed. Institutions need to be sure that in making the difficult
choices about allocating scarcer resources that those groups who historically
have not been invited to the table will not find themselves disproportionately scrambling against each other for the leftovers. It is a decade in which we
will have to rely on the imagination and energy of the entire academic community and place student learning at the center of our common commitments. Women's studies has much to contribute to this discussion, as *The
Courage to Question* testifies.

We expect our research to be a watershed for women's studies and dispel
many misconceptions now circulating in the highly politicized attack on educational reform movements, especially those that call for diversity and multiculturalism in the curriculum. While critics of women's studies characterize
the field as imposing a rigid, monolithic ideology on its students, the research in our three-year study presents a dramatically different picture. Cap-
turing the complexity of student learning, one Wellesley student describes
women's studies as generating "learning that does more than fill your brain.
It fills your body, it fills your heart, [and] it makes you grow." According to
our research, instead of reducing intellectual and political options, women's
studies expands them. In differentiating between women's studies and non-
women's studies courses, one Hunter College student explained, women's
studies courses "open with questions…that's really the biggest
difference…you question all the time, all the time."

In that spirit of questioning, we offer some of what we discovered about
student learning through our FIPSE project. We hope it begins a fruitful dialogue between a broad community of educators and students committed to
generating both the yearning and the courage to question.

---

1. For an overview of the more general hostility to women and the women's movement, see Susan
Faludi's *Backlash* (New York: Crown Publishers, 1991), especially chapter 11, "The Backlash Brain
Trust: From Neocons to Neofems." For examples of specific attacks on women's studies, see re-
ports of the National Association of Scholars'(NAS) 1988 conference as reported in the *New York
Times*, November 15, 1988, A22, and in *The Nation*, December 12, 1988, 644; see also a full page
ad from the NAS in *The Chronicle of Higher Education*, November 8, 1989, A23, or an article on
pages 8–10 in the July 20, 1990, issue of Washington, D.C.'s *City Paper*, on the Accuracy in
Academia conference. Most recently, these efforts to discredit women's studies and other educa-

tional reform efforts have been collapsed into one catch-all and misleading phrase, "political correctness."

2. *NWSA Directory of Women's Studies Programs, Women's Centers, and Women's Research Centers* (College Park, Md.: NWSA, 1990), ii. Subsequent statistics on the number of majors and minors as well as the graduate programs in women's studies are taken from pages ii–iii in that same volume.

3. See the report and recommendations about the women's studies major in *Reports From the Fields* (Washington, D.C.: Association of American Colleges, 1990), 207–24.

4. Our language was inspired by Jill Mattuck Tarule, a member of the National Assessment Team and one of the authors of *Women's Ways of Knowing* (New York: Basic Books, 1986). In *Women's Ways*, they refer to "passionate knowing" as "a way of weaving…passions and intellectual life into some recognizable whole" (p. 141).

■

UNIVERSITY OF COLORADO
PERSONALIZED LEARNING

BY MARCIA WESTKOTT AND GAY VICTORIA

The University of Colorado takes an approach to "The Courage to Question" that is more descriptive than evaluative. Rather than ask, "What are our goals for student learning, and how well are we achieving them?" the program asks a more basic question: "From the standpoint of student learning, what do we actually do?" The report includes a history of the program's experience with assessment; an explanation of their descriptive focus and results of the process; and current and ongoing implications of the project. The report also places the project within the context of recent reports on reform in higher education.

HISTORY OF ASSESSMENT
IN THE WOMEN'S STUDIES PROGRAM

The University of Colorado is located in Boulder, Colorado, with an enrollment of 25,571 students. Its student body is primarily white (87.5 percent), middle class, and native to Colorado. Women constitute 46 percent of the student population. Sixty-one percent of the undergraduate students at CU–Boulder receive some type of financial aid. CU–Boulder employs 1,094 full-time faculty members and is considered the leading comprehensive research university in the Rocky Mountain region and among the top public universities in the country in gaining federal research support. The campus has several active women's organizations and clubs, although it has no women's center. The major campus program identified with women is the Women's Studies Program.

The Women's Studies Program was founded in the early 1970s by a group of faculty members, students, and community members. By the fall of 1974, a full-time director had been appointed. The curriculum reflected a national pattern, which the program has since maintained: interdisciplinary core courses with a women's studies rubric and courses offered by departments and cross-listed with women's studies. In 1979, the Women's Studies Program was subsumed with eleven other programs under the Center for Interdisciplinary Studies, which was maintained as an umbrella unit until

Student demand for courses reflects both the
expanding scholarship and the social concerns
that scholarship addresses

1985 when the center was abolished. Since 1985, women's studies has grown considerably as an independent program, increasing the number of majors from twenty-five in 1984 to seventy in fall of 1991 and employing four full-time and one part-time faculty members.

The growth of the Women's Studies Program during its eighteen-year history is the result of both national trends and local circumstances. First, the dramatic expansion of feminist scholarship has generated a surge of intellectual excitement in women's studies nationally and internationally. Student demand for courses reflects both the expanding scholarship and the social concerns that the scholarship addresses. Concomitantly, as the new scholarship on women generated academic attention within the traditional disciplines, more departments sought to hire faculty members whose scholarly or creative work focused on women or gender. Thus, while the 1974 proposal to establish the Women's Studies Program identified fifteen faculty members across campus who were interested in teaching women's studies in their departments, a 1991 survey identified forty-two core and affiliated full-time faculty members who have *actually taught* these courses during the past three semesters.

Local circumstances also have promoted the growth of women's studies at the University of Colorado. A core faculty known for its outstanding teaching has developed an excellent reputation among students. Students drawn to women's studies courses are among the most articulate and capable on campus. "Affiliated" faculty members (that is, those who are listed in other departments and whose courses are cross-listed with women's studies) have given generously of their support and influence at crucial moments in the program's history. While administrative support has been uneven from office to office, over the years a general acceptance of and support for women's studies prevails (for example, approval to conduct national searches for directors at three separate times). And finally, the Boulder community—with its numerous feminist organizations—is a setting that supports women's studies activities.

In 1988, with the hiring of the present director, the program moved from a basement location to its present site in Cottage Number One, the original women's dormitory. In addition to the director's position, the program received four full-time, tenure-line faculty positions. In academic year 1991–92, a full-time senior instructor and a one-third time instructor—as well as seven part-time instructors—round out the core teaching faculty.

Today, the Women's Studies Program does more than meet its original

aim of offering courses on the new scholarship on women. Since 1983, it has
provided a major area of academic concentration for 190 undergraduates
who have been awarded the major under the American Studies designation;
the program also has granted a certificate to approximately 100 students. In
addition to providing an integrated curriculum in women's studies for its major and certificate students, the program also seeks to foster an intellectual
feminist community on campus through its numerous programs and activities, to support the work of faculty members who are engaging in feminist
scholarship in their disciplines, to contribute to feminist discourse through
scholarly and creative work, and to promote enlightened and responsible
leadership for women in the community.

When the Women's Studies Program at the University of Colorado was
invited in 1989 to participate in the assessment project, "The Courage to
Question," we initially regarded it as an opportunity to refine and expand assessment procedures that we had already developed. Our campus, like other
institutions of higher education in Colorado, had been mandated by the
state to assess student learning in all academic units beginning in 1987–88.
Following the advice of those in the Office of Academic Affairs who were
coordinating the effort, we developed a rather standard procedure. The faculty identified the knowledge and skills goals that we thought our students
should attain and devised an instrument for measuring them.

In the first year, the women's studies faculty selected one knowledge goal
and two skills goals to assess. Because the required survey of feminist theory
served at that time as a type of capstone course for majors, we decided to
embed the assessment of these goals in a requirement for the course. The
knowledge goal we selected was knowledge of major paradigms of feminist
thought. The skills goals we selected were: (1) the ability to write a focused
and coherent analytical essay that is based upon and sustained by evidence;
and (2) the ability to analyze arguments and interpretation for internal con-
sistency and underlying assumptions. The final examination in the course
was to be assessed for these student learning goals. After the instructor graded the examination for the purpose of the course, three faculty members—
including an outside evaluator from another institution—evaluated the student exams according to the assessment goals.

The outcome of the assessment project was not especially illuminating.
In fact, it did not tell us much beyond what the course instructor had discovered in the process of grading the exams for the class: overall, the students
did relatively well in meeting these goals. This experience, however, led us to

Our students were, in effect, telling us that their
education in women's studies produced the learning experience that higher education reformers
have been advocating for the last several years

question the approach we had taken to assessment, which eventually led us
to redefine our project for "The Courage to Question."

We were dissatisfied with the process we had developed for several reasons. First, the state mandate created an atmosphere that encouraged com-
pliance rather than enthusiasm. Our selection of knowledge and skills goals
as well as the methods of assessment emerged from a desire for efficiency. We
regarded assessment as one more bureaucratic requirement for evaluation
that impinged on our time. Like most faculty members in women's studies
programs, we were already overworked. We resented yet another requirement
for self-evaluation that interfered with our real work: teaching and research.
Thus, we formally complied with the mandate by following campus guidelines and embedding the assessment in course requirements. As a result, our
goals and the process of assessing them looked very much like standard academic fare: one could not tell much difference between the women's studies
assessment plan and those of traditional arts and sciences disciplines. We
were resigned to the process; we did not "own" it, and we didn't learn much
about ourselves as teachers and learners.

Participation in the NWSA/FIPSE project gave us an opportunity to re-
examine our attitudes toward assessment. First, the situation was dramatically different. We chose to participate in the project. The attitude of the national assessment team (as advisors to us) was flexible, helpful, and respectful
of the educational experience of women's studies students and faculty. We
were encouraged to take a more comprehensive look at assessment, its purposes, and its possibilities for self-reflection. Through biannual meetings we
were given the opportunity to engage in dialogue with faculty members from
other women's studies programs as a means of clarifying our individual campus approaches as well as raising the larger question of assessing women's
studies. The setting for our process was supportive and intellectually exciting. The audience for our reports was not a state bureaucrat but other wom-
en's studies programs and educators interested in assessment.

In this setting, we began to question other aspects of our previous approach to assessment. We realized that we had selected particular goals not
simply because they might be important but also because they were conve-
nient—that is, relatively easy to evaluate given our resources. Moreover, we
realized that even when these understandably pragmatic motives were not
operating so explicitly, our program goals reflected certain intentions by particular individuals at a specific time. We saw that our program could identify
a variety of combinations of goals, depending on who was asked and when.
Given this shifting context of goal identification, we decided to push back

the question from intention to the context itself and look at what we were actually doing in our women's studies courses. With help from our students, we started looking for answers.

In April and May of 1990, we held a series of potluck dinners with women's studies majors and certificate students, faculty members, and the staff advisor. We asked the students, "What actually happens for you as a learner in women's studies courses and as a women's studies major/certificate student?" and "What do you learn and how do you learn it?" The discussions were lively, intense, thoughtful, and fun. In an interesting way they reproduced the best of our classroom experiences: a student suggesting an idea; another picking up on it, confirming it, elaborating on it, taking a different slant; still another disagreeing with part of it, clarifying both the agreement and disagreement; another student mediating the disagreement, searching for some paradox that might illuminate the discussion. The faculty members and staff advisor took notes on these discussions and met to interpret them. We concluded that while students may have taken different slants on this theme, they were telling us that women's studies was an exciting learning experience because they as learners were personally, actively engaged in their learning experience.

STUDENT LEARNING
AND HIGHER EDUCATION REFORM

Our students were, in effect, telling us that their education in women's studies produced the learning experience that higher education reformers have been advocating for the last several years. Reports on undergraduate education have stressed the importance of students' involvement in their learning process. Although the specific goals varied from report to report or among institutions, the condition best suited to achieve those goals—active student learning—was clearly the current educational ideal.

In 1984, the Study Group on Excellence in Higher Education sponsored by the National Institute of Education (NIE) sounded the new emphasis for improving undergraduate education.

> There is now a good deal of research evidence to suggest that the more time and effort students invest in the learning process and the more intensely they engage in their own education, the greater will be their growth and achievement, their satisfaction with their educational experiences, and their persistence in college, and the more likely they are to continue their learning.[1]

The NIE report specified involvement to include devoting energy to studying, working at jobs on campus (rather than at off campus jobs), participating in student organizations, and interacting frequently with faculty members and other students. In his 1985 study, Alexander Astin confirmed the importance of the last item: frequent student-faculty interaction was the most influential factor affecting students' satisfaction with their undergraduate experience.[2] Subsequent reports issuing from organizations such as the Association of American Colleges (AAC), the Carnegie Foundation for the Advancement of Teaching, the American Association for Higher Education (AAHE), and the Education Commission of the States reiterated the importance of improving active student involvement and faculty engagement in teaching and learning.

These reports, while underscoring the ideal, identified impediments to its realization. Involvement in learning requires time, and both students and faculty members find themselves pressured by competing demands. Cutbacks in federal funding require more students to work off campus and to work more hours. A Carnegie Commission study found students were much more engaged by their social life and jobs outside of class than they were by academic or intellectual interests.[3] Faculty members also feel the pressure or the lure of competing demands. A Carnegie survey of five thousand faculty members found that at research universities, the reward system encourages research over teaching.[4] Prestige within a discipline nationally also is associated with the degree to which a faculty member engages in published research.[5] Although faculty members and administrators frequently affirm the principle that teaching and research need not necessarily be at odds with one another, the higher education reports reflect a growing uneasiness with this nostrum; they suggest or directly state that in practice the time demands of research impinge upon faculty involvement with teaching. The consequence of these tugs on student and faculty time, interests, rewards, and mutual perceptions—tugs that interfere with active involvement in teaching and learning—is the creation of what the authors of the AAC report on general education called the "two cultures in academia":

> On many campuses, students view faculty with the ambivalence of respect and resentment, admiration and disappointment. Depending on the institution and the department, relations between students and faculty can range from harmony and colleagueship through mutual avoidance to antagonism and undeclared conflict. On such campuses, the rhetoric about an "intellectual community" is belied by the reality of these two separate cultures.[6]

The report suggests that the two cultures in academia foster an attitude of detachment on both sides. Students don't make demands on faculty members in exchange for faculty members not making demands on students. Students put in the time they think is necessary to get the grades they want and then turn to more exciting interests. Faculty members put in the time they think is necessary to teach, hold office hours and attend meetings, and then, if time permits, turn to the real work of research. Neither side makes too many demands, yet each harbors complaints. Students contend that faculty members are aloof and condescending; faculty members complain that students can't write or think or analyze. Each manages to find one or a few exceptions to what they take to be the pattern of the other's disinterest or incompetence.

This, of course, is an exaggeration. Obviously, there are faculty members and students who are actively engaged in intellectually exciting teaching and learning experiences. But the concerns that these various reports raise converge in a portrait of a university culture that fosters isolation, resignation, and discontent on the part of students and faculty.

The consequences are experienced not simply in the separation of students and faculty (and, indeed, among students and among faculty members) but in the curriculum as well. In *A New Vitality in General Education*, AAC's task group on general education cites the problem with the disorganized general education curriculum and attributes it to the faculty's focus on their specialized research within their discipline. "We have specialized to such a degree that we have lost interest in and the capacity for integrating knowledge."[7] In *The Challenge of Connecting Learning*, another AAC task force finds coherence lacking even "within arts and sciences majors." The authors call for "connected knowing"; that is, making links among courses and ideas within the major but also encouraging students to connect personally with the material they were learning.[8]

The reports, thus, describe a problem that did not appear in our students' accounts of their women's studies learning experience. While some components described in the reports were acknowledged—for example, competing tugs on students and faculty time demands and interests—they did not emerge as central themes. To the contrary, students reported that faculty members were generally accessible and responsive to their questions and concerns and that faculty-student activities bridged the two cultures. They reported that through taking women's studies courses, they were challenged to carry the knowledge gained in their classes into their social life and into their work experience, giving them a language and a critical framework for evaluating their experience. They described their classes as demanding and supportive experiences that fostered connected learning. As one student stated, "We have wonderful teachers who care about us, are telling us something real and tangible. They validate our existence as women, and they are great role models, something women don't have much of."

TEACHING AND LEARNING IN WOMEN'S STUDIES CLASSES

Our students were responding to their women's studies classes in a way that confirmed recent studies on feminist pedagogy. Grounded in feminist scholarship and theories of knowledge that have challenged academic disciplines, feminists have questioned traditional teaching practices. As Culley and Portuges note, "changing what we teach means changing how we teach."[9] Traditional practices take an approach to teaching that presumes that objective knowledge is possible, "mastery" of universal truths is desirable, the teacher is the uncontested expert, and students learn through competing with one another. In contrast, feminist pedagogy assumes an approach that views knowledge as contingent, open, and interconnected and learning as more effective in a setting that is non-hierarchical, student-centered, and collaborative.

Most of the writing on feminist pedagogy has documented the non-traditional practices that feminist teachers use in the classroom. We were interested in learning more about feminist pedagogy from the perspective of our students. What in particular were our students responding to when they described their learning experiences so positively? Was it the teaching techniques? the material? some combination? How did they interpret their active engagement in the classroom?

To try to answer these questions, we turned to studying women's studies classes more systematically. At the potluck dinners, the students indicated several dimensions to their active connection within their classes. We subsequently grouped these dimensions under three categories: course content, course structure, and classroom dynamics. While at times these categories may overlap and influence one another, basically they refer to the subject matter of the course (what students read, discuss, think about, research); the structure of the course (format, requirements); and classroom dynamics or pedagogy (teaching style, student participation, faculty-student interaction).

Our research was built on these informal student impressions and the categories we derived from them. Specifically, we were interested in answering two questions: (1) were all three of these categories equally important in fostering active learning or was one component more important than the others? and (2) was the active learning experience that our students identified with their women's studies courses unique or could it be found in other classes?

We decided to answer these questions from the perspective of illuminative evaluation, an approach used in educational research to evaluate innovative educational programs where traditional approaches have proven inadequate.[10] Evaluation traditionally has been inextricably linked with testing—testing to provide quantitative data from which statistical inferences can be drawn. However, test-oriented evaluation presents a number of problems when conducting an evaluation of an educational innovation. It is often difficult to articulate and specify complex goals, to account for idiosyncratic influences, even to formulate precise research questions—all issues which this project presented.

Illuminative evaluation offers an alternative "social anthropology" paradigm. Whereas traditional evaluation procedures tend to operate in isolation, illuminative evaluation attempts to incorporate the wider context in which educational programs operate. The goal of illuminative research is to "unravel [the complex scene encountered]...[and to] isolate its significant features."[11] Illuminative evaluation is, in fact, a general research strategy rather than a standard methodological package. The tactics used to conduct the research are chosen to fit the particular subject at hand. After making initial observations, the researcher identifies certain phenomena, events, or opinions as topics for more intensive inquiry: "As the investigation unfolds...problem areas become progressively clarified and re-defined."[12] This "progressive focusing" permits unique and previously unidentified phenomena to be examined.

The illumination approach seemed best suited to the rather open-ended nature of our questioning. In the initial discussions our students identified the importance of their own active engagement, and we derived the categories that might foster that experience. We then used these categories to inform a series of classroom observations and to analyze course syllabi. We used the information that we gathered from these sources to create a questionnaire (see pages 38–42).

Because we wanted to compare learning experiences in women's studies classes with those in classes in other departments, we initially conducted observations in three different courses—one women's studies course, "Women and Religion," and two non-women's studies courses (an English course, "Advanced Shakespeare," and an American Studies course entitled "American Autobiographies"). We selected these courses through a process of purposive sampling that allowed us to control for class level, class size, academic discipline, and instructor evaluations.

Because we wanted students who had sufficient time as undergraduates to enable them to reflect upon their educational experiences, we limited the comparison classes to upper-division courses. Because class size significantly affects classroom atmosphere and student engagement, we selected classes with roughly the same number of students. "Women and Religion" had thirty-two students, "Advanced Shakespeare" had twenty-five students, and "American Autobiographies," had twenty-one students. Academic discipline was another area of consideration. Because content to a large extent affects style of teaching, we selected courses from the humanities and social sciences, academic disciplines considered most similar to women's studies. Since the teaching ability of women's studies instructors is rated consistently high in faculty course evaluations, teaching excellence of the instructor also was a criterion for selection of comparison classes.

Gender was a factor that could not be controlled because of limitations inherent in our study. Women's studies classes are exclusively taught by female faculty members and most often the majority (if not all) of the students are female. This was true for the "Women and Religion" class: it was taught by a female, and all of the students were female. The "Advanced Shakespeare" class was taught by a female and comprised twelve female and thirteen male students. The "American Autobiographies" class was taught by a male and had thirteen women and eight men. The gender profile is an important difference, one which we recognize has significant implications, given our eventual findings.

All three professors teaching these three courses agreed with considerable interest to participate in the project. On the first day of observation, Research Assistant Gay Victoria introduced herself to the students and gave them a brief description of the project and the reasons for wanting to make the observations. She subsequently observed three seventy-five-minute class periods in each of the three classes during the periods of November 15–16 and November 26–December 4, 1990. She audiotaped all of the classes with the consent of the instructor and the students.

The class observations were directed by the three components, which

students and faculty members had identified as contributing to active learning in women's studies classes—content, structure, and dynamics. *Content*
was, of course, an obvious area of difference between the women's studies
and non-women's studies classes. Although both the "Advanced Shakespeare" class and the class on "American Autobiographies" presented multicultural approaches to the course material (incorporating discussions regarding race and class as well as gender whenever appropriate), neither of them
had women as their primary focus. In contrast, the content of the "Women
and Religion" class was focused solely on women.

All three courses contained many *structural* similarities: all appeared to
incorporate similar types of course requirements (critical thinking and writing skills were stressed in all three classes); all were generally conducted in a
discussion rather than lecture format; and all formally structured some aspects of the class to be determined by students. Interestingly enough, the
women's studies class was conducted in a seating arrangement which was
more or less traditional: for example, rows of seated students, with the instructor in front. The other two classes, in contrast, were conducted in a less
traditional circle arrangement.

Dynamics presented a number of interesting observations. The pedagogy most often associated with feminist approaches—such as student-centered or dialogic teaching—was not unique to the women's studies class.
All three instructors involved students in discussion and responsibility for
directing the class. While all three classes had active participation rates,
the average response rates for the "Advanced Shakespeare" course (83.3
percent of the students spoke) and the "American Autobiographies" course
(70.3 percent) were somewhat higher than the average participation rate in
the "Women and Religion" course (46.6 percent). This was an interesting
finding, given students' reporting on their active learning in women's studies classes. One way to interpret the difference was to speculate that the
slightly larger class size affected the participation rate. Another explanation
was that this class was an anomaly and that students were, in fact, not actively involved. Yet another interpretation suggested that active learning is
not the same as, or confined to, student responses to professors' questions.
Students may be actively involved without necessarily verbalizing their responses in class. When we looked at *how* students engaged the material, we
discovered something that supported the latter interpretation. The students
in the "Women and Religion" course related classroom material to their
own lives, a process that did not take place in the other two classes.

We thus concluded that content was more
important to fostering personalized learning
than pedagogy alone

For example, during a discussion of the relationship between war and ritual and war as ritual, a student of the "Women and Religion" class observed:

> *Over Thanksgiving, my dad and I got into a lot of conversations about*
> *the war.... He tried to justify it to me...you know, thinking that we*
> *should go to war.... I asked him a question, "Well, how do you think*
> *things would be different if there was a matriarchy instead of patri-*
> *archy?" The way he saw matriarchy is—and this is where the shock*
> *was—that, all of the sudden, men would follow one woman's orders.*
> *Like there would be the one woman on the top and then it would be*
> *exactly like it is right now.*

Class members empathized with this student but also discussed the reasons
why someone might automatically think of that model of matriarchy, given
popular examples of women heads of state.

Students in the "American Autobiographies" and the "Advanced
Shakespeare" class did not engage in this type of dynamic. Admittedly, the
subject matter of these two classes may have offered fewer opportunities to
make personal connections with the course material than "Women and
Religion" did. However, even when opportunities did present themselves in
these other classes, students (male or female) did not make the connections—for whatever reason. It was unclear at this point why this dynamic
was present only in the women's studies class. One possible explanation
could have been the fact that the professor in this class actually "modeled"
the integration of the personal with the intellectual by using examples from
her own religious upbringing and those of family members to illustrate various points about the influence of religion.

Yet "modeling" did occur during observations of one of the other classes.
The female professor in "Advanced Shakespeare" made at least two attempts
to encourage students to connect the themes of war in Henry V (the play under discussion) to the Gulf War (which had escalated at the time). She herself volunteered that she had a difficult time reading the play without thinking about contemporary parallels. Each time she encouraged students to
reflect on a connection (without directing them how to reflect), the students
quickly returned to a discussion of the text itself. Thus, although the professor herself modeled making contemporary connections to the material, the
class resisted. There may be many reasons for this resistance: for example,
students (with friends or loved ones at risk) may have felt too closely affected

by the Gulf War to discuss it. Nevertheless, only the students in the women's studies class volunteered connections between the material, themselves, and their present contexts.

The observations of the three classes suggested some interesting initial answers to our questions. Pedagogy alone did not foster a personal connection to the material. Indeed, those techniques most often associated with feminist pedagogy—that is, student-centered learning, discussion emphasis, a democratization of responsibility—occurred more frequently in the two classes which were *not* the women's studies course. However, although these pedagogical techniques fostered active student learning in the classroom, student engagement was not "personal" in the way that it was for women's studies students. This distinction required our clarifying the difference between "active" engagement and "personal" engagement. It also required our exploring more fully what "personal" connection meant in the classroom. Surely the students actively involved in "Advanced Shakespeare" and "American Autobiographies" were learning in a way that could hardly be called "impersonal." They obviously were intellectually excited by the material and the class discussions. They were not detached; they were "turned on" by learning. This description was true also of the women's studies students. Yet for them, something additional was happening. They were connecting the *content* of the material with their lives, and they were connecting themselves with the content of the material.

We thus concluded that content was more important to fostering personalized learning than pedagogy alone. It was not enough that a professor modeled a personal connection to the material or that she fostered student involvement through discussion. The students in the women's studies class were also actively involved because the material touched them deeply. They read about the history of women in the Judeo-Christian tradition, and they wanted to know historically what it was like for women to be excluded from certain religious practices. They read theological tracts and reflected on their own spirituality. They read about women's involvement in contemporary religious cults and spoke with concern about women they knew who were involved in these organizations. Content itself, it would seem, sparked the personal connection.

We decided to test our speculation about the centrality of content through observing additional classes. We selected five courses for this second phase of the project: two women's studies courses ("Feminist Theory" and "Fathers and Daughters"); two English classes ("American Women Writers" and "Readings in American Poetry"); and a course from the Religious Studies Department on "Sufism." The same criteria used in the first phase of the project (upper division, teaching excellence, size, and academic discipline) were used in selecting classes for the second phase. The second phase, however, included an additional consideration not included in the first. Because we speculated that content was one aspect of women's studies courses that uniquely informed student engagement in learning (through personalizing knowledge), we included "American Women Writers," a course with a content focus on women but not offered through the Women's Studies Program. Although some students from other departments were enrolled in the course, most were English majors. Therefore, this course enabled us to compare the responses of women's studies students to those of non-women's studies students in a course focusing exclusively on women.

Three of the classes were taught by female faculty members ("American Women Writers," "Feminist Theory," and "Fathers and Daughters") and two by male faculty members ("Readings in American Poetry" and "Sufism"). The students in the two women's studies classes were once again either exclusively or predominantly female (the "Feminist Theory" class had two male students). The three non-women's studies classes had a mixture of male and female students. All five classes were upper-division classes with anywhere from seventeen to twenty-six students. Three separate observations consisting of one class period (either fifty or seventy-five minutes) were carried out in each of these five classes during the period from March 5 to April 10, 1991, using the same procedure as in the first phases.

With regard to *structure* (requirements, skills, classroom format), all five classes in phase two had similar course requirements and were conducted either through discussion or a combination discussion/lecture format. All five of the classes placed a great deal of emphasis on critical thinking and writing skills. All were conducted in a circular seating arrangement. In terms of pedagogy or *dynamics*, all but one of the five classes formally incorporated students into various aspects of designing and/or running of the class. The class that was most traditionally structured (designed and led by the faculty) was a women's studies course, "Feminist Theory." Again, the two English classes—"American Women Writers" and "Readings in American Poetry"—were the most highly student-centered, delegating much of the responsibility for designing questions and leading class discussion to the students. This pattern did not surprise us. Influenced by one of its faculty members, the English Department has been known on campus for innovation in fostering student-centered learning.[13]

The most interesting findings concerned the personalization of knowing. Again, students reproduced the earlier pattern of personalizing learning in their women's studies classes. And, again, for the most part, students resisted personalizing learning in the three courses that were not women's studies. However, two exceptions to the earlier pattern proved to be especially illuminating. The first anomaly was a lengthy and intense personalized discussion in one class period of the religious studies class, "Sufism." The professor had just returned student papers and, to the class as a whole, made a personal response to material in one of the student's papers, a response validating a point the student made. Several other students—first a male, then a female—followed by also connecting personally to the point the professor made. The discussion continued to weave in and out of academic and personal reflections on love and piety.

The second exception involved the lack of modeling of, or formal requirement for, engaging in personalized learning during our observation of the "Feminist Theory" course. Although it is possible that the professor modeled personalized learning in other class sessions, it did not occur during our observations. Yet, even in this class which was also the most traditionally structured, students made personal connections to the material. This finding was especially interesting when compared to our observations of student engagement in the English Department's "American Women Writers" class. Despite modeling on the part of the female instructor, in this class the students resisted connecting the material to their personal lives. In contrast, despite the absence of the professor's modeling in the women's studies "Feminist Theory" class, students repeatedly made connections between their lives and the material under discussion. It seemed as though these junior- and senior-level students, most of whom were women's studies majors, had developed an approach to their women's studies courses in which they expected personal connections to be made, even when such connections were not formally encouraged.

These findings suggested further comparisons. The professor in the religious studies class was especially skillful in eliciting students' personal responses. Not only did he model it himself but he did so in a way that was directed to specific issues that encouraged particular students to respond. He appeared to know his students well and directed his questioning to them personally. For example, through his questioning of a student musician, the student was led to reflect on a parallel between his experience of playing the violin and stages of spiritual growth. In the session we observed, however, students in the religious studies class did not volunteer personal connections on their own. Unlike the women's studies students, they did not initiate personalized learning but waited until the professor gave them permission to do so or explicitly requested it.

As we reflected on these differences, we were struck by what appeared to be a unique atmosphere among students in the women's studies courses. Many of these students—especially majors—knew one another; they met for events and activities outside of the classroom, and they had taken other classes together. This core (sometimes consisting of only three or four students) created an atmosphere of trust and mutual respect. They also were the ones who took a leadership role in initiating discussions about their personal responses to the material. They helped to create, in effect, a student culture. It was this student culture that appeared to function whether or not men were present (there were two men in the "Feminist Theory" class) and whether or not students received formal faculty encouragement for personalized learning. Our gradual unravelling of our questions, therefore, led us to the conclusion that the women's studies students themselves played a major role in creating their classroom experience.

The patterns we discovered in class observations were confirmed by our initial analysis of the questionnaires administered to the students in all five classes. Given our observations of the salience of the personalized connection to the course content, we were especially interested in student responses to the questions addressing this issue:

☐ How often does course content relate to you personally?

☐ How often in the classroom does it feel acceptable to relate course material to your personal life?

☐ How often do you feel "encouraged" by the instructor to relate course material to your personal life?

☐ How often in the classroom do you verbally express a personal connection to course content?

☐ How often does course content actually affect you or your life in some significant way?

Applying a simple t-test, we found that students in the women's studies classes scored significantly higher than students in the other classes on all of these questions. Moreover, we found that students in the English Department course "American Women Writers" scored significantly higher than students in the other non-women's studies classes but lower than students in the women's studies classes. This appeared to confirm our supposition that both content and student culture contributed to the personal connection, but we are looking forward to conducting a more elaborate statistical analysis of the questionnaire before drawing conclusions from these data.

Nevertheless, the students' written responses to the open-ended questions certainly confirmed the patterns of the initial class observations and the answers to the questions on personal connection to the material. When asked how the course content affected their lives, students in the English and religious studies classes responded generally by referring to what they learned, "It gave me a new perspective on American literature and life." "It gave me a broader perspective on literature." "It has helped me to understand a religion and culture different from my own." Very few students from these classes stated that the course helped them to think differently about or reevaluate their lives (the majority of these comments came from women students in "American Women Writers"). And one male student responded angrily to the question itself, "Although courses in religious studies (including this one) touch me deeply, I have little or *no* interest in sharing my 'personal life' (in regards to religion) with my classmates. Spirituality and academia do not go together very well. The mind often cannot relate to the heart. I don't really want to talk about it here."

In contrast, the responses from many of the students in the women's studies class indicated an ease with and desire for making a personal connection to the material, "This course will stay with me for the rest of the summer." "I apply everything I learn in women's studies classes to my life." "My women's studies courses have strengthened me." "I tend to read theories and think about how they apply to my life." "This class pushes me to self-examination and reevaluation and opens new avenues of thought." A political science major who had taken numerous women's studies classes noted, "Without women's studies classes half of my sanity would be missing in my educational experience. I think my education was extremely enhanced through taking women's studies classes."

The comments on the questionnaires helped us to clarify more fully the difference that we had noted earlier between students' active and personal engagement in their classes. When the students in the non-women's studies classes were intellectually involved with the material, they were excited by the ideas and enjoyed the learning process itself. We noticed this same process with the women's studies students, but they also expressed another dimension that could best be described as ethical. The women's studies students were concerned with drawing the implications of their learning for

Our students become excited by this material not
only because it is intellectually innovative and
compelling but especially because it explains
their own experiences

guiding their own actions in the world. They wanted to learn about the
world: its history; its political, economic, and social structures; its cultural
forms; its irrationalities and its positive possibilities. They also wanted to
learn about themselves in relationship to the world in order to help them
make judgments about making choices and interacting with others.

The ethical concerns that our students bring to their women's studies
classes reflect the conditions that bring them to these classes in the first
place—an experience of the world in which the traditional expectations for
women and men are challenged. They want to understand the traditions and
the challenges, not in order to discover some new "politically correct" mode
of behavior, but to explore the possibilities for change and to revalue parts of
their own past.

CONCLUSION

Our two major discoveries—the importance of course content in promoting
active, personalized learning and the culture of women's studies that assumes
personal/intellectual connections—raise for us many additional issues and
questions. The influence of content (over either course structure or teaching
dynamics) in creating a personally and intellectually exciting learning experience cannot be overemphasized. It suggests the powerful influence of simply exposing students to works on women's history and literature, to analyses
of the economic, social, and political structures influencing women's lives, to
feminist theory, to the psychology of women, to women's art and music and
theatre. Our students' positive responses to the content of women's studies
remind us of our own personal and intellectual excitement in "discovering"
the works that eventually came to define women's studies as a new field. It
also suggests the importance of the efforts of the past ten years to create curricular reform. The current backlash against that reform reflects the power
that the new scholarship wields. Women's studies is a new perspective that
challenges traditional structures and beliefs. Our students become excited by
this material not only because it is intellectually innovative and compelling
but especially because it explains their own experiences. These are the "aha"
moments when students understand their personal lives in the context of
wider, overlapping, and interlocking fields.

We suspect that the culture of personalized learning created by women's
studies students is grounded in this compelling connection. In the absence of
a dominant cultural discourse that would validate their lives, and in the context of prevailing cultural forms that undermine them, our students often

seek out their first women's studies classes as avenues to self-understanding.
The desire for the intellectual is deeply rooted in the personal. When they
do encounter the material that helps them to make sense of their lives—and
those issues and problems that were hitherto "nameless"—they establish an
expectation that women's studies course content will pertain to women's
lives in general and to their lives in particular. We suspect that the student
culture of personalized learning emerges from this shared expectation for the
intellectual to explain the personal. It appears, also, that the expectation is
reinforced not only by course content and faculty support and modeling but
also by students' mutually supportive interaction.

We would like to learn more about this student culture. Ideally, we
would like to follow a cohort of student majors longitudinally from their first
introductory women's studies course through graduation. We would want to
learn why—of all the students enrolled in "Introduction to Women's
Studies"—some choose to become majors. We would want to follow their
initial encounter with the material—and with the struggle with it that Lee
Knefelkamp identifies as the tension between support and challenge.[14] By
observing middle-range classes, we would want to learn how individual expectations for personalized learning develop into a student culture that fosters it. Are there certain student-teacher interactions that support it? Are
there other components to this student culture? other activities that promote
it? What is the influence of an all-female class in promoting a culture of personalized learning? We would also want to know more about the culture itself. Are certain voices and perspectives privileged? Are some groups silenced
or intimidated? Are there assumptions about what constitutes a personal
connection that are culturally limiting? Is there a tension between what
Belenky et al. have called connected knowing and separate (for example, analytical) knowing?[15] What happens when students encounter material that is
difficult or "inconvenient" to know? These are the questions that we are
starting to ask in phase three, which extends our work from "The Courage to
Question." We have begun to study "Introduction to Women's Studies," using classroom observation, student journals, questionnaires, and interviews.

Meanwhile, we still are required by the state to conduct a yearly assessment of student learning. Our experience with "The Courage to Question"
has led us to abandon our previous approach and to adopt a portfolio
method. Our approach rejects a method whereby faculty members alone
measure student learning and proceeds from the assumption of an equal part-
nership between students and faculty in assessing student learning.

Our portfolio process is embedded in a new capstone course for majors and certificates. A major requirement for the course is a ten-page paper, a reconstructive narrative of the student's journey as a women's studies major. To help prepare to write the narrative, students are asked to pull together materials from their women's studies courses (in the future, newly declared majors will be asked to keep a portfolio of these materials). As another building block, students are asked to write short memoirs of their individual courses, addressing questions such as, "Why did I take this course? What did I learn? How? Was I challenged? How? Was I supported? How? How would I change the class? What questions did I have going into the class? Were they answered? Were any left unanswered?" Building from these class memoirs and portfolio items, the students write narratives that make sense of their learning experience as women's studies majors and certificates. By sifting through memories, papers, exams, and personal journals, students must remember themselves as they were before they became women's studies majors and reconstruct their development. In doing so, students are required to recognize the interplay between personal connections and intellectual experience.

The second capstone course requirement involves students' extending their narratives to a project, the "next step." The definition of the project is flexible. It might be an artistic expression that interprets their learning experience, an analytical paper that pursues an unanswered question, an investigation of an intended career, a short story. When students present their narratives and "next step" projects, they may invite other faculty members and students to the class. Through her presentation and dialogue with those present, each student will be encouraged to reflect on her learning (both product and process) and to link her learning experience to her future plans. The assessment report will draw from these presentations, narratives, and portfolios. Authored by a subcommittee of faculty and student participants, the report will be submitted as the Women's Studies Program's yearly assessment of student learning.

Creating an assessment method that is more informative and useful to students and faculty members is only one of the benefits of our participation in "The Courage to Question." The process itself has encouraged us to reflect more fully on our classroom experiences. It has helped us with redefining our requirements for the major (to include new courses on critical thinking and a capstone course). We also have revitalized connections with faculty outside of women's studies. Other faculty members who participated in the project have expressed an interest in our focus on personalized learning. We, on the other hand, have learned from them useful techniques to foster student-centered learning. Our participation also has introduced us to new scholarship on assessment, student learning, and curricular reform, enabling us to assume some leadership in recent campus efforts to revitalize undergraduate education.

Although our approach to "The Courage to Question" looks more like research than assessment, we are pleased that we have taken this direction. It has allowed us to gain some perspective on classroom learning in women's studies that will enable us to clarify our goals both individually and collectively. Our discovery of the personalization of knowledge is not exactly new. Women's studies from the beginning has made the connection between the personal and the intellectual. What is new for us is to begin to consider what this connection means specifically for teaching and learning.

1. *Involvement in Learning: Realizing the Potential of American Higher Education* (Washington, D.C.: National Institute of Education, 1984), 17.

2. A. W. Astin, *Achieving Educational Excellence: A Critical Assessment of Priorities and Practices in Higher Education* (San Francisco: Jossey-Bass, 1985).

3. *Campus Life: In Search of Community* (Princeton: The Carnegie Foundation for the Advancement of Teaching, 1990).

4. *The Condition of the Professoriate: Attitudes and Trends* (Princeton: The Carnegie Foundation for the Advancement of Teaching, 1989).

5. E. L. Boyer, *College: The Undergraduate Experience in America* (New York: Harper and Row, 1987).

6. *A New Vitality in General Education* (Washington, D.C.: Association of American Colleges, 1988), 42.

7. *A New Vitality*, 23.

8. *The Challenge of Connecting Learning*, Liberal Learning and the Arts and Sciences Major, Vol. 1 (Washington, D.C.: Association of American Colleges, 1991).

9. M. Culley and C. Portuges, eds., *Gendered Subjects: The Dynamics of Feminist Teaching* (Boston: Routledge & Kegan Paul, 1985), 2.

10. M. Parlett and G. Dearden, eds., *Introduction to Illuminative Evaluation: Studies in Higher Education* (Cardiff-by-Sea, Calif: Pacific Sounding Press, 1977); M. Parlett and D. Hamilton, "Evaluation as Illumination: A New Approach to the Study of Innovative Programs," in *Beyond the Numbers Game*, D. Hamilton, et al., eds., (London: Macmillan, 1978), 6–22; J. P. Shapiro and B. Reed, "Illuminative Evaluation: Meeting the Special Needs of Feminist Projects," in *Humanity and Society* (November 1984): 432–41; M. A. Trow, "Methodological Problems in the Evaluation of Innovation," in M. C. Wittrock and E. E. Wiley, eds., *The Evaluation of Instruction* (New York: Holt, Rinehart and Winston, 1970), 289–305.

11. M. Parlett and D. Hamilton, "Evaluation as Illumination: A New Approach to the Study of Innovative Programs," in D. Hamilton et al, eds., *Beyond the Numbers Game* (London: Macmillan, 1978), 6–22, 17.

12. Ibid, 18.

13. Martin Bickman, "Active Learning in the University: An Inquiry into Inquiry," in Mary Ann Shea, ed., *On Teaching*, Vol. 1 (Boulder: The University of Colorado Faculty Teaching Excellence Program, 1987): 31–66.

14. L. Lee Knefelkamp, *Developmental Instruction: Fostering Intellectual and Personal Growth of Students* (Doctoral dissertation, University of Minnesota, 1974).

15. M. F. Belenky, B. M. Clinchy, N. R. Goldberger, and J. M. Tarule, *Women's Ways of Knowing* (New York: Basic Books, 1986).

STUDENT QUESTIONNAIRE
UNIVERSITY OF COLORADO

Provide three responses to each question below:

A. answer in regard to courses from your major area of study
B. answer in regard to courses from outside your major area of study
C. answer in regard to this course

1. *On the average*, how often do you miss class sessions?

	Never	Rarely	Occasionally	Frequently	Always
A.	1	2	3	4	5
B.	1	2	3	4	5
C.	1	2	3	4	5

2. What is the usual reason for missing class?

A.
B.
C.

3. How many fellow students do you usually know by name?

	None	A Few	About Half	Most	All
A.	1	2	3	4	5
B.	1	2	3	4	5
C.	1	2	3	4	5

4. How often do you meet with fellow students outside of class?

	Always	Never	Rarely	Occasionally	Frequently
A.	1	2	3	4	5
B.	1	2	3	4	5
C.	1	2	3	4	5

5. What is the usual purpose of meeting with students outside of class?

A.

B.

C.

6. How many fellow students would you say you have friendships with?

	None	A Few	About Half	Most	All
A.	1	2	3	4	5
B.	1	2	3	4	5
C.	1	2	3	4	5

7. How often do you think about or "mull over" course or course related material outside of class (other than for class preparation or for class assignments)?

	Never	Rarely	Occasionally	Frequently	Always
A.	1	2	3	4	5
B.	1	2	3	4	5
C.	1	2	3	4	5

8. How often do you discuss aspects of the course material with someone outside of class?

	Never	Rarely	Occasionally	Frequently	Always
A.	1	2	3	4	5
B.	1	2	3	4	5
C.	1	2	3	4	5

9. With whom do you generally have these discussions? (e.g., friends, mother, roommate, etc.)

A.

B.

C.

10. How often does course content motivate you to do additional reading?

	Never	Rarely	Occasionally	Frequently	Always
A.	1	2	3	4	5
B.	1	2	3	4	5
C.	1	2	3	4	5

11. How often do you find yourself getting "interested" in the course material?

	Never	Rarely	Occasionally	Frequently	Always
A.	1	2	3	4	5
B.	1	2	3	4	5
C.	1	2	3	4	5

12. How often do you find yourself getting "absorbed" in the course material?

	Never	Rarely	Occasionally	Frequently	Always
A.	1	2	3	4	5
B.	1	2	3	4	5
C.	1	2	3	4	5

13. How often does course content relate to you personally?

	Never	Rarely	Occasionally	Frequently	Always
A.	1	2	3	4	5
B.	1	2	3	4	5
C.	1	2	3	4	5

14. How often in the classroom does it feel acceptable to relate course material to your personal life?

	Never	Rarely	Occasionally	Frequently	Always
A.	1	2	3	4	5
B.	1	2	3	4	5
C.	1	2	3	4	5

15. How often do you feel "encouraged" by the instructor to relate course material to your personal life?

	Never	Rarely	Occasionally	Frequently	Always
A.	1	2	3	4	5
B.	1	2	3	4	5
C.	1	2	3	4	5

16. How often in the classroom do you verbally express a personal connection to course content?

	Never	Rarely	Occasionally	Frequently	Always
A.	1	2	3	4	5
B.	1	2	3	4	5
C.	1	2	3	4	5

17. How often does course content actually affect you or your life in some significant way?

	Never	Rarely	Occasionally	Frequently	Always
A.	1	2	3	4	5
B.	1	2	3	4	5
C.	1	2	3	4	5

18. Describe how course content has affected you or your life?
A.
B.
C.

19. In the space below or on the back, write any additional comments you might have regarding any of the question(s) in this questionnaire.

20. Age:

21.   Sex: Female/Male

22. Which one of the following race groups do you identify with and feel you belong to?
1.   American Indian
2.   Black (or Afro American)
3.   Hispanic (or Mexican American/Chicano, etc.)
4.   Asian (or Oriental)
5.   Anglo (or Caucasian)

23. How much education was completed by your parent who went to school longer?
1.   junior high
2.   high school
3.   vocational/technical
4.   college (4 year degree)
5.   graduate school (doctor, lawyer, Ph.D., etc.)

24. In which social class would you say that your family is located?
1.   lower class
2.   working class
3.   middle class

4. upper middle class
5. upper class

25. Your current student classification:
1. Freshman
2. Sophomore
3. Junior
4. Senior
5. Unclassified

26. Your academic major: _____
Second major/certificate: _____

27. If you would be willing to participate in further discussion regarding your learning experiences at the University of Colorado, please list your name, current address, and permanent address below.

LEWIS AND CLARK COLLEGE
A SINGLE CURRICULUM

BY LAURIE FINKE, ELAINE MAVEETY, CAROL SHAW, AND JEAN WARD[1]

Lewis and Clark College bases its assessment on the three questions that summarized their program goals: How effectively do
students learn and apply gender analysis? What impact, if any,
has gender studies had on the classroom and institutional climates at Lewis and Clark? And, what impact, if any, has gender
studies had on the personal growth of students and alumnae?

Since its founding as Albany Collegiate Institute in 1867, Lewis and Clark
College has been committed to an equal education for women and men
within a single curriculum. Martha Montague's centennial history of Lewis
and Clark includes a report on those early days:

> During the year 1869–1870, the student body numbered eighty-six:
> forty-three women and forty-three men. Albany always received
> women on equal terms with men, never keeping them separate in aca-
> demic work or making special rules for them, as in some neighboring
> colleges. Both were "scholars" or students, and often the scholastic
> records of the women were higher than those of the men.[2]

Today, 125 years after its founding, Lewis and Clark, a private liberal arts
college located in Portland, Oregon, remains committed to a single curriculum for the 1,850 women and men enrolled in the College of Arts and
Sciences. In 1990–91, 55 percent of these undergraduates were women and
45 percent were men. Undergraduates represented forty-five states and forty
nations, and 12 percent of these students were minorities.

THE GENDER STUDIES PROGRAM
AT LEWIS AND CLARK

In the early 1970s, Lewis and Clark offered some women's studies courses,
mainly in literature and history, and, with the assistance of faculty members,
a number of students designed interdisciplinary majors in women's studies.
Instead of establishing a formal women's studies program, however, the col-

lege sought to meet its historic commitment to "balanced exploration of the perspectives, traditions, and contributions of women and men" by integrating scholarship by and about women across the curriculum and creating an interdisciplinary minor that examined women and men in relation to one another.

Progress in curriculum integration was spurred by an intensive faculty development seminar on women's studies held in the summer of 1981 and supported by a grant from the National Endowment for the Humanities. Male and female faculty members, representing fourteen academic disciplines, studied for a month with four visiting scholars from history, psychology, anthropology, and literature. Gender studies was approved as the first interdisciplinary minor at Lewis and Clark by unanimous vote of the College of Arts and Sciences Curriculum Committee on February 20, 1985. A Gender Studies Program that spoke to all students—women and men—and addressed the intersections of gender, race, class, and culture was seen as central to the mission of the college.

The Gender Studies Program provides an interdisciplinary minor, promotes ongoing efforts to integrate scholarship by and about women and minorities across the curriculum, serves as a critical element in the core curriculum, and sponsors an annual symposium. The Gender Studies Symposium, begun in 1982, brings together Lewis and Clark students and faculty members, scholars from other institutions, and representatives from community organizations to share scholarship and concerns. A unique feature of these symposia is the full involvement of Lewis and Clark students.

WHAT IS GENDER STUDIES?

Gender studies is an interdisciplinary field that examines the biological, social, and cultural constructions of femininity and masculinity, as well as the ways women and men locate themselves within gender systems. Gender defines relationships among women, among men, and between men and women. Interacting with factors such as race, class, and culture, gender studies examines the relationships between biological differences and social inequality, explores the construction of sexual identity, and analyzes the variations in gender systems that have occurred across cultures and over time. It also illuminates the images of femininity and masculinity that shape cultural representations and explores the similarities and differences in women's and men's communication and artistic expression. Finally, gender studies involves the political and philosophical exploration of strategies for change that can transform coercive and unequal gender systems and enhance both individual choice and our common humanity.

The gender studies minor at Lewis and Clark consists of a minimum of six courses (thirty quarter hours): four required courses and two electives drawn from a list of over fifty approved electives offered by eighteen departments. The four required courses include: GS 231, "Gender in Cross-Cultural Perspective" (formerly GS 210, "The Social and Cultural Construction of Gender"); GS 300, "Gender and Aesthetic Expression"; GS 310, "Sex Differences and Social Inequality"; and GS 440, "Feminist Theory." GS 200, "Women and Men in American Society," is an introductory course but is not required for the minor.

The gender studies minor differs in several ways from Lewis and Clark's ongoing efforts to integrate gender across the curriculum. Integrating gender issues is not the same as focusing on them. A gender-balanced course, for example, might include the experiences, perspectives, and voices of women, as well as men, without making the similarities and differences between them the central question; the primary focus of a gender-balanced course might be a historical or literary problem, of which gender is but one dimension. Although there is heuristic value in approaching any inquiry with the assumption that gender and culture matter, to be aware of these dimensions of inquiry is not the same as undertaking a systematic investigation of the differences that gender makes.

KEY QUESTIONS

Participation in "The Courage to Question" has been timely for Lewis and Clark. After six years of experience with a gender studies minor and a decade of curriculum integration efforts and annual Gender Studies symposia, we welcomed the opportunity to pause and focus on student learning. Three key questions that summarized our program goals (see page 78) and informed our study are:

☐ How effectively do our students learn and apply gender analysis?

☐ What impact, if any, has gender studies had on the classroom and institutional climates at Lewis and Clark?

☐ What impact, if any, has gender studies had on the personal growth of students and alumnae(i)?

METHODOLOGY

Throughout the process of data collection, data analysis, and writing this report, four of us—one student, one staff member, and two faculty members/administrators—have worked collaboratively as a team and brought different disciplinary perspectives to our work (see note 1). For our study, we relied on three significant data collections: questionnaires, student papers and projects, and selected course syllabi. In addition, we relied on previously collected materials, such as computer conversations, symposium papers and programs, student journals and diaries, student honors projects, and practica reports.

QUESTIONNAIRES
Anonymous questionnaires distributed to students, faculty members, and alumnae(i) in 1990–91 provided both quantitative and qualitative data about the Gender Studies Program, including student learning, integration efforts, and personal growth. For student questionnaires, we used random sampling, stratified by distribution of majors. Respondents, whose ages ranged from eighteen to forty-six, represented twenty-one named majors and twenty minors. Faculty questionnaires were sent to all undergraduate teaching faculty members; alumnae(i) questionnaires were mailed to all alumnae(i) who had participated in the gender symposia over the past five years and for whom we could obtain mailing addresses. A total of 210 questionnaires were returned and analyzed: 145 student questionnaires (41 percent males and 59 percent females), 41 faculty questionnaires, and 24 alumnae(i) questionnaires. These questionnaires reflect an unusually high return rate of 48 percent for students and alumnae(i) and 46 percent for faculty members.

PAPERS AND PROJECTS
To gain information about students' gender analysis (knowledge base and learning skills), we collected and analyzed sets of papers and projects from three gender studies classes (five sections). Where possible, longitudinal materials, including journals, were used. Papers and projects were collected from two courses required for the gender studies minor and one elective gender studies course.

As a comparison with students' gender analysis in gender studies classes and to gain information about curriculum integration of gender issues, sets of student papers were collected and analyzed from fall term 1991 core curriculum courses: "Basic Inquiry," "Critical Inquiry," and "Advanced Inquiry." For the "Basic Inquiry" classes, longitudinal information was obtained through examination of first and last portfolios written during the term. A scoring sheet (see pages 80–81) was developed for knowledge base and learning skills. All student work was scored independently by two readers and by a third if there were disagreement.

SYLLABI FROM DISCIPLINE-BASED, NON-GENDER STUDIES CLASSES

To obtain more information about curriculum integration efforts, we began with a list of more than one hundred courses generated by the student questionnaires. We were interested in courses that were neither required nor elective gender studies courses but that students claimed incorporated a gender perspective. We then selected twenty courses from the student-generated list, divided proportionately among the three divisions of the College of Arts and Sciences (humanities and fine arts, mathematics and natural sciences, and social sciences) and between male and female professors, and requested syllabi and course materials to assess gender content.

As was the case for student papers and projects, all syllabi were scored independently by two readers and by a third if there were any disagreement between the first two readers. The evaluation system used for curriculum integration was adapted from Mary Kay Thompson Tetreault's "feminist phase theory."[3]

PERSONAL GROWTH DATA

Finally, to assess students' personal growth in the Gender Studies Program, we turned to student and alumnae(i) questionnaires. Qualitative analysis of questionnaire comments and narrative statements complemented our quantitative analysis of questionnaires and revealed a number of personal growth themes.

KNOWLEDGE BASE AND LEARNING SKILLS

When asked on the questionnaire to rate their overall learning in required gender studies courses on a scale of 1 to 5—with a 1 being poor and 5 being excellent—students rated their courses at 4.4, while alumnae(i) who had taken one or more required courses rated their learning at 4.7. Of students who had taken required gender studies courses (N=42), seven said these courses were the most intellectually challenging courses they had taken. One sophomore international affairs major wrote that the program is "one of the most academic, theoretical, and demanding. Something that is lacking in most departments."

To answer our first key question, we needed to determine what knowledge and skills students were learning that enabled them to analyze gender effectively. To confirm students' self-reporting, we developed a system of coding for student portfolios, papers, and journals. Our articulation of our knowledge

While we recognize that feminism, and hence feminist teaching, is ideological and even political, we also contend that it is no more so than other so-called "objective" and "apolitical" teaching

---

base had to include the first five goals listed in the Gender Studies Program Goals (see page 78). While knowledge about gender is potentially limitless, we can articulate at least a provisional structure of knowledge.

Feminist inquiry is at the core of knowledge in gender studies. We do not see gender studies as a retreat from a commitment to feminism either as a political or an intellectual movement. While we recognize that feminism, and hence feminist teaching, is ideological and even political, we also contend that it is no more so than other so-called "objective" and "apolitical" teaching. Indeed, it is the goal of feminist inquiry to expose the political agendas that lurk behind inquiry in the sciences, social sciences, arts, and humanities. Furthermore, since feminism has been an intellectual, social, and political movement for almost two centuries, it is a legitimate area of inquiry in and of itself.

Therefore, we want our students minimally to understand feminism both historically and theoretically. This is a major content area, the foundation of the knowledge base of gender studies that grounds other areas of inquiry within the field. As one student, a senior in "Feminist Theory," put it:

> Women are not born inherently submissive, inferior objects. Society teaches these roles. It is the goal of feminist theorists to bring this fact of socially constructed roles into direct scrutiny, and attempt to clarify their destructive force, eliminate them and thus change the world.

KNOWLEDGE BASE PLOTS

> [A] good course, like a novel, has a plot, or an underlying framework which gives coherence to the more specific detail.[4]

To make some sense of the boundless content of gender inquiry, we had to construct a flexible scheme to give coherence to the knowledge base of our Gender Studies Program. We were inspired by the remarks above by Barrie Thorne, Cheris Kramarae, and Nancy Henley that the structure of knowledge resembles the narrative plot of a good book. Following an idea suggested in a 1986 essay by Paula Treichler, we defined eight basic "plots," or narratives, which represent current intellectual activity in gender studies.[5] We adapted Treichler's "plots" to create an underlying framework for the knowledge base of gender studies. Those eight plots are:

☐ *The politics of sex/gender*: Who benefits from a social and political construction that subjugates women? What social and political relations exist and have existed between men and women, among women, and between women and other disempowered members of society? How do the oppressions built into a given social structure relate to economic, political, and sexual practices? What kinds of analyses and activism are needed to bring an end to the subjugation of women?

☐ *Cultural images of sex/gender*: How is gender represented in both high and mass culture? How do words, images, and patterns of discourse intersect to construct our notions of femininity and masculinity? How are these systems of representation linked to cultural "facts" and internalized as cultural knowledge? How do those oppressed by such representations create more empowering representations?

☐ *Nature/nurture*: Are there any foundational biological differences between the two sexes or are all differences socially constructed? Are there any biological differences between heterosexuality and homosexuality or have these differences been socially constructed? What difference does it make if we ask why people become heterosexual rather than why they become homosexual?

☐ *Diversity*: The category "woman" cannot erase the differences among individual women's lives. What are the relationships of other social differences— which include but are not limited to class, race, ethnicity, sexual preference, age—to gender?

☐ *The body*: How do both men and women understand their embodiedness differently? How can we describe and interpret female sexuality on its own terms and in relation to male sexuality? How do scientific theories of the nature of female sexuality reflect and construct social, economic, religious, and medical policies and practices?

☐ *Communication*: What does it mean to say that language is patriarchal? Through what processes do women learn to use language? Do they have equal access to linguistic resources? How are women represented within the symbolic order? How do women make meaning? By whose authority are particular meanings "authorized"?

☐ *Interpersonal relationships*: This plot examines the structuring, maintenance, and termination of dyadic, family, and work relationships and other small group interactions. How do socially constructed gender roles contribute to the dynamics of relationships? What are the dynamics involved in dysfunctional relationships?

☐ *Women's creation of knowledge*: How have women contributed throughout the disciplines to the creation of knowledge? How does the inclusion of women in all disciplines change the ways in which those disciplines constitute knowledge?

Students must grasp…the social and political
relations that exist between men and women…
before they can begin to articulate possibilities
for change

DISCUSSION
When we devised our system of eight "plots" to describe the knowledge base
of gender studies, we had assumed that these plots were more or less equal and
accessible to all students at every level. Therefore, the presence or absence of
a plot would tell us whether or not those cultural narratives were being effectively taught. We expected that students given a choice of topics for research
and writing would distribute themselves across this range of potential narratives. The results of our scoring, however, prompted us to rethink this assumption (see Table 1). (The courses referred to are Gender Studies 200, "Men and
Women in American Society"; Gender Studies 300, "Gender and Aesthetic
Expression"; and Gender Studies 440, "Feminist Theory.") One unexpected
outcome was that student papers clustered around the first four plots. This
finding was corroborated by the results from the non-gender studies inquiry
courses (see Table 2) in which, once again, the first plot (politics) and the
fourth (diversity) were heavily represented.

TABLE 1: KNOWLEDGE BASE IN GENDER STUDIES COURSES

Plots	GS 200	GS 300	GS 440	Totals
politics	11	8	9	28
cultural images	2	18	10	30
nature/nurture	7	0	3	10
diversity	4	0	8	12
body	2	1	1	4
communication	1	4	2	7
interpersonal relationships	6	0	3	9
women's creation of knowledge	0	3	8	11

TABLE 2: KNOWLEDGE BASE
IN NON-GENDER STUDIES INQUIRY COURSES

Plots	Basic Inquiry	Critical Inquiry	Advanced Inquiry	Totals
politics	2	2	18	22
cultural images	2	5	0	7
nature/nurture	0	0	2	2
diversity	31	7	14	52
body	0	1	0	1
communication	3	0	0	3
interpersonal relationships	3	0	0	3
women's creation of knowledge	2	0	0	2

Our results suggest that knowledge in gender studies is not chaotic or random. Certain key concepts precede others, laying foundations for other narratives. While limitations on space prohibit a detailed discussion of the results for each plot, certain patterns emerge from the data. The first four plots—the politics of sex/gender, cultural images of sex/gender, nature/nurture, and diversity—seem to be both more general and perhaps more basic than the last four. In GS 200 ("Men and Women in American Society"), the ratio between the first four and last four plots is twenty-four to nine; one of the first four plots was almost three times more likely to show up than the last four. In GS 300, the ratio is 26 to 8; in GS 440, 30 to 14. By the time students reach GS 440 ("Feminist Theory"), the ratio has dropped to 2 to 1. In the non-gender studies inquiry courses, the disparity is much more pronounced: eighty-three to nine, which means that in inquiry courses the first four plots are nine times more likely to show up than the last four.

Our results suggest that students need to feel comfortable with the first four plots before they are ready to move on to the final four plots. Students must grasp the political ramifications of gender inequality, the social and political relations that exist between men and women, and the oppressions built into social structures, before they can begin to articulate possibilities for change. It makes sense that students would move from an analysis of sexual inequality to explore the cultural images that create and reinforce that inequality, and then to question whether or not such inequalities are natural or

Students ought to move from a position in which
they are repeating knowledge to one in which
they are producing knowledge

socially created. The frequency of the diversity plot in non-gender studies
inquiry courses may suggest that the integration of gender into the core curriculum at Lewis and Clark is being accompanied by at least some consciousness of the importance of race and class as complementary categories of analysis. It also suggests that students might come to understand gender as a
social issue by first understanding other kinds of inequalities, primarily racial
inequalities. The politics of diversity—racial, class, and sexual—may provide
yet another "gateway" into gender studies.

The virtual absence of the final four plots in non-gender studies inquiry
courses is perhaps the most telling finding, suggesting that these topics may
not be fully covered anywhere in the curriculum outside of gender studies
classes. Taken together, these findings suggest that integrating gender into
the disciplines in itself is not sufficient remedy to women's past exclusion
from the academy. The focus on certain issues—the body and sexuality, gender and communication, interpersonal relationships, and most importantly
women's creation of knowledge—may require the kind of focus only a gender
studies minor allows.

LEARNING SKILLS
Our second task in answering the first key question was to determine what
learning skills we hoped students would acquire in gender studies courses.
After considerable discussion, the following six learning skills emerged:

☐ *Analyzing gender as a social construct.* Students should not only understand
that gender is socially constructed but should be able to analyze the implications of that assertion as well. They should understand that masculinity and
femininity are relational and not essential qualities which can simply be la-
belled as either "good" or "bad."

☐ *Questioning the adequacy of traditional form.* Since the traditional academic
essay, with its stance of distanced objectivity, does not encourage self-
revelation, students ought to understand and question the relationships between form and content in their own and others' writing. They ought to experiment with forms beyond the traditional academic essay, including (but
not limited to) poetry, epistolary, or journal writing—forms that reveal more
directly the situatedness of knowledge (see below).[6]

☐ *Establishing positionality.* Students should become increasingly aware of
what we might call their own positionality in relation to knowledge about
gender. Positionality is the point at which intellectual curiosity becomes
personal engagement with the material studied, often experienced by the

student as a sense of self-awareness or sudden epiphany. We see this move-ment most strikingly recorded in student experiments with nontraditional forms of writing once the student has become aware that his or her experi-ence may contribute to the ongoing knowledge that constitutes the study of gender. The student is no longer objectively reiterating the history of gender relations but has become a contributor. This personal engagement, once ar-ticulated, moves the student toward a recognition of agency and the ability to produce rather than repeat knowledge.

☐ *Recognizing agency as well as oppression.* Students in gender studies courses should move from an analysis of power, oppression, and victimization to one that accounts for the agency of all oppressed peoples.

☐ *Producing rather than repeating knowledge.* In keeping with our notion that knowledge in gender studies is without boundaries, students ought to move from a position in which they are repeating knowledge to one in which they are producing knowledge.

☐ *Understanding the social construction of knowledge.* Students ought to move from the specific analyses of the various "plots" to a meta-analysis of how knowledge is socially constructed and not simply "there" to be discovered.

Unlike the knowledge-base plots, learning skills were rated on a 5-point scale with 1 being the weakest and 5 the strongest. If a reader saw no evi-dence of a particular skill, it was not scored. We scored essays from the same three gender studies courses and, for comparison, the same set of non-gender studies inquiry courses. The results of scoring for learning skills are recorded in Tables 3, 4, and 5.

TABLE 3: LEARNING SKILLS IN GENDER STUDIES COURSES

Skill	GS 200	GS 300	GS 440	Average
social construction of gender	3.3	4.0	4.0	3.8
form	0.8	2.3	0.8	1.1
positionality	1.3	1.6	1.6	1.5
agency	1.6	2.5	2.2	2.1
producing knowledge	1.3	2.5	2.1	1.5
social construction of knowledge	0.0	2.2	3.1	1.8

TABLE 4: LEARNING SKILLS IN CRITICAL
AND ADVANCED INQUIRY COURSES

Skill	Critical Inquiry	Adv. Inquiry	Average
social construction of gender	1.8	0.73	1.27
form	0.11	0.5	0.31
positionality	0.25	1.26	0.76
agency	1.19	0.86	1.03
producing knowledge	0.0	0.4	0.2
social construction of knowledge	1.47	1.18	1.33

TABLE 5: LEARNING SKILLS FOR BASIC INQUIRY PORTFOLIOS

Skill	A1	A2	B1	B2	C1	C2	Avg
social construction of gender	0.07	0.0	0.09	0.47	0.0	0.0	0.11
form	0.0	0.0	1.84	1.3	2.8	2.4	1.39
positionality	0.07	0.64	1.69	1.77	2.7	1.8	1.45
agency	0.0	0.14	0.38	0.5	0.0	0.0	0.17
producing knowledge	0.0	0.0	0.0	0.43	0.28	0.22	0.16
social construction of knowledge	0.0	0.0	0.0	0.33	0.11	0.05	0.08

Looking at learning skills in related clusters suggests the ways in which students build on previously acquired skills. Cluster One includes only the understanding that gender is socially constructed. Cluster Two includes experimentation with traditional form as a vehicle for understanding the knower's positionality. Cluster Three (recognizing agency, producing rather than repeating knowledge, and the understanding of the social construction of knowledge) is an interrelated third cluster that leads toward a greater integration of self-knowledge within a wider social context.

☐ *Cluster 1*: The results indicate that the skill students in gender studies courses learn most effectively is the social construction of gender, suggesting that this skill may be foundational. The results confirm many student responses on the questionnaires that ranked the social construction of gender and/or sexuality as their most significant learning experience. For instance, a female political science major who had taken two required courses wrote, "To be frank, when I first came to L&C and enrolled in the Social and Cultural Construction of Gender [GS 210], I thought there were *huge* biological differences between men and women. I wouldn't have articulated that but, deep down, I didn't move beyond that social construction until taking a gender course." Students in gender studies courses are much more likely to understand and write about the implications of gender as a social construct than students in non-gender studies courses, perhaps another indication of the differences between gender integration and gender focus.

☐ *Cluster 2*: A second cluster of skills, which also might be characterized as a part of the foundation of gender studies, includes form and positionality. Gender studies courses scored somewhat higher on these two skills in comparison with most non-gender studies courses. Gender studies courses averaged 1.1 on experimentation with form and 1.5 on positionality—with GS 200, as we would expect, the lowest on both skills. The results compare, however, with an average in "Basic Inquiry" classes of 1.39 for experimentation with form and 1.45 on positionality. This finding might suggest that BI is at least as successful in introducing these skills as any gender studies course but that these skills are not reinforced in other parts of the core curriculum. BI introduces students to thinking and writing by encouraging them to experiment with different forms of writing. In addition, BI portfolios often rated high on positionality because, once again, the course asked them to think about themselves in relation to the knowledge they were acquiring.

Unlike the BI portfolios, which show student development in thinking and writing over time, the gender studies papers we looked at can only give us a snapshot of a student's learning at a particular moment. Because most of the papers we scored—with the exception of BI portfolios—were responses to fairly traditional assignments, it was difficult for students to demonstrate experimentation with nontraditional form and even, in many cases, positionality. With the exception of GS 300 (which is a course about aesthetic form), experimentation with form did not seem to be a major concern in these papers. There are, however, other places in which students in gender studies courses are encouraged to experiment with form and to write about their own epiphanies. Most gender studies courses require some combination of journals, diaries, daily logs, computer conversations, and reflective and exploratory writing—material reviewed but not scored for this study. This nontraditional writing contributed significantly to the outcomes of the papers we did score. Here we run up against the limits of the quantitative method we chose. The data from the questionnaires and from informal student writing tell us that students in gender studies courses experience all sorts of connections, clicks, epiphanies and the like, but because we did not score the kinds of writing in which they are revealed, we must turn to a more textured qualitative analysis as evidence for those skills.

A representative illustration demonstrates the powerful longitudinal self-discovery our students claim gender studies promotes. This example comes from the journal of a male student who took "Communication and Gender," which serves as a gender studies elective. At the beginning of his notebook, this student writes that some of the authors of course readings have "chips on their shoulders" and offend and anger their readers. He goes on to say, "So I have some problems trying to understand and deal with all of the 'complaining,' as I think of it, that women are doing these days." At the beginning, he does not see the relevance of the examples given by the authors in support of their arguments. He says, "Who is coming up with all of this? It kind of comes across like these people are of a communist type of thinking." He believes that there really is no cause for change and that "women see only what they want to see." Later on, this student becomes less defensive, yet he still says, "I don't see the male sex as ever changing." Furthermore, he does not see anything wrong with using generic terms such as "he" or "man."

However, he begins to see that "culture has a big effect on the roles of men and women and their conversational differences." His comments about an incident he saw on ESPN reveal his growing awareness of how certain off-hand comments can affect others who hear them. He even begins to value so-called feminine traits and says that homophobia and expectations of "masculine" behavior stand in the way of gender communication. He becomes aware that socialization influences gender ideals and communication. Finally he says, "Bate describes what feminism is and what it wants to accomplish. I have been kind of vague about what feminism is, but this chapter has helped me develop a much better understanding of the actions and goals of the movement." Perhaps the most remarkable feature of this student's development is the movement from vague assertions and attacks—"Who is coming up with all this?"—to specific analyses of readings which have particular authors, "Bate describes what feminism is." Not only has this student begun to understand what the social construction of gender means in his own

life, he has begun to engage intellectually with the material as well. This
same student is currently enrolled in a second gender studies course.

☐ *Cluster 3*: The second cluster of skills focuses on students' abilities to see
the relationships between knowledge about gender and their personal lives, a
connection that turned up repeatedly in our questionnaires as one of central
importance. The next level of learning skills would involve integrating this
newfound personal engagement with a wider social context of which the self
is a part. This stage involves the integration of intellectual knowledge and
political activism for change.

Students' understanding of the agency of the oppressed tended to be
lower than we might have hoped, particularly in the upper-level courses.
Gender studies courses on the whole, however, did better than non-gender
studies courses on this skill, suggesting that students in gender studies courses
are more likely than students in other classes to be able to move from an
analysis of oppression and victimization to an understanding of how oppression is resisted.

Students in gender studies courses, especially in upper-level courses,
scored consistently higher on the fifth learning skill—producing rather than
repeating knowledge. This is perhaps because students do not see knowledge
as isolated and fragmentary. Instead, again and again, they remark that their
understanding of gender connects the various parts of their lives and education.

Deciphering the social construction of knowledge may be the most difficult of all the skills to acquire. Not surprisingly, it was not addressed in GS
200, the introductory course, but received the highest score in the upper-level courses, particularly GS 440, a course that investigates the social construction of knowledge. Non-gender studies courses consistently scored lower
than equivalent gender studies courses, a finding that puzzled us since the
goal of understanding knowledge as socially constructed is not unique to gender studies. However, our findings suggest that feminist inquiry may be more
committed than other nontraditional pedagogies to a social constructionist
perspective.

CONCLUSIONS

The first and most significant conclusion from the data is that there is a crucial difference between the integration of gender into the curriculum and the
kind of systematic investigation of gender that the minor allows. The in-
depth inquiry into gender as a system allows for an analysis of issues that a

We hope that our discoveries suggest not a rigid
and hierarchical curriculum, not a *typography*, but
a *topography*, or a map, that might help students
find their way around in the field

---

course which is gender-balanced but not gender-focused usually cannot
achieve because the students have not yet grasped the key assumptions on
which gender studies is based. Without such a basis, students will be impeded
in their discussions of, say, sexuality or language and gender because they will
be struggling to understand the politics of the issue. All of the non-gender
studies inquiry courses we examined were relatively gender-balanced. Yet the
relative infrequency of the final four plots and the low scores on the last cluster of skills in non-gender studies courses suggest that students acquire some
knowledge and skills from gender-focused courses that they cannot acquire
from even the most well-integrated non-gender studies courses.

A second conclusion we might draw from these data is that the sequence
of courses in our minor is well designed to lay the groundwork required for
students to advance to more in-depth and critical analysis of gender. The
elective introductory course, GS 200, focuses primarily on the politics of
sex/gender while introducing elements of the next three plots—cultural images, nature/nurture, and diversity. While in the past elements of the last four
plots have been included in the course, our results might suggest that this is
not necessarily a good idea. We might do better using the course to integrate
the first four plots more fully. In addition, this course is the place to work on
the development of the first two clusters. Faculty members designing this
course in the future may want to think more about how writing in the course
can be designed to enable students to track discoveries about themselves more
fully and to experiment with a greater variety of writing forms.

We do not mean to suggest that students encountering this model of
knowledge base and learning skills must move through it in a lockstep fash-
ion. Indeed, that is hardly ever the case at Lewis and Clark College, where
students often do not take courses in sequence. Students enter gender studies
courses at several points in the curriculum and for very different reasons. We
hope that our discoveries suggest not a rigid and hierarchical curriculum, not
a *typography*, but a *topography*, or a map, that might help students find their
way around in the field, allowing movement in a variety of directions but
still enabling students to forge connections and to build on previously acquired knowledge and skills.

INSTITUTIONAL CLIMATE

There is support for being a man [at Lewis and Clark].
MALE, HEALTH AND ECONOMICS, JUNIOR

Lewis and Clark is a comparatively safe and supportive place to be a woman.
FEMALE, ENGLISH, SENIOR

[The Gender Studies Program] defines L&C as a safe place for people, where they can express their gender as they see fit.
FEMALE, ENGLISH/COMMUNICATIONS, JUNIOR

To assess the impact of gender studies on classroom and institutional climates at Lewis and Clark, we looked at three areas: 1) efforts to integrate gender analysis into disciplinary and interdisciplinary courses; 2) whether or not there is such a thing as feminist pedagogy and if so whether it has been integrated into the institutional culture; and 3) the effectiveness of the Gender Studies Symposium as a means of integration and connected learning for our students. Due to space constraints and a focus on pedagogy by other reporting institutions, we will not report here the results of our study in that area.

The qualitative evidence from our questionnaire demonstrates that students perceive that the Gender Studies Program has a significant impact on the institutional climate. A transfer student describes the impact as "profound": "[the Gender Studies Program] is why I transferred here.... I know many people for whom it has been transformative.... Also, because gender is put on the line here, I feel more comfortable dealing with my professors openly on the issue as well as bringing it into class.... Each class (even outside Gender Studies) heightens my awareness about these issues.... L&C seems to be a safe atmosphere for women to speak out and not worry about being disregarded. Although I'm sure it's not perfect...I feel that in comparison to other schools I've attended, L&C is a 'gender haven'."

Even relatively new students notice an institutional climate that permeates the classroom. At the end of her first year, an eighteen-year-old who had taken no gender classes reported these observations: "One thing I have noticed at Lewis and Clark is that all professors, from sociology to physics, are aware of their language as it applies to gender. This awareness is perpetuated and enforced by students who will stop a professor or another student if s/he says something inappropriate.... [E]very male should be required to attend Lewis and Clark for a year.

Men here cannot get away with slander against women commonly used by men
at other schools."

CURRICULUM INTEGRATION:
COURSE SYLLABI EVALUATION
Students singled out integration of gender in non-gender studies courses as a
significant dimension of their educational experience. When asked on the
questionnaire to rate their overall learning in other general college curriculum courses that included a focus on gender issues, the average student rating
was 4.3. Most of these students commented in positive terms about their experiences in these courses, placing them into the categories of "excellent/
best/favorite/good/better/more interesting/more personal/more challeng-
ing/more discussion-oriented/more diversity of issues/more student participation." Typical comments were: "They were more interesting and intellectually stimulating than most" and "Better than average. Generally more
thorough, thoughtful, and demanding."

To document this student assessment of gender integration across the curriculum at Lewis and Clark, we took the list of courses students identified in
the questionnaire as having a gender focus and eliminated those which were
either required or elective courses for the gender studies minor. We were left
with eighty-one courses which students claimed incorporated a gender perspective. The distribution among the three college divisions was remarkably uneven. In Fine Arts and Humanities there were forty-seven courses named; in
Social Sciences, twenty-seven; and in Natural Sciences, only seven.

We were surprised, however—even astonished—by the number of courses on this list and the diversity of course titles. A focus on gender issues in
"Labor Economics"? "Europe in Crisis"? "Old Testament"? To examine the issue more thoroughly, we chose twenty of these courses, divided among the
three divisions and between male and female professors (see page 79). Using
an adaptation of Mary Kay Thompson Tetreault's "feminist phase theory," we
scored syllabi and course materials for curriculum integration.

Based upon our evaluation of syllabi and course materials submitted,
each course received a numerical score for its stage of curriculum integration,
according to the following scale:
☐ 0: *Women Invisible*. Who are the truly great actors/thinkers in history? At
this stage, they are overwhelmingly, perhaps exclusively, male, white, and
European. The need to maintain "standards of excellence" is stressed either
through a "back to basics" core curriculum or through an emphasis on up-

holding the great Western tradition.

☐ *1: The Search for Missing Women.* Who were the great women, the female Shakespeares, Napoleons, Darwins? At this stage, new data about women are added to the conventional paradigms of knowledge in the disciplines as a kind of affirmative action program. You would expect to see "exceptional women" on the syllabus or as subjects of student writing.

☐ *2: Women as Disadvantaged, Subordinate Group.* Why are there so few great women thinkers/actors? Why are women's contributions devalued? The incentive at this phase might be anger or a desire for social justice. At this stage, one is protesting the existing paradigms but within the perspective of the dominant group. Here we would include "images of women" courses, women in politics, the beginnings of women-focused courses.

☐ *3: Women as Agents/Actors.* What were/are women's experiences? What are the differences among women? Here we expect inquiry to take place outside existing disciplinary paradigms, challenging the dominant perspective. Women-focused courses would predominate, along with interdisciplinary or discipline-challenging courses. Links with ethnic and cross-cultural studies are explored.

☐ *4: Women's Experiences as Epistemological Challenge to Disciplines.* How valid are current definitions of historical periods, greatness, norms for behavior? How must our questions change to account for women's experience, diversity, and difference?

☐ *5: Transformed, Gender-Balanced Curriculum.* How can both women's and men's experience be understood together, in relation to each other? How do class, race, sexual preference, and age intersect with gender? This course would present an inclusive vision of human experience, which would seek to transform paradigms of knowledge and reconceptualize the "core curriculum."

Our analysis of syllabi is confirmed the students' perceptions about gender focus in the courses they had identified. Table 6 shows our findings on stages of gender integration listed by division.

TABLE 6: AVERAGE STAGE OF CURRICULUM INTEGRATION,
BY DIVISION

Division	No. of Courses Evaluated	Average Stage of Curriculum Integration
Arts & Humanities	9	3.6
Social Science	9	3.2
Natural Science	2	3.5

TABLE 7: TOTAL COURSES IN EACH CURRICULUM STAGE (N=20)

Stage	0	1	2	3	4	5
No. of Courses	None	None	2	12	2	4

The average stage of curriculum integration for all twenty courses ana-lyzed in the three divisions was 3.4. In no case did we identify a syllabus that scored lower than 2 on the scale. Although we had expected to find some de-gree of gender integration in these course syllabi, we were pleased by the depth of integration which emerged from this analysis. It is worth pointing out, however, that in the natural science division we scored only two of the seven courses named, so that the average score of 3.5 for the natural sciences may be skewed. The fact that out of eighty-one courses only seven named by students as being gender balanced were from this division suggests that con-tinued curriculum integration is necessary for mathematics and the natural sciences.

CURRICULUM INTEGRATION:
STUDENT INQUIRY PAPER EVALUATION
To add another dimension to our analysis, we scored a collection of student papers from five core curriculum inquiry courses using the same integration stage scale developed for the course syllabi above. We found that student pa-pers scored consistently lower than course syllabi (see Table 8).

TABLE 8: GENDER INTEGRATION IN CRITICAL
AND ADVANCED INQUIRY PAPERS

Integration Stages	Critical Inquiry	Advanced Inquiry
0-Women Invisible	2	0
1-Search for Missing Women	0	9
2-Women as Disadvantaged	4	6
3-Women as Agents	0	1
4-Epistemological Challenge	10	1
5-Balanced Curriculum	2	2
Average Integration	3.22	2.0

Papers from the critical inquiry course showed an average of stage 3 on the integration scale, with most of the papers clustered at stage 4. The syllabus for this course was at stage 5. In the advanced inquiry course, papers were predominantly clustered at stages 1 and 2, while the course syllabus scored at stage 3 of integration.

One conclusion we can draw from this analysis is that it again points to the difference between courses with a gender focus and those which are gender integrated. While an integrated course may contain a gender-balanced presentation in its course materials, it will contain many other agendas as well. When students choose paper topics, gender is only one of many possibilities for further exploration. In a course with a gender focus, however, students cannot ignore the issue of gender.

Having looked at course syllabi and student papers in some core curriculum courses, we moved to consideration of longitudinal effects by scoring the first and final portfolios from three sections of "Basic Inquiry" using the integration stage scale. By the end of the term, all three sections gained approximately a percentage point in integration, although variation across sections occurred. This finding suggests significant longitudinal growth for first-year students across their first term. In the initial portfolios, women were invisible in nineteen cases; by the end of the term, there were no portfolios in this category.

Table 9 shows the average gender integration scores for each section's portfolios.

TABLE 9: GENDER INTEGRATION IN BASIC INQUIRY
SECTIONS A, B, AND C

Average Integration Score	1st Portfolio	2nd Portfolio	Longitudinal Gain
Section A	.29	1.7	1.41
Section B	1.13	2.0	.87
Section C	.55	1.3	.75

In summary, we concluded that the strength of gender integration in non-gender studies courses confirms the observations of the sophomore who told us on the questionnaire: "I've not taken a gender studies course, but I've been exposed to gender issues through other classes. My time commitments to my major and minor don't allow for elective gender classes, so I'm truly glad and appreciative of the focus that gender receives in my other classes."

INTEGRATION: THE GENDER STUDIES SYMPOSIUM
In 1982, the first Lewis and Clark Gender Studies Symposium was composed of one community presentation and papers by two Lewis and Clark faculty members and one student. It has grown each year. Table 10 shows the growth in symposium presenters over the last ten years.

TABLE 10: NUMBERS OF PRESENTERS AT GENDER STUDIES SYMPOSIA

Year	LC faculty	LC students	Community	Other
1982	2	1	1	1
1983	4	4	0	2
1984	13	13	0	14
1985	4	42	5	25
1986	9	40	0	21
1987	8	28	4	10
1988	23	40	17	10
1989	17	53+	4	13
1990	17	50+	26	4
1991	25	100+	16	23

In 1991, our tenth year, attendance and participation set all-time records. The symposium had a total of fifty-three events spread over four days. Attendance at the three keynote addresses by Gerda Lerner, John

Stoltenberg, and Carter Heyward ranged from five hundred to seven hundred people per evening. Attendance at the panels and workshops throughout the four days was also very high, occasionally "standing room only." The range for panel attendance was from a minimum of thirty-five to a maximum of two hundred fifty, with an average of seventy-five to eighty for panels, theatre performances, and workshops.

We do not know of another annual symposium where student papers are presented with those of faculty members and visiting scholars. During the 1991 Gender Studies Symposium, more than one hundred Lewis and Clark students presented scholarly papers, read original poetry or fiction, exhibited artwork, or participated in theatre productions. This is in addition to the students who moderated panels or introduced speakers and the members of the planning committee who worked behind the scenes in many capacities, including hosting keynote speakers and Fulbright scholars. In addition to the number of students who are actively involved in planning the symposium and presenting their work, many students receive their initial "introduction" to the discussion of gender issues through attendance at symposium events. Many faculty members integrate symposium sessions into their syllabi.

We hoped to learn whether the symposium is reaching the general college population in any significant ways or if it merely "preaches to the choir." Of the 145 students responding to our questionnaire, 109 had attended one or more symposia, and 42 of these students had taken at least one required gender studies core course. When asked, "What was the effect of symposium attendance on your understanding of issues of gender, race, and class?" the average rating from those who attended was 4.2 on a scale of 1 to 5. The twenty-four alumnae(i) respondents rated their learning in the symposia at 4.3. In describing their participation in the symposium, students frequently used adjectives such as "challenging," "revolutionary," "inspiring," "excellent," "amazing," "transforming," "informative," "educational," and "empowering."

Twenty-one students had been symposium planners, presenters, or moderators and rated their learning experience at 4.6. Symposium presenters scored their learning the highest, illustrating their stronger sense of learning through the experience of direct involvement. They commented: "I spoke on campus attitudes regarding rape.... It seemed to define my position as a feminist more clearly for me. I was very glad that I spoke. I learned a lot about my feelings on the issues." "Being asked to present my paper and doing it was frightening and exhilarating as a woman afraid of public speaking."

Of the students who had taken no required gender studies courses, seventy-three had attended at least one symposium, and five had participated in presenting, planning, or moderating. Clearly, the symposium attracts students who are not enrolled in gender studies courses. One first-year student commented: "Although I have not taken any *classes* in the Gender Studies Program, I have gone to three of the symposium events. I was pleased with all of them; I can't believe how much a few hours can change one's perspective.... Not all of us have enough interest or time to take the classes, but we still want to learn. The symposium is perfect for this objective.... Everything I saw at the symposium reminded me of what I can do or not do to make the world between men and women easier to cross."

Many other students commented on the intellectual excitement and new awareness generated by attending symposium sessions: "Woke me up! I just attended and listened and listened and thought and questioned. I'm beginning to see new perspectives on things." "It was so incredible to see people (staff and students) present things they had worked on. There were so many varied issues that it made me really think about a variety of subjects, not just my own area of concentration." "Learning from my peers, through their papers is a rare and valuable experience, in that it generates a sense of community among us." "I gained a new perspective on the sometimes angry and/or defensive pose developed by many lesbians as a result of society's rejection and condescension about their lifestyle/sexual orientation."

Because of the excitement surrounding symposium discussions, various groups have formed that meet year round and are ancillary to or spin-offs from the Gender Studies Symposium. In 1991, students initiated a computer conversation program for gender issues, which included topics such as rape, gay, lesbian and bisexual issues, abortion, and "survivor stories." Also in 1991, students conceptualized and published the first issue of *Synergia*, a gender issues journal.

PERSONAL GROWTH

As the New York Times etc. whips up hysteria nationwide about alleged "indoctrination" by feminists, "leftists," and anti-Bloomites, I am bemused by the retro-stupidity of it all and grateful that at Lewis and Clark the people who mattered understood that a mono-cultural, androcentric, hetero-sexist education was not an education! I didn't learn how to be "politically correct" at LC—I learned how to take my-

*self and other people seriously and to value complexity. If that's "PC,"
thank god for it! And, as a teacher now, I value the example of LC
faculty who understood and showed that they understood their own responsibility to be self-critical and generous.*

A LEWIS AND CLARK COLLEGE GRADUATE

Of the students (N=145) and alumnae(i) (N=24) who responded to the
questionnaire, most saw learning about gender, race, and class as essential to
their education and called for more institutional support of the Gender
Studies Program. A typical comment was, "Gender studies is a necessity in a
liberal arts education." One first-year male student, who had taken gender
studies elective courses and attended one symposium, wrote: "It is the *responsibility* of a liberal arts college to provide gender education to its students.
Never let gender studies at Lewis and Clark be ended. It is one of the most
important programs here."

The Lewis and Clark alumna above who referred to political correctness
in her 1991 questionnaire response has completed her Ph.D. and currently is
a professor at a large midwestern university. She writes that when she arrived
at Lewis and Clark, in the early 1980s, she was already "a committed feminist" and was thrilled by the "extraordinary proliferation of feminist perspectives across the curriculum, not just in gender studies classes." While the
majority of students who arrive at Lewis and Clark are not typically self-proclaimed "committed feminists,"[7] data collected for our study suggest similar
personal growth themes introduced in this alumna's questionnaire: heightened awareness through intellectual community, increased self-esteem, empowerment, and agency. To understand how learning through the Gender
Studies Program affects the personal growth of women and men, we asked a
number of open-ended questions in our questionnaires, which invited students and alumnae(i) to reflect on what impact, if any, the program had on
their lives.

HEIGHTENED AWARENESS THROUGH
INTELLECTUAL COMMUNITY
The first personal growth theme that emerged was heightened awareness
through intellectual community. The annual Gender Studies Symposium was
the vehicle which provided intellectual community for many students. An
alumna recalled: "Learning from my peers, through their papers, was a rare
and valuable experience...that...generated a sense of community among us."

Another graduate wrote: "The symposium ratified my sense that the world of gender scholarship was a *big place* with enormous complexity and that any denial of that complexity—in the name of 'excellence' or 'unity' or even 'sisterhood'—was dangerous and counterproductive." Heightened awareness through intellectual community was underscored by the woman student who reflected on her symposium participation:

> *The most significant experience I have had at Lewis and Clark was participating in the Gender Studies Symposium.... Much of what I learned changed my attitudes and beliefs and gave me new concepts to examine. Many of the ideas deeply moved me, making me aware of unfulfilled desires in my personal life and in the world as a whole.*

Respondents noted that the symposium promotes heightened awareness by reaching students who, due to enrollment demands, frequently are denied access to gender studies courses. Seventy-five percent of our random, stratified student sample had attended one or more symposia. A senior who had attended four symposia observed, "The Gender Studies Symposium was, I believe, the most well-attended event on campus this year. You don't have to have taken gender courses or be a gender minor to be affected by the Gender Studies Program on this campus." This observation was confirmed by a first-year student's comment: "I've become aware of gender discussions that I've been completely blind to before." For a graduate, the gender symposium had "an eye-opening effect [and was] an entrance to an unfamiliar *and* very familiar world of issues." Another graduate reflected, "I always learned more about other races, especially during the symposium and felt more aware and sensitive to people of color."

As an example of heightened awareness through intellectual community, we turn to a narrative provided by a male student, a double major in international affairs and economics, who wrote: "As a white male, who thought I was open-minded and aware, feminism and my own sexist behavior have shattered that illusion. I'm thankful for it; I just wish it had occurred earlier." After attending his first symposium in 1991, he wrote:

> *Until April of this year, I would not have labeled myself a feminist, nor was I even aware of what it meant. The impetus for me was hearing [in a class] an LC woman tell about her rape. I was deeply moved and disturbed by this. I did not think that rape was so pervasive, so I*

*decided that I was not as informed about what was happening in the
world. I went to the International Woman's Day at [Portland State
University] and...I signed up for the Portland Women's Crisis Line
training for men.... The Gender Symposium brought all the information and more into the core of my being.... The pornography presentation on Wednesday drilled home my internalized sexism and made me
internalize all the other information that had been previously left out of
my life....The experience was extreme, but I would want it no other
way. I'm thankful to those women who have helped open my eyes. I
realize that the issues must become a responsibility of men to correct.
My actions and behavior in the future will show the impact that the
gender symposium had on me. Gender studies and the symposium
must keep growing so that we may, one day, see a world of equality.*

For those who enrolled in gender studies courses, awareness is heightened even more. After taking GS 440, "Feminist Theory," a senior male student wrote: "It has made me open my eyes and see more clearly the complex-
ities concerning gender, race, and class in our society. It has made me
examine myself much more critically." Another student found that gender
studies courses had "an incredible impact" on her "gender *awareness* and *sensitivity*." After taking GS 231, "Gender in Cross-Cultural Perspective," a
male student majoring in biology and chemistry wrote: "I used to be really
homophobic. Presently, several of my friends are admitted homophiles. I love
them!"

Fourteen alumnae(i) rated their gender courses at the 5 level, three at
the 4 level, and one at the 3 level. One alumnus, now a graduate student in
international affairs, commented: "Before coming to LC, I had not been exposed even to the idea that gender was a subject in and of itself.... I started to
recognize what little I knew and what I still had to learn." Another graduate
wrote: "They [the gender courses] completely revolutionized my understanding of life on this planet, and more specifically, my life. They were the most
important part of my education." "Not until I got in law school," wrote another alumna, "did I realize the everyday understanding and sensitivity that I
had gained about gender, race, and class was so unusual."

EMPOWERMENT AND AGENCY

For male students, heightened awareness was the most frequent and dominant personal growth theme. As one male senior put it, "We men have a lot

70

The majority of respondents did not see gender studies as an isolated retreat…but as an integral part of their experience at Lewis and Clark

to learn." But while men most frequently cited heightened awareness, women were much more likely to point to empowerment and agency as personal outcomes of their education. For many women, the presence of female professors in gender studies was empowering. One student recalled: "Some of the profs really served as mentors—strong women role models are *so* important to *all* students." After taking "Rhetoric of Women," a gender studies elective, a woman who plans to pursue graduate study in psychology wrote: "The experience of studying women who worked to make changes in our country was empowering, giving me new role models to admire and emulate. I developed a new confidence in myself as a woman. I want to be a part of the continuation of spreading new knowledge and research, and making a difference in people's lives."

Movement from heightened awareness to empowerment and agency was apparent in many student and alumnae(i) statements, again particularly those of women. One woman student described this personal growth as "a sense of pride in who I am and what I can do as an individual in society." Another student felt empowered with "the ability to question what I see happening" and able to act as an agent to "change what I am doing." "For me personally," wrote one student, "this awareness within the classroom validated my experience as a woman (so that it was just as real and valued as male experience), as a lesbian, and as a powerful person. In many ways, it has been and continues to be very empowering." Another student wrote: "Getting in touch with my feminist voice put me in touch with a lot of issues around me. It also helped me to get involved with the symposium planning committee and the Portland Women's Crisis Line." For another woman student, gender studies courses "let me learn to think critically and be more confident and challenge oppressing situations…."

Finally, the narrative provided by a forty-six-year-old student is a moving reflection on personal growth through gender studies courses. This student excelled as a major in English and a minor in gender studies, and she celebrated a June graduation with her husband and children. In her student questionnaire, she wrote:

> When the Women's Movement was prominent in the late '60s and '70s, I was raising my two children and didn't get involved at all. I lived in a very conservative state (Nevada), and I was ignorant. At thirty, I thought I was too old to go to college. When I was forty-two, I realized I couldn't go on being a secretary. I started college for the

first time—at the community college here in Portland. After I had sev-
enty-two credits, I transferred to Lewis and Clark because (1) they
emphasize writing and critical thinking, and (2) they have a Gender
Studies Program. I had felt a lack over the years because I didn't have
the knowledge to put into words what I'd experienced, felt, or thought.
I wanted to know women writers and see if I could become a better
me. Being an older student was very difficult the first term.... This
year, my senior year, I spoke out against unfairnesses and supported
friends and issues. This year, I realize I'm smart, strong, worthy,
thoughtful, analytic—yes, I'm what I always wanted to be—Me. I
used to be afraid to be me; now I feel I can stand taller.

CONCLUSIONS

The exploration of our three key questions and the conclusions suggested by
our data can be broken down into four findings:

☐ Student and alumnae(i) enthusiasm for gender studies translates into enthusiasm for Lewis and Clark as an institution. The majority of respondents
did not see gender studies as an isolated retreat from the rest of the college
but as an integral part of their experience at Lewis and Clark. Many felt gender studies defined Lewis and Clark. This finding has, we think, important
implications for recruiting and retaining students and faculty members.

☐ Although many respondents spoke about the integration of gender into
the curriculum along with the minor as interdependent components of the
Gender Studies Program, the study shows that there are important differences between attempts to integrate gender into the curriculum as a whole
(including the symposium) and the minor with its focus on gender. The
study reminds us that while both elements of the program are essential, they
serve different ends and often reach different audiences. One could not, and
should not, be substituted for the other. Gender integration enables the program to heighten awareness of gender issues on campus, introduce new information about women's contributions to the disciplines, and generally to improve the institutional climate, while the minor creates a space for in-depth
analysis of gender and for exploration of the full range of cultural narratives
articulated in our knowledge base. Without the minor, many of the knowledge plots and learning skills would not be available to students; without the integration component, the program would risk becoming isolated.

☐ It follows from the second conclusion that the Gender Studies Program at

Lewis and Clark should not expand to become a major. The interrelationships between integration efforts and the minor provide the best possible
combination for our students at this time. The data indicate that the minor
enables students to forge connections not only between their academic studies and their personal experiences (as we would also expect a women's studies
major to do) but also between the gender minor and other coursework they
do, including their majors. The breadth of majors represented both in our
minors and in other students who enroll in gender studies courses is striking
and contributes enormously to the interdisciplinary nature of the program.
This conversation among various disciplines might be lost if the program
were institutionally isolated as a department or major.

□ Based on our own analysis of the knowledge base and learning skills of gender studies, we might conclude that the sequencing of courses within the minor is well designed to take students through the various knowledge plots and
learning clusters, enabling students to build upon previous learning; but we are
not able to guarantee that students take the courses in the designed sequence.
One recommendation might be to require GS 200, "Men and Women in
American Society," of all gender studies minors and make it a prerequisite for
other gender studies courses. We plan to initiate a discussion of the feasibility
of such a move and its impact on staffing and student accessibility.

Most significantly, our study validated our own sense of the importance
of gender studies at Lewis and Clark. In all our investigations for this study,
only one respondent (a male who had never participated in gender studies)
called for the abolition of the program. Most representative were the responses of two students who wrote:

> I think one of the best things about the L&C Gender Studies Program
> is that it does attempt and has had some success in getting an integrat-
> ed body of students (I mean men and women) in the classroom. When
> the issues can be discussed between men and women, different per-
> spectives can be offered, and everyone can learn something.

> I like men being in the classroom. (They are, since they feel included.)
> I get to know them in a different way.

It seems, in a delicious irony, that we have come full circle. At the
founding of Lewis and Clark over a century ago, women were to be included
along with men in a curriculum that recognized that the presence of women

in the classroom could contribute significantly to the quality of the academic conversation. As the twentieth century draws to a close, the Gender Studies Program at Lewis and Clark College provides a space in which men can work side by side with women to formulate more effective strategies for promoting social equality, justice, tolerance, and diversity.

---

1. We are indebted to a number of people who contributed to the structure and content of Lewis and Clark's study. Mary Henning-Stout, Assistant Professor of Counseling Psychology at Lewis and Clark, provided advice about research design in the early stages of our work. Joan Poliner Shapiro, Lee Knefelkamp, and Caryn McTighe Musil, along with other members of the National Assessment Team, provided valuable suggestions throughout the process. Finally, we are indebted to the faculty, students, and administrators at Lewis and Clark who contributed in so many ways and made this study possible.

2. Martha Frances Montague, *Lewis and Clark College, 1867–1967* (Portland, Ore.: Binfords and Mort, 1968), 11–12.

3. Mary Kay Thompson Tetreault, "Integrating Content About Women and Gender into the Curriculum," in *Multicultural Education: Issues and Perspectives* ed. James A. Banks and Cherry M. McGee Banks (Boston: Allyn and Bacon, 1989).

4. *Language, Gender, and Society* (Rowley, Mass.: Newbury House, 1983).

5. Barrie Thorne, Cheris Kramarae, and Nancy Henley, "Teaching Feminist Theory" in *Theory in the Classroom*, ed. Cary Nelson (Urbana: University of Illinois Press, 1986), 58–66.

6. For the literature on situated knowledge, see Donna Haraway, "Situated Knowledges: The Science Question in Feminism and the Privilege of Partial Perspective," *Feminist Studies* 14 (1988): 575–99.

7. Review of several years of comparative data on entering first-year students at four-year, private, nonsectarian colleges shows that Lewis and Clark students are more likely to enter with higher interest in political and social action than their counterparts at other institutions and are more likely to take "liberal" positions on issues such as the death penalty, military spending, and homosexual relations. Lewis and Clark students report that they arrive with high interest in obtaining a "general education" and less interest in attending college "to make more money." For detailed information, see: "The Astin Study," data collected by the Cooperative Institutional Research Program and sponsored jointly by the American Council on Education and University of California–Los Angeles.

STUDENT QUESTIONNAIRE
LEWIS AND CLARK COLLEGE

Male:
Female:
Age:
Year in School:
Major:
Minor:

Part I: Gender Studies Program

1. What do you think are the objectives of the Gender Studies Program at Lewis and Clark?

2. How well do you believe these objectives are being met? (What particular strengths and weaknesses do you perceive?)

3. What difference, if any, do you see between a gender studies program and a women's studies program?

4. What impact, if any, do you believe the gender studies program has had on Lewis and Clark?

5. In your opinion, should Lewis and Clark have a gender studies program? Why or why not?

Part II: Gender Studies Core Courses

1. Indicate which, if any, of the following gender studies core courses you have completed and in which courses you are currently enrolled:
C = completed course E = enrolled course
[list of courses followed on original questionnaire]

2. Circle the number on the scale that best represents your overall learning in the above gender studies core courses:

1	2	3	4	5
poor	fair	average	good	excellent

3. What do you consider to be your most significant and least significant learning experiences in these courses?

4. How do these gender studies core courses compare with other courses you have taken at Lewis and Clark?

5. Was the learning/teaching climate in these gender studies core courses different from your non-gender studies classes? If so, how?

6. What effect, if any, have these gender studies core courses had on your understanding of issues of gender, race, and class?

7. Which of these courses would you recommend to other students? Why?

Part III: Practicum/Internship in Gender Studies
If you completed or are currently involved in a practicum/internship in gender studies, describe the practicum and comment on the experience:

Part IV: Other Courses with a Gender Focus
1. What other courses have you taken in the Lewis and Clark general college curriculum that included a focus on gender issues?

2. Circle the number on the scale that best represents your overall learning in these courses:

1	2	3	4	5
poor	fair	average	good	excellent

3. What do you consider to be your most significant and least significant learning experience in these courses?

4. How do these courses compare with other courses you have taken at Lewis and Clark?

5. Which of these courses would you recommend to other students? Why?

Part V: Gender and Overseas Programs

1. Have you participated in a Lewis and Clark overseas program?   Yes   No
   If yes, what was the program?

2. How did gender issues figure in the program—in preparation, during the course of
the overseas study, after return to campus?

Part VI: Gender Studies Symposium

1. Have you ever attended any of the Lewis and Clark Gender Studies Symposium
events? Yes   No
   If yes, circle the year(s) of your participation in the symposium?
      1982   1983   1984   1985   1986   1987   1988   1989   1990

2. Which events do you recall attending, and what was your evaluation?

3. What effect did your attendance at the symposium have on your understanding of
issues of gender, race, and class?

4. Circle the number of the scale that best represents your learning experience in the
symposium?

1	2	3	4	5
poor	fair	average	good	excellent

5. Have you ever been involved as a planner, presenter, or moderator in a Lewis and
Clark Gender Studies Symposium?
      Yes   No
   If yes, circle the year(s) of your participation:
      1982   1983   1984   1985   1986   1987   1988   1989   1990

6. Describe and comment on your participation in the symposium:

7. What effect did your participation in the symposium have on your understanding
of issues of gender, race, and class?

8. Circle the number of the scale that best represents your learning experience as a
symposium planner, presenter, and/or moderator:

1	2	3	4	5
poor	fair	average	good	excellent

Part VII: What Else?

What else would you like to communicate to us about the Gender Studies Program at Lewis and Clark as we plan for the future?

CHARACTERISTICS OF CONNECTED AND SEPARATE KNOWING

Aspect	Connected Knowing	Separate Knowing
The name of the game	The "Believing Game": looking for what is right—accepting	The "Doubting Game": looking for what is wrong—critical
Goals:	To construct meaning—to understand and to be understood	To construct truth—to prove, disprove, and convince
The relationship between the knowers:	Collaborative: reasons *with* the other	Adversarial: reasoning *against* the other
The knower's relationship to the known:	Attachment & closeness	Detachment & distance
The nature of agency:	Active surrender	Mastery and control
The nature of discourse:	Narrative & contextual	Logical & abstract
The role of emotion:	Feelings illuminate thought	Feelings cloud thought
Procedure for transcending subjectivity:	"Objectivity" achieved by adopting the other's perspective	"Objectivity" achieved by adhering to impersonal and universal standards
Basis of authority:	Commonality of experience	Mastery of relevant knowledge and methodology
Strengths:	Expansive, inclusive	Narrowing, discriminating
Vulnerabilities:	Loss of identity and autonomy	Alienation and absence of care

Based on Belenky, Clinchy, Goldberger & Tarule, *Women's Ways of Knowing: The Development of Self, Voice, & Mind* (New York: Basic Books, Inc., 1986); and Elbow, *Writing Without Teachers* (New York: Cambridge University Press, 1973), with thanks to Hilarie Davis for her suggestions.

PROGRAM GOALS
GENDER STUDIES PROGRAM

Theory, Content, and Praxis Goals

1. To examine feminist theories concerning the social and historical constructions of gender, both locally and globally, including:

a. the relational rather than essential nature of women/femininity and men/masculinity;

b. how gender defines relationships among men, among women, and between men and women;

c. how gender defines sexuality, sexual identity, social inequality, and the family.

2. To improve upon our model of gender studies, including a critique of Western feminist theory.

3. To recognize that women's lives have been under-represented in traditional disciplines and to identify women's as well as men's roles in cultural, social, and scientific endeavors.

4. To study, compare, and evaluate an array of disciplinary constructions of gender including, but not limited to, aesthetic, cross-cultural, psychological, and biological perspectives.

5. To identify the intersections of gender with race, class, age, sexual identity, and ethnicity, both locally and globally.

6. To integrate gender analysis into students' academic programs, including:

a. the Core Program (general education program);

b. the other College mission foci—International Education and STV (Science, Technology, and Values);

c. other interdisciplinary programs;

d. disciplinary curricula.

7. To involve students and faculty in a critical appraisal of how institutional and classroom climates affect the learning of women and men.

8. To provide classroom and institutional climates that encourage synthesis as well as questioning, connection as well as criticism, action as well as thought, practice as well as theory.

COURSES SCORED ON
CURRICULUM INTEGRATION SCALE

Fine Arts and Humanities
English 205 (Medieval and Renaissance Literature)
English 206 (Seventeenth & Eighteenth-Century Literature)
English 315 (American Literature, WWII–present)
History 232 (Europe in Crisis, 1890–1950)
History 270 (India: Past and Present)
Art 224 (Painting)
Philosophy 354 (Aesthetics)
Philosophy 421 (American Ideology and Culture)
Religious Studies 222 (Old Testament)

Mathematics and Natural Sciences
Biology 111 (Perspectives in Biology)
Health and Physical Education 350 (Mental Health)

Social Science
Communications 101 (Introduction to Interpersonal and Organizational)
Communications 330 (Communication and Culture)
Economics 335 (Labor Economics)
Education 305/550 (Historical/Ethical Perspectives on Education)
International Affairs 230 (African Politics)
International Affairs 237 (Third World Politics)
Psychology 218 (Abnormal Psychology)
Sociology/Anthropology 110 (Introduction to Cultural Anthropology)
Sociology/Anthropology 350 (Global Inequality)

SCORING SHEET
FOR KNOWLEDGE BASE
AND LEARNING SKILLS

Reader _____ File _____
Paper _____
Date _____ Female _____ Male _____

I. Plots for Knowledge Base for Gender Studies

___ 1. **Politics of sex/gender plot** (economic, political and sexual subjugation of women built into social structures; activism for change)

___ 2. **Cultural images of sex/gender plot** (representations of gender—masculinity and femininity—in art and the media, both high and mass culture)

___ 3. **Nature/nurture plot** (biological to socially learned differences)

___ 4. **Diversity plot** (recognition and respect for racial, ethnic, cultural, sexual, class, and age differences)

___ 5. **Body plot** (female sexuality and male sexuality; heterosexuality and homosexuality)

___ 6. **Communication plot** (verbal and nonverbal; discursive and nondiscursive; the making and authorization of meaning)

___ 7. **Interpersonal relationships plot** (the structuring, maintenance, and termination of dyadic relationships, family relationships, work relationships, and other small group relationships, etc.)

___ 8. **Women's creation of knowledge plot** (women's contribution throughout the disciplines to the creation of knowledge)

II. Learning Skills

___ 1. Social construction of gender

     1   2   3   4   5

___ 2. Agency of the oppressed

      1   2   3   4   5

___ 3. Form and content: questioning adequacy of traditional forms of expressions; experimentation with non-traditional forms

      1   2   3   4   5

___ 4. Knowledge in gender studies seen as interminable; producing rather than repeating knowledge

      1   2   3   4   5

___ 5. Positionality—self-awareness, self-empowerment, "clicks," and "epiphanies"

      1   2   3   4   5

___ 6. Social construction of knowledge

      1   2   3   4   5

—■—

OLD DOMINION UNIVERSITY
MAKING CONNECTIONS

BY ANITA CLAIR FELLMAN AND BARBARA A. WINSTEAD

Old Dominion University examines four areas for the assessment
of program goals—knowledge base, critical skills, feminist pedagogy, and personal growth—asking the following questions:
What are the key concepts in women's studies? Are learning
skills developed in women's studies any different from learning
skills developed in other disciplines? Are students' voices heard
and respected in the classroom? Is personal growth different for
women's studies students? Finally, a fifth area of assessment was
established: How has participating in women's studies influenced
faculty members?

Old Dominion University is a state-supported institution with seventeen
thousand students in Norfolk, Virginia, the site of the nation's largest naval
base and a bustling port. These two factors assure that many local residents,
in fact, may have spent part of their lives in other locations. The university
is largely nonresidential, with an undergraduate student body whose average
age is twenty-three. A high proportion of students hold part- or full-time jobs
while going to the university; 17 percent of undergraduates attend ODU part
time. Typically, 30 to 40 percent of the students in the introductory women's
studies course are married and/or have children. All these factors mitigate
against student involvement in campus activities and intensify the responsibility of courses to embody the institution's educational mission.

In women's studies specifically, student engagement with or attachment
to the program has ebbed and flowed over the years, depending largely upon
fortuitous combinations of students. It is always a struggle to make incoming
students aware of a program that exists only at the 300- and 400-level in
time for them to plan to become women's studies minors. At the time of this
assessment, and perhaps aided by it, student involvement in women's studies
was once again on the rise, with about thirty-five students enrolled as minors. Some of the same centrifugal forces exist for faculty members involved
in the Women's Studies Program. They are spread among nine or ten departments or programs in four of ODU's colleges. Because there are no institu-

tional incentives or rewards, those who serve on the Women's Studies
Advisory Council (WSAC) do so purely out of interest and feminist solidarity.

We decided to participate in "The Courage to Question" for two basic
reasons. Since we had a loosely structured minor, we wanted first to find out
just what we were teaching our students and what they were learning.
Second, we wanted our participation in the assessment project to create
stronger connections among the WSAC.

Founded in 1977, with its first director appointed in 1978, Old Dominion University's Women's Studies Program is well established. The administration of the College of Arts and Letters, where the program is located,
firmly supports women's studies; in fact, the college's contribution to the university emphasis on urban issues is interpreted to mean a focus on gender and
ethnicity. Many women's studies and women's studies cross-listed courses fill
university-wide, upper-division general-education requirements.

Nonetheless, the resources put into the program are modest: the director
is still its only permanent faculty member. In recent years, however, the
provost of the university and the deans of the relevant colleges have contributed funds to permit release time for a visiting half-time faculty person
lent, on a rotating basis, from other departments in the university. The director, this annual joint appointee, and an occasional adjunct instructor teach
the two core women's studies courses. Instructors usually are lent to the program from the English department to cover two other popular women's studies courses. The remainder of the twelve to fifteen courses that we offer each
semester are cross-listed from other departments—mostly within the College
of Arts and Letters—where the majority of feminist scholars on campus is located. In addition to the one women's studies required course, students have
a choice of about thirty other courses to apply to a fifteen-credit (five-course)
women's studies minor. While this wide selection bespeaks a strong interest
in feminist scholarship, especially among arts and letters faculty members, it
does highlight the director's lack of formal control over the content of the
courses from other departments. It also contributes to a smorgasbord education in women's studies, a situation we will rectify as we plan for a baccalau-
reate degree in women's studies.

SETTING GOALS

From the beginning, assessment of the Women's Studies Program at ODU
was a collaborative and hands-on learning project. Those women's studies
faculty members and students willing and able to participate, numbering

about twenty-five over the course of the project, were involved at all levels: deciding whether or not to engage in assessment, setting goals, defining goals, developing assessment tools, using those tools (administering questionnaires and tests, conducting interviews), and interpreting results of data collected. Only this final report can be said to be the work of a few rather than many. While inclusiveness can be cumbersome, its virtues are the richness of diverse opinions and perspectives and the commitment of the participants.

Having decided to assess the Women's Studies Program, we faced the initial question of *what* to assess. "The Courage to Question" grant suggested four areas: knowledge base, learning skills, feminist pedagogy, and personal growth, with the proviso that we could delete, add, modify, or substitute according to our institutional and programmatic needs. Although we used these four as a framework for establishing specific assessment program goals, we established a fifth area to assess: women's studies impact on women's studies faculty members. This target acknowledges the reflexive nature of teaching women's studies—or any academic discipline. The assumptions, methods of inquiry, and styles of discourse of a discipline, as well as the social relationships established around a common purpose, affect faculty members, their teaching, and, consequently, student learning.

With five areas to assess we established five subcommittees to develop specific objectives for each area. The meetings of these subcommittees resulted in lively conversation and debate. Critical questions were raised: Is there a canon in women's studies? "No, let there not be!" most of us said, but we did agree that there is a knowledge base. Are or should learning skills developed in women's studies be any different from learning skills developed in other disciplines? We concluded that even though making connections between personal experience and academic knowledge is to be expected in most disciplines, this skill has a special significance in women's studies. What is feminist pedagogy anyway? We are still investigating this question but have gained some valuable insights. Is personal growth different for women's studies students? We decided to look particularly at students' friendships. Finally, how has participating in women's studies influenced *us as faculty members*?

METHODS

We were determined that our goals and objectives not be method-driven. Whenever anyone said, "But how will you measure that?" someone always answered, "We don't need to worry about that yet." Eventually, of course, we did have to choose methods to measure our objectives.

We were guided by the National Assessment Team to use data that we already collected (journals, papers, finals) and measures that can be used for multiple purposes (interviews, questionnaires). We found, too, that others had developed measures that we could use. Thus, the questionnaire sent to ODU graduates who minored in women's studies and the exit interviews with seniors graduating with a minor were adapted from an alumnae questionnaire used by Wellesley College. For some objectives, we developed our own instruments. Although it was tempting to limit our research subjects to the manageable number of women's studies minors, we decided ultimately to use some instruments that would enable us to learn something about all students in women's studies, including many who were minors. The objectives for each area and the methods used to measure them are reviewed in the next section.

KNOWLEDGE BASE
To define our objectives for the first area, knowledge base, we asked instructors of women's studies or cross-listed courses to identify five key concepts that they attempted to convey to students. These were summarized as: the systematic, interlocking oppression of women; women's varied relations to patriarchy; the social construction of gender; the social construction of knowledge; and the redefining and reconceptualizing of women's power and empowerment. To ascertain change in knowledge, each instructor was asked to develop and administer a short, ungraded test at the beginning of the semester (pre-test) and then give the same test at the end of the semester (post-test). Instructors then compared answers and prepared a report describing ways in which student knowledge had and had not changed. The tests, used in fifteen classes representing nine different courses over two semesters, were given to 630 students for the pre-tests and 525 students for the post-tests. Thirty-six of these students identified themselves as women's studies minors. With the exception of the short answer test given in four sections of one course, the tests were multiple choice in nature.

The courses were:
- ☐ WMST 301 Women in a Changing World (offered twice)
- ☐ WMST 460 Feminist Thought
- ☐ WMST 495 Gender and Ethics (offered twice)
- ☐ PSYCH 323 Psychology of Women (offered twice)
- ☐ CRJS 325 Women and Crime
- ☐ ENGL 463 Women Writers (offered four times)

☐ ENGL 477 Language, Gender and Power
☐ HIST 495 Women in Latin American History
☐ HIST 495 Women and Work in American History

Many of our conclusions from these tests about student knowledge are based on the entire class. However, "Women in a Changing World," "Feminist Thought," "Women and Work in American History," and "Women Writers" had sufficient numbers of women's studies minors to enable us to make meaningful generalizations about the knowledge base of minors as opposed to non-minors in those classes.

While these tests were the most efficient way to take a reading of students' awareness of some key points for each course, they were not a refined instrument for ascertaining what students understood. It was not always easy to distinguish between wrong answers based on students' lack of knowledge and those that were a function of imprecise or confusing questions. Sometimes wrong answers were a product of a little knowledge, rather than of no knowledge, but it was difficult to tell from the results exactly where the gap lay in transmission. For instance, in "Psychology of Women," on the basis of the first semester's post-tests, the instructor attempted (throughout the following semester) to correct a widely held misconception; nonetheless, the test results were virtually the same the second semester.

Much more time-consuming, but more useful, was the analysis of final exams for a few courses. In retrospect, this may have been the single most valuable instrument for knowledge-base objectives. Perhaps we would have benefitted from having each instructor design one compulsory exam question for the final exam that would test students' mastery of one key concept. The portfolio of papers from women's studies courses submitted by graduating minors was another good means of gauging student comprehension of important ideas.

Finally, graduating minors (twelve) and alumnae (fifteen) were asked in an interview or by questionnaire to identify the three most important concepts that they had learned in women's studies courses (see pages 107–108). The open-ended nature of this request yielded somewhat general answers that were only moderately instructive. Furthermore, our alumna questionnaire called for a considerable investment of time and thought on the part of the respondent. Despite our suggestion that alumnae answer as little or as much of it as they wished, we probably would have gotten a better return with a shorter questionnaire.

We turned to our students and asked them what
was most critical about how they are taught....
Without hestitation or qualification they said
having their voices heard and respected

LEARNING SKILLS

Our objectives for the learning skills area were to assess connected learning
as well as students' ability to examine the assumptions underlying culturally
accepted work, studies, and literatures; and their ability to redefine and de-
fend questions, problems, and issues. We used course papers and exams and
students' submissions to the annual Women's Studies Student Essay Contest.

FEMINIST PEDAGOGY

To decide on objectives for assessment for feminist pedagogy, we turned to
our students and asked them what was most critical about how they are
taught. Without hesitation or qualifications they said having their voices
heard and respected. We designed a questionnaire to ask simply, "Was your
voice (that is, your questions, concerns, and opinions) heard and respected
in this class?" and distributed it to students in women's studies and cross-listed courses. We also asked questions concerning "voice" in the minors' exit
interviews and the alumnae questionnaires.

PERSONAL GROWTH

Our objective was to measure the sense of "we-ness" students feel in the
women's studies classroom. We designed a questionnaire asking students to
estimate the number of female and male acquaintances, friends, and close
friends they had in their classes—both women's studies and non-women's
studies (see page 106). The questionnaire was administered at the beginning
and the end of the semester, and changes in friendships over time were analyzed. Questions also were asked in the minors' exit interviews and in the
alumnae questionnaires about changes in friendships that occurred as a result
of participation in women's studies.

IMPACT ON FACULTY

We assessed how the women's studies program has affected the teaching and
scholarly lives of women faculty members associated with the program. To
accomplish this, we interviewed one another; this process served both to encourage us to examine our own lives as they are affected by participation in
women's studies and to explore and discover how women's studies has influenced our colleagues.

RESULTS

KNOWLEDGE BASE

We should make clear at the outset that we were not measuring the information that our students had acquired but rather the distillation of that information into a series of complex concepts with which to interpret the world. For example, when students learn from lectures, readings, and research projects how little reliable knowledge we have on diseases and physical conditions specific to women, we wish them also to understand the larger point about the devaluation of women in our culture and about the social construction of knowledge. If we convey to students that domestic service lost its place as the primary occupation for African American women almost forty years after it ceased being the most common job for white women, we want them to realize that not all women experience a patriarchal system in the same way. It was student understanding of the larger concepts that we had defined as the desired knowledge base.

Social construction of gender

Based on our evaluations, it is apparent that students come to understand that gender is socially constructed. Over the course of the semester, students move from a reliance on individual or biological explanations to sociocultural ones. Hence, students in "Women in a Changing World" were less likely to agree by the end of the semester that women mother because of a maternal instinct; women's studies minors were even less likely to think so than their classmates. Students also came to see workforce jobs as a reinforcement of gender identity rather than as a natural outgrowth of feminine abilities. In "Gender and Ethics," an increased percentage of students ceased accepting individualist justifications ("I meant no harm" or "She chose this freely") in favor of understanding how choices are constrained by less visible, and less conscious, structural barriers. Several minors who had taken the sociology of sexuality course taught by a feminist instructor retained as a key concept the realization that sexuality, too, is socially constructed. In "Psychology of Women," students switched to sociocultural as opposed to biological explanations of gender-related behaviors. The troubling exception to this was the persistence in the belief that violence against women is best explained by the pathological impulsivity and aggressiveness of some males.

Students ordinarily come into our classes convinced that all impediments that stand in women's way are a result of restrictive socialization of both male and female children. The degree of their passionate interest in this subject can be demonstrated by which questions students chose to answer on a midterm in "Women in a Changing World." Ninety percent selected an essay question that asked them, on the basis of the course reading they had done on socialization, to describe how they planned to socialize their daughters. The instructor saw her task as deepening their understanding of how lifelong this process is and how pervasive the gendering of our culture. Students' capacities to analyze gendered cultural messages increased by the end of the course. Most of those with children, for example, wrote of looking at children's cartoons and television shows with new eyes. In analyzing what they had learned from committing an assigned gender role violation, the vast majority of women students marvelled at how deeply they had been socialized as females despite their initial belief that they were free individually from the confining aspects of femininity.

Interlocking oppression of women
When it comes to the more challenging issue of the systemic devaluation and subordination of females, of the interlocking forms of oppression of women, we do see a difference in understanding between minors and non-minors. For instance, most students come to understand that rape and sexual harassment are crimes of violence, not of uncontrollable desire, and represent an attempt to subjugate and control women. On the "Women and Crime" post-test, 100 percent of students understood correctly that rape victims are less likely to be believed by the police and prosecutors than victims of other crimes. They are less clear, however, on how society encourages and perpetuates such violence.

Minors are more likely, judging from their final exams and their exit interviews, to see patriarchy as an overarching framework, a system, as opposed to a series of random discriminations against women. One minor, in analyzing her gender violation for "Women in a Changing World," observed wryly that given the power of males in our social system, even her attempt at role reversal (she offered to buy a male stranger a drink) resulted in his still wresting control of the situation from her. "I find that male-dominant societies are everywhere," observed a minor in the "Women Writers" course, while one of her classmates indicated that she was completing the course with an increased awareness of power relations illustrated in literary works. In their exit interviews, seven women's studies minors, including one male, identified the existence of a patriarchal system as one of the three most important concepts they had learned. They commented on the "extensiveness of male domination—far beyond what is noticeable to the eye" and on "law as an expression of patriarchy." The alumnae in the questionnaires also referred expressly to patriarchy as an important concept or wrote of recognizing "power inequalities and their impact on our lives."

Women's varied relations to patriarchy
As we anticipated, instructors have made differential progress in emphasizing women's varied relations to patriarchy. We are gratified to learn, however, that students in at least four courses not focused exclusively on minority women all indicate strong interest in African American women and show marked increases in their knowledge by the end of the semester. Of the thirty white students in "Women in a Changing World" during one semester, twenty-four chose to answer at least one short-answer (100–120 words) question on the final exam on African American women; most did well. On the other hand, when they were asked in an essay question on that same exam to integrate the history of African American women into their summary of the history of the American feminist movement, every student ignored that aspect of the question. In addition to telling us something about their learning skills, this tells us that our students are not yet mainstreaming their knowledge of minority women into the overall picture they have of American women. Corroborating our belief that minority students, like women in general, are eager to see their individual or group experiences reflected in the curriculum, four of the five African American students in that same course answered an essay question that gave them the option of comparing the situation of African American women with women in the developing world.

The courses in which the subjects of sexual orientation and homophobia are raised also produce apparent changes in student knowledge and attitudes, as evidenced in class discussion and written assignments in "Women in a Changing World." Students are wrestling with the general homophobia that pervades this geographic area but are open to understanding lesbians' points of view or answering exam questions with knowledge and empathy on the historical experience of lesbians. Our female students' commitment to non-coercive socialization of children makes them receptive to criticisms of homophobia because they see it as imposing rigid gender guidelines on children. Letty Cottin Pogrebin's article on this topic, "The Secret Fear That Keeps Us from Raising Free Children" (Ms., October 1980, 51–54), was selected by 90 percent of the students in "Women in a Changing World" for discussion in their journals in the year previous to our study.

Social construction of knowledge
Virtually all our women's studies and cross-listed courses emphasize the social construction of knowledge. Most of our students begin to grasp this fundamental concept. They understand that what they learn in women's studies classes has been excluded knowledge. "Why haven't we been taught all this before?" is the most common query in the introductory women's studies class. Quite a few alumnae mentioned as one of the key concepts they had learned that important women had been unfairly hidden from history, a perspective voiced by both male and female students in every women's history course we have ever offered.

Judging by their responses to the short-answer questions on the post-test, a modest minority of students in the "Women Writers" course took the next step as well in understanding that human beings create knowledge. They were especially drawn to the concept of the resisting reader: identifying the subjective element in the supposedly universal; situating famous authors as writing from their gender, race, and class; and learning not to acquiesce as a reader in what Judith Fetterley has called "the endless division of self against self."[1] In one "Women in a Changing World" class, all eight minors chose to answer the question on the final exam that asked students to indicate how feminism has taught us to rethink or redefine rape, the generic pronoun, sexual intercourse, or domestic violence. Not only were they more likely to answer that question than the other students in the class, they also gave more sophisticated answers, some of them focusing on the relation between world view and resulting change in definition.

While our students see that feminists might organize or define knowledge differently than non-feminists, they often do not assimilate the fact that feminists themselves construct a view of the world in a variety of ways. In "Feminist Thought," minors did significantly better on the post-test than did other students in the class in differentiating the main ideas among varieties of feminism, possibly because these other students were still simply pitting a monolithic feminism against non-feminism. Based on what we discovered about students' developmental needs intellectually, the Women's Studies Program now requires at least one previous women's studies course as a prerequisite for "Feminist Thought."

Women's power and empowerment
The redefining and reconceptualizing of women's power and empowerment come through in a number of ways. Many of the pre- and post-tests asked

students to define feminism. One of the shifts over the course of the semester in those definitions, among a minority of the respondents, was the move away from a strict equal rights perspective (feminism as women's efforts to be treated equally with men) to one that was more woman-centered (an appreciation of women's distinctive attributes, contributions, and perceptions). This insistence that women should not have to be identical to men to be valued was especially evident in the minors' exit interviews. About half of them spoke of the importance of validating one's own perceptions as a woman, of not needing to see women as just like men, of the desirability of reorganizing the public sphere to accommodate the place of childbearing and child rearing in women's lives.

LEARNING SKILLS

We set out to assess two things about students in women's studies or cross-listed courses. First, do they become connected knowers, individuals who use self-knowledge and empathy to learn? Second, do they acquire the ability to examine and evaluate assumptions underlying culturally accepted "fact" and theory?

A brief review of Belenky, Clinchy, Goldberger, and Tarule's exposition of "women's ways of knowing" will help in the discussion of our results.[2] Along the path to constructed knowledge, and just past the positions of silence and received knowledge (listening to and learning from authorities), is subjective knowledge. According to Belenky et al., "The subjective knower...sees truth as subjectified and personal. The subjectivist discovers that each person's life experience gives a different view of reality from that of any other person. What is more, truth is necessarily a private matter and, at least from the point of view of these women, should not be imposed on others."[3]

Beyond subjective (or received) knowledge is procedural knowledge, the understanding that there are procedures, skills, and techniques for obtaining knowledge. A person can acquire procedural knowledge through separate knowing (learning directly about the rules, standards, methods, and logic used to "know" something) and/or connected knowing (learning by becoming familiar with and understanding other people and their ways of thinking). Finally, constructed knowledge is reached when knowers attempt "to *integrate* knowledge they felt intuitively was personally important with knowledge they had learned from others. They told of weaving together the strands of rational and emotive thought and of integrating objective and subjective knowing."[4] The constructivist knows, "All knowledge is constructed, and the knower is an intimate part of the known."[5]

Our emphasis on connected knowing and the ability to examine assumptions highlights essential ingredients of constructed knowledge: the empathic connection with others and the objective analysis of the bases of knowledge. Although we did not identify these criteria to the judges of the annual Women's Studies Student Essay Contest, which draws entries from all over campus, all six winning entries in 1990 displayed evidence of learning these skills. Some of the undergraduate essayists attempted to see the world through the eyes of their subjects (as in the case of the two papers based on interviews with contemporary local women), and others used conventional forms of scholarship to ask unorthodox questions of their material (for example, a study of the discontent with the female sex role expressed in the poetry of an Argentinean woman poet).

Connected learning is an implicit goal in many women's studies classes. It is a common practice in the introductory women's studies course to ask students on take-home exams to describe the world view of someone mentioned in a course reading—for example, a lesbian in Buffalo in 1940 or a Southern black domestic servant in the 1950s. At other times, students in that course have been asked to compare their mothers' options and ambitions with their own. These are assignments on which students generally do well if they are asked to do a narrative or recreation. Given information about the circumstances in which other women live, students can empathically place themselves with others and describe what other people's thoughts and feelings would be.

It is likely that many of our students are subjective knowers as described by Belenky et al.[6] As subjective knowers they are thrilled at the opportunity provided in women's studies classes to express their personal feelings and opinions and to hear those of others. As subjective knowers, however, they understand "point of view" to be an opinion or perspective based on personal life experience and, therefore, not open to examination (without being intrusive) or criticism (without appearing hostile). They do not readily see that "point of view" represents a model or theory that can be understood in terms of its internal logic and the external forces that influence it.

Based on a careful reading of final exams in both "Women in a Changing World" and "Feminist Thought," we conclude that some students also find it hard to apply the ideas or insights of an analytic article to a description of personal experience: for example, exploring whether Chodorow's insights about mother-daughter relations might apply to their mothers and themselves. If a descriptive phrase or example used in the analysis is similar to their own experience, then this may be seen as validating the analysis. If, however, their own experience appears to contradict the analysis, they are unable to use their experience to form an alternative analysis or to place their experience along a continuum to which the analysis might apply. In other words, these students do not consider how or why they or others have certain feelings or opinions.

Similarly, students' abilities to identify with the subject of study is related to how well they acquire and/or retain information. For example, in the pre- and post-tests for "Women and Crime," the instructor discovered that of the three categories of questions—employment, victimization, and female criminality—students did best on the first category, in which the "relational distance" was the smallest. Students identify with trying to work in the criminal justice system; hence, by the post-test, 100 percent of the respondents correctly answered the question dealing with the relatively low percentage of women working in criminal justice. If, as we suspect, connecting with the subject matter enhances learning, then stimulating students' empathic skills also will enable them to learn more about subjects distant from their own experiences.

Summarizing information, identifying point of view, and applying the information or perspective to another source are all skills that come hard to a majority of our students. Short-answer questions on exams in several courses revealed that more students—a bare majority—are able to focus on key bits of information than can master the second two skills.

Not surprisingly, the identification of the assumptions underlying a piece of literature, research, or scholarship is difficult for our students. Also, they often are unable to compare points of view or apply the insights of one writer to another. In "Feminist Thought," very few students, whether women's studies minors or not, chose to answer questions on the final exam that asked them to link the ideas in any two pieces of assigned reading. Our impression is that in many majors, students are required only to pluck information—not point of view—from the course readings. It is possible that we in women's studies may be insisting to students that the identification of point of view is important but that our courses by themselves are inadequate to teach students the skill of reading critically. On the other hand, our very best students do learn these skills. In an oral summary of an assigned piece of reading in a sociology course cross-listed with women's studies, one graduating minor (sociology major) explicitly incorporated readings done for a women's studies course in a previous semester. In a paper for a history course taken in her last semester, another women's studies minor synthesized paradigms from both women's studies and political science (her major).

Our challenge as instructors is to use students' abilities as subjective knowers to appreciate the diversity of points of view expressed in class and to encourage their curiosity about why such differences exist. The analytical material can then be presented as hypotheses about these differences and about where points of view come from. Further, we might use their empathic skills to help them understand not only the feelings and thoughts of others but also the historical, social, and intellectual contexts that influence them.

The minors' exit interviews indicate that we are meeting this challenge with about 25 percent of the students. One student remembered being "asked to think about why an author chose to write about this subject, why she had the perspective she did, how her work connected with her life." Another said, "In other courses, ideas are posed to us as 'this is the way it is,' but in women's studies courses an idea would be given to us to evaluate. I learned to question things I read for the first time.... You gave your opinion, but you were also asked for evidence. It's a good thing. You have a tendency to spit it out without thinking much about it."

FEMINIST PEDAGOGY

Our goal was to assess whether students feel able to speak when they want to in women's studies classes and whether their voices are heard and respected. Despite the fact that we originally formulated a much more complex goal about shared authority in the classroom, the student members of our assessment committee were adamant that, to them, the ability to speak freely and confidently in class was the key element of feminist pedagogy. To assess "voice," we used a short questionnaire in women's studies classes and questions on the minors' exit interviews, and the alumnae survey.

The results were reassuring. All the minors, without exception—both African American and white—indicated that they felt welcome to speak in class and that various points of view were respected. "Discussion, not confrontation" was the way one minor described the exchange in the typical women's studies classroom. "I talked more than I've ever talked," commented another. "It's not that I was restricted in my expression in other classes," observed yet another student, "it's just that I knew that my opinions would be welcome in women's studies classes." Two-thirds of the alumnae also remembered women's studies classes as those in which their voices were heard and respected. Although some of them felt male students to be scornful at times, the alumnae commented that the instructors were always supportive. "My point of view was as important as the teacher's," reflected one graduate certificate holder. Another student observed that she found herself and found her voice through the kind of supportive criticism offered in the women's studies classroom.

Since the majority of our students are subjective knowers, they revel in the opportunity to express what they *know* from their own experience and have that understood and validated in the classroom (as opposed to being *told* what to *know* and being expected to express only that received information). They also are willing to hear others and acknowledge that what others have to say is equally important. They are most likely to criticize other students when they speak about things they have not personally experienced (males talking about women; women talking about men; whites talking about African Americans; an individual talking about rape survivors if she/he has not experienced or been threatened by rape). Some students are able to discuss the process or background from which these personal views arise; in other words, to address how subjective knowledge is *constructed*—and this certainly is the level at which instructors hope to bring the discussion. We believe, however, that both students and instructors are cautious about "analyzing" a view whose expression and validation is a personal victory of sorts for the student.

We asked the "voice" question of students enrolled in women's studies courses at the end of the fall 1990 term: "Was your voice (your questions, concerns, and opinions) heard and respected in this class?" In three of the nine classes surveyed, *all* of the students responded "yes." Positive responses in the other six classes ranged from 78.5 percent to 97 percent. In all of the classes, students remarked that questions and comments were encouraged and that diverse opinions were respected. Sample comments were:

> *The class fostered participation and personal stories from everyone in relation to the works being examined.*

> *I never felt judged or criticized, although frequently I encountered disagreement as well as agreement.*

> *The instructor was very tolerant of opinions.*

While a popular misconception is that a women's studies class is an alienating environment for males, our data suggest that men form new and close friendships with females in women's studies classes

---

Students expressed appreciation of the willingness of the instructor and other students to listen to many perspectives.

In the few instances where students felt their voices were not heard, they offered their own explanations in terms of the size of the class (one had an enrollment of 150), their lack of interest in the class, and their own unwillingness to speak out. In some cases, students expressed the feeling that the class atmosphere was not conducive to their voice being heard.

The number and quality of positive responses indicate that women's studies instructors accomplish their goal of letting students' voices be heard in the classroom. Students find that their own opinions and feelings are respected and that the opinions and perspectives of others are instructive. Among the courses surveyed, smaller classes and classes that focused more on class discussion and students' participation were the ones in which the highest percentage of students felt they had a "voice."

Another indication of the emphasis on student voices in women's studies classes comes from the results of the "Friendship Questionnaire." Students in women's studies classes were asked, in addition to information about friends, to describe their women's studies class and other classes that they were taking concurrently in terms of number of students, style of teaching (lecture, lecture plus questions/comments, lecture and discussion, mostly discussion), and whether group projects were recommended or required. Even considering only classes with fifty or fewer students, women's studies classes still were less likely to be all lecture (2 percent versus 15 percent), more likely to be lecture plus discussion (55 percent versus 26 percent), as opposed to lecture plus students' questions/comments (34 percent versus 53 percent), and more likely to be mostly discussion (9 percent versus 6 percent). These results demonstrate that there is a greater structural emphasis on student voices in women's studies classes. Women's studies courses also were more likely to recommend or require group projects (72 percent versus 41 percent), suggesting that students also are more likely to learn in these classes that they have something of value to share with one another.

PERSONAL GROWTH
Our initial goal here was to measure the sense of "we-ness" students felt in the women's studies classroom. We were especially interested in how women's studies affected students' friendships. Because ODU has essentially a commuting student body and its students are older, often with family and job responsibilities, it is difficult for students to create friendship networks. In

the minors' exit interviews and the alumnae questionnaires we asked, "Did women's studies courses change your friendships or social network (make friends, lose friends, change nature of friendships)? If so, how?" Seventy percent of the minors and 73 percent of the alumnae answered "yes". Several mentioned making new friends: "Women's studies enlarged my circle of friends just by the nature of the open, honest classes"; "I found kindred souls whom I could associate with in a comfortable atmosphere"; "It gave me a new and different network of friends who fuel my intellectual pursuits." Others mentioned that the quality and depth of their relationships had improved. One minor stated, "It has changed the nature of all our [old friends'] friendships. [They are] at a deeper level now. It's almost like a spiritual bond." Two minors stated that they had made "lifelong" friends in women's studies classes. Others found that some old friendships suffered. One male minor said he was "weeding out old friends" but also that his friendships were "not so superficial now." A woman minor said, "I now have more women friends and fewer men friends. Before it was just the opposite."

Students in women's studies courses were also asked at the beginning of the semester and then again at the end of the semester to estimate their number of female and male acquaintances, friends, and close friends in their women's studies classes and in the other classes that they were taking concurrently. At the end of the semester, students were asked to indicate the extent of their interaction with their best friend in class. Whatever classes they take at ODU, students in general report knowing more students in class, at all levels of friendship, at the end of the semester. The results, however, indicated that both female and male students show a greater increase in the number of *close* female friends from the beginning to the end of the semester in women's studies than they do in other classes. Interestingly, male students (but not females) also show a greater increase in the number of female friends (as opposed to close female friends) in women's studies classes than they do in other classes. It may be that a women's studies class provides a context in which men are freed from any heterosexual incentive to pursue women and are allowed to view them as friends.

Since the teaching styles characteristic of women's studies classes may encourage students to get to know one another, additional data analyses (analysis of covariance) were done to compare friendship patterns while controlling for teaching style. Even then, women's studies classes continued to enhance and alter friendships more than non-women's studies classes did.

The results suggest that the friendship process that distinguishes women's studies classes from other classes is the deepening of friendships with women (that is, more close female friends). While a popular misconception is that a women's studies class is an alienating environment for males, our data suggest that men form new and close friendships with females in women's studies courses. Although the style in which women's studies courses are taught (for example, more discussion) might have accounted for these findings, covariance analyses indicated that it did not. This suggests that something else about women's studies classes—the content, the opportunity to share personal information (not just opinions), or the discovery that others have similar points of view on important issues—encourages the development of close female friendships and, for males, new female friendships.

Although our initial goal was to focus on friendships, the data we received from the minors' exit interviews and the alumnae questionnaires encourage us to speak more broadly of the changes women's studies produced in students' lives. Among the minors, the student who spoke most forcefully about this indicated that feminism is a way of life for her, that women's studies and feminism focused not only her academic life at ODU but her plans for future education and for employment. In her interview she said that women's studies courses had affected "every aspect" of her life, making her rethink her "cultural, religious, family values, friendships, romantic relationships, every relationship I have and the decisions I make. As far as intellectually, it's focused my academic career—the questions I ask in class, the perspectives I use on the material, what I agree and disagree with." Other students also indicated that women's studies affected their work plans. One student now knows that she wants to work more closely with people, another wishes to work specifically with women, and yet another has switched her field for prospective graduate studies from psychology at ODU, with its limited number of women's studies courses, to sociology, with its numerous feminist scholars.

The alumnae responses to the questions asking whether women's studies affected their personal, professional, and intellectual lives were even more pronounced. They had more to say on this subject than on any other that we asked. Women's studies affected everything about them, three women indicated, from the way they thought to the nature of their livelihood. Another woman declared, "What I learned in those classes will never cease to affect every aspect of my life." Yet another said that the program completely changed her life, and without women's studies, she would not have developed her writing and expertise about women. "I sometimes felt as if I had a completely new brain," declared a graduate.

Two other alumnae specifically indicated that they apply what they learned to the workplace and volunteer activities. Several women stressed that the program helped them to empower themselves, to tap what was inside, with one woman remarking that women's studies satisfied a longing she did not realize she had. Another noticed that she had become less intimidated by male authority figures: "Awareness leads to growth," she commented, "and so I grew." A Japanese graduate certificate holder, now wrestling with the role demands of marriage and motherhood, asserts her determination to make her domestic life egalitarian and to treat her daughter and any future sons the same. The one alumna who declared the program to have had minimal impact on her—merely reinforcing what she already knew and believed—is now getting a graduate certificate in Jungian studies, focusing on perceptions of men's and women's roles. "Not everybody is discontent as a woman," she reminds us. Others used their acceptance of the feminine to increase their self-confidence and to help empower other women. For many alumnae, political beliefs were not changed by women's studies as much as they were sharpened and firmed up.

In addition to learning about themselves and shaping their life choices, students and alumnae told us that they had learned about others, especially other women. One minor indicated that having heard other students talk about their lives in women's studies courses, she is now more sensitive to the needs, thoughts, and feelings of others. Another student, an African American woman, thought that women's studies courses stand out in their awareness of the variations among human beings. On the alumnae questionnaire, three women wrote that they learned tolerance and patience in women's studies classes because they realized that not everyone's life experiences are the same.

IMPACT ON FACULTY

Because a number of us had come into feminist scholarship through our participation on the Women's Studies Advisory Council, and others of us viewed the WSAC as an oasis from exasperating departments, we decided to examine the impact of women's studies on ourselves as faculty members. Our method was to pair off and to interview each other. All but one of the ten who participated had taught at least one women's studies or cross-listed course.

Each of the remaining nine faculty members interviewed mentioned the exhilaration of teaching women's studies courses. For many of us, these are our favorite courses because they touch on the subject matter of our research; they offer a respite from a heavy diet of service courses; students are more engaged in women's studies courses; or we are able to experiment with teaching techniques. We find that teaching women's studies courses inevitably influences what and how we teach in other courses. We bring more material about women into our standard courses, and we often introduce more discussion or joint student projects into those courses as well. One faculty member observed that teaching in the ODU Women's Studies Program had stimulated her interest in the theory and practice of feminist pedagogy, while another commented that she had garnered material for her mainstream philosophy courses from her women's studies courses. "And when I teach logic," she added, "I move beyond the traditional approach—logic as criticism, and usually negative criticism—to its constructive and creative role." Another faculty member attributed the dramatic shift in her linguistics courses to the women's studies faculty development sessions on minority women. These resulted, she said, "in valuing (verbally and nonverbally) contributions of women and gay students. No more chilly climate in my classes."

Involvement in women's studies also has had a positive effect on research and scholarship. Two faculty members commented that they had not really enjoyed doing research until they began doing feminist research. Women's studies "made me actually *want* to publish," one woman observed, while another recalled that the first time she submitted a feminist paper to a conference, shortly after she arrived at ODU, she did "the first draft in a single weekend, on a topic I'd been hoarding notes on for years.... That may have been my first experience of joy in writing. I now find writing my most rewarding professional activity." Still another faculty member concludes that it was her respect for the bravery of a former director of women's studies who, through mentoring, gave her the courage to do feminist research. She added, "My growing familiarity with feminist scholarship has given me more realistic, less inflated expectations of what is involved in doing that and more conventional scholarship. Now I am more willing to give an interesting project a try rather than assuming that much more knowledge and experience would be required on my part."

Another woman first encountered the now-influential feminist scholarship in her discipline through agreeing to teach a women's studies cross-listed course in her department because no one else was available to offer it. Two faculty members, neither in fields where this is customary, undertook joint book-length projects with graduate students, one of which has been published. One of those faculty members also has used our annual Work in Progress conference on feminist scholarship to spur herself into doing research, giving a presentation and submitting an article on a topic new to her.

A majority of those interviewed indicated that involvement on the WSAC, in combination with participation in the ODU Women's Caucus, had been significant socializing forces into the political climate of the university. As one woman put it: "I feel that I have benefitted from watching other feminist women maneuver as academics, after trying unsuccessfully myself to find role models among male professors.... This has given me the opportunity to be more myself in academic settings, rather than maintaining a low profile, as I had done at other institutions where I had taught." Another, who characterizes her department as "almost oblivious to university politics," maintains that "whatever I have learned about the political life of the university has come from my women's studies friends." A third remembered her early days at ODU, before there was a comparable organization for black faculty members, when participation on the WSAC introduced her to a core group of sympathetic faculty members.

Finally, everyone cites the importance of the friendships they have formed with other women's studies faculty members. Often our closest and most significant university friendships are with one another. While we also have university friendships based along departmental lines, the combination of shared values (if not disciplinary interests) and absence of intradepartmental competitiveness among WSAC members gives our relationships a distinctive sunniness. Like our students, we find that our shared feminist perspective yields true and lasting friendships.

EFFECT OF PARTICIPATION IN "THE COURAGE TO QUESTION"

Participating in "The Courage to Question" has permitted us to accomplish our two initial overriding goals: to determine what we are teaching our students and what they are learning and to reinforce bonds among members of the Women's Studies Advisory Committee. Because the project required us to articulate our educational goals and objectives, we were obliged to meet as a committee (plus additional faculty and student representatives) repeatedly. Although the Women's Studies Program has sponsored excellent colloquia and faculty development workshops throughout its history, this was the first time we had faced one another and asked, "What are our goals?" Also, for the first time we have on paper a comprehensive and clear statement about

Many of us needed to be reminded that there
often is a difference between what is said by
the instructor in the classroom, no matter how
clearly, and what is heard by students

what we are doing in women's studies, a description of our women's studies
program goals that we can share with others interested in developing wom-
en's studies courses in their departments. It was a validating and reassuring
experience to discover that each of us does have a clear picture of what she is
trying to communicate to students and that, when put together, these individual views reveal a shared vision of what the Women's Studies Program is
about. We have found words to describe what we are trying to do in our
classroom, and we have discovered in one another resources, knowledge, and
skills that previously we may have overlooked.

On an individual level we already have planned alterations to our courses based on which ideas or concepts students are not grasping and which
skills students still need to develop. Many of us needed to be reminded that
there often is a difference between what is said by the instructor in the classroom, no matter how clearly, and what is heard by students. Without being
negligent about the content of the course materials that we so carefully put
together, we must nonetheless pay more attention to whether and how students are processing lectures, discussions, and reading assignments. In some
classes this has resulted in more group discussion or more feedback from students. In general, we are talking much more about classroom dynamics, for
the FIPSE project revealed just how starved we were for discussion about
teaching. We have built upon the project's assessment of teaching by spon-
soring a feminist pedagogy workshop each of the last two springs, during
which we refined teaching strategies and extended our investigation of the
connection between teaching and learning.

Another new shared activity initiated by the FIPSE project is the annual
WSAC retreat. In 1990, we met for a few days late in the spring to talk about
assessment tools. That meeting, which produced our institutional research
design, also produced a new cohesiveness in the faculty and renewed our
spirits. As a consequence, we held our second annual retreat the following
spring, extending its length by two days. That time we talked over the preliminary findings from the assessment project, planned the next year's wom-
en's studies activities, and started some long-range planning for the program.
At this year's retreat, we will discuss the findings from this report and share
ideas about both knowledge base and learning skills. We have focused on
ourselves as participants in a women's studies program more than ever before
in our history, and, as a result, we feel we have achieved a sense of identity
and community as women's studies faculty members.

Participation in the project also has led to closer ties with students. We do not think it a coincidence that a women's studies student group started up again last year after a several-year lapse. Its network is expanding all the time. In addition to women's studies minors, it now includes those who have graduated, current graduate students, and friends from the community. Their activities even extend to occasional student-faculty potlucks. Spurred by updating our alumnae mailing list for our alumnae questionnaire, we held a women's studies reunion a year ago and plan to hold a second one to commemorate the fifteenth anniversary of the program.

The amount of voluntary labor to accomplish this project was enormous. At times it seemed to WSAC members that they would drown in assessment materials. Nonetheless, our involvement has made us a more cohesive faculty and, at the same time, has initiated a period of critical reassessment of what we are teaching, how we are teaching it, and what students have gained from the whole enterprise.

1. Judith Fetterley, *The Resisting Reader: Feminist Approach to American Fiction* (Bloomington: Indiana University Press, 1978).
2. M. F. Belenky, B. M. Clinchy, N. R. Goldberger, and J. M. Tarule, *Women's Ways of Knowing* (New York: Basic Books, 1986).
3. Belenky, et al., *Women's Ways of Knowing*, 69–70.
4. Belenky, et al., *Women's Ways of Knowing*, 134.
5. Belenky, et al., *Women's Ways of Knowing*, 137.
6. Belenky, et al., *Women's Ways of Knowing*.

STUDENT QUESTIONNAIRE
OLD DOMINION UNIVERSITY

Name:
Social Security Number:
Women's studies major/minor:
Course name and number:
Instructor:
Number of students in the class:

1. Style of teaching:
☐ all lecture
☐ lecture and students' questions/comments
☐ lecture and discussion
☐ mostly discussion

2. Does the instructor recommend or require group discussion or group projects?

3. Currently, how many students do you know in class (including acquaintances and friends)?
___ number of female acquaintances and friends
___ number of male acquaintances and friends

4. Currently how many students in class are friends?
female friends / male friends

5. Currently how many students in class are close, personal friends?
female close friends / male close friends

6. Think of the person whom you know *best* in this class. Check all of the following activities that apply to your interactions with this person:
☐ I see her/him only in class.
☐ I see her/him before and/or after classes but only at ODU.
☐ I see her/him for social occasions away from ODU.
☐ I talk with her/him outside of class about course assignments.
☐ I talk with her/him outside of class about topics mentioned or discussed in class.

7. How did being in class together change (if it did) your relationship with this person?

ALUMNAE QUESTIONNAIRE

INTRODUCTION: In order to learn more about Old Dominion University's Women's Studies Program and its impact on students, we ask that you respond to the following questions. We are interested in anything and everything that you have to share with us about your women's studies experiences, but feel free to skip questions that are not relevant to your situation. Women's studies include all cross-listed courses, not just WMST courses.

Background Information

1. What year did you graduate?

2. What is your age?

3. What is your race/ethnicity?

4. What was your major?

5. After leaving ODU did you earn any advanced degree(s)? In what fields?

6. Are you currently earning any advanced degree? In what field? Please provide us with an employment and volunteer activity history:

7a. First job (since graduation from ODU); number of years at the job

7b. Second job; number of years at the job

7c. Third job; number of years at the job

8. List volunteer activities since graduating from ODU

9. How were the learning environments structured in your women's studies courses (e.g., lecture, small group discussions, group projects)?

10. Did the size of the class make a difference? If so, how?

11. Were the learning environments different from non-women's studies courses? If so, how?

12. Was there much discussion in women's studies classes? Did students debate or argue with each other? Did you feel that your voice was heard and respected? If not, why not?

13. Did you discuss course readings and lectures outside the classroom? If so, with whom? (specify relationship: roommates, female friends, male friends, family)

14. Were different points of view encouraged by the instructors in your courses? If so, how did instructors teach you about different points of view? (give examples)

15. Did you participate in women's studies activities other than courses? If so, describe these and their impact on you.

16. How did your participation in the women's studies program make you feel about yourself?

We are interested in all of your thoughts and feelings about women's studies courses and the women's studies program at ODU. Please share any that have not been addressed by these questions.

WELLESLEY COLLEGE

COUNTING THE MEANINGS

BY ROSANNA HERTZ AND SUSAN REVERBY[1]

Wellesley College's overall query for the project was: what makes
women's studies at a women's liberal arts college different?
Comparing women's studies and non-women's studies courses,
Wellesley focuses on three questions: Did the courses change or
affect students' personal lives, their intellectual lives, and their
political beliefs? Did students feel pressure to give politically correct answers and identify only with feminist ideas? And, was the
pedagogy different?

Wellesley College, founded in 1870 and opened in 1875, is one of the traditional "seven sister schools" dedicated to the education of women. Located
in a suburb just outside of Boston, it has a diverse student body of more than
2,200 women who came last year from every state in the U.S. and from sixty-
one different countries. Nearly 70 percent of the students receive aid from
some source, and the college admits on a "need-blind" basis.[2] The college
also has had a traditional commitment to gender equity on its faculty. The
male/female ratio on the faculty is about 50/50, even at the tenured level,
and the president of the college has always been a woman. The college in recent years also has made an effort to hire more faculty members of color with
"target of opportunity" hiring positions and other incentives to departments.

Somewhat ironically, Wellesley, like most women's colleges, was somewhat slower than larger coeducational universities in making a firm commitment to women's studies. Throughout much of the first century of the college's existence, Wellesley built and supported what Bryn Mawr's first
president, M. Carey Thomas, labeled a "male curriculum." Wellesley, as with
many of its sister institutions, was dedicated to proving that gender did not
matter in education and that women could do the work thought only appropriate for men.

When the first stirrings of women's studies began in other colleges and
universities across the country in the late 1960s and early 1970s, a 1971 report to the college's trustees entitled "Committee on the Future of the
College" considered, among other issues, the question of women's studies. At

"If Wellesley teaches our students that they can
do anything, women's studies helps them to
understand that if they cannot, it is not their
fault"

---

that time, the report's faculty authors concluded that specific courses on
women in the coeducational schools "seem intended to provide counseling
services as well as factual information to students often in desperate need of
advice and moral support." They unanimously rejected the idea of a special
institute on women and referred interested students to courses in the existing
curriculum "that dealt in large measure with women's problems." At that
time, a survey showed that students could find such coverage in 3 courses,
with women as sub-units in 4 other courses, and receiving some thematic
mention in 9 others out of a total curriculum of 493 courses.[3]

Despite other similarly inhospitable pronouncements, the elements necessary to create a women's studies program coalesced in the interstices of the
college. The availability of outside funding and support from the college's
president and dean led to the founding in 1974 of a Center for Research on
Women, a mile away from the main campus (although in a college-owned
house) and staffed with researchers almost all of whom were *not* members of
the faculty. But as interest on the part of students and faculty members for
courses in women's studies grew, a small group of intrepid faculty members
created the beginning of a coherent program and voluntarily directed its early students. These respected women faculty members, both junior and senior
and drawn from the humanities and social science departments, were able to
give the initial program intellectual substance.

The program's viability became less problematic after 1981 when a well-
respected feminist scholar, Nannerl Keohane, became the college's president.
In 1982, it became possible for students to major in women's studies without
special petitioning, and the president authorized hiring one junior faculty
member (part-time the first year, then full-time and tenure track from then
on) with an appointment solely to the Women's Studies Program. In 1986,
another half-time faculty appointment was made available, which became
full-time in 1989. A year later, another half-time faculty member (with a
joint appointment in another department) became part of the program.[4]

Ten years later, the program is still small in terms of control over faculty
lines but large in terms of student interest, course loads, and majors. There
are now nine overcrowded core courses, two-and-a-half faculty members
whose appointments are to the program (including one tenured), more than
sixty cross-listed courses, and more students majoring in women's studies
than in half the departments at the college. More than 40 faculty members
(out of approximately 225) teach the cross-listed courses and consider themselves part of the broader women's studies community. Women's studies at

Wellesley functions as a department with faculty members, separate office space, majors, budgets, a secretary, and a director who is treated administratively as a department chair. In March 1992, Academic Council, the college's faculty-administration governing body, voted to make *de jura* what was *de facto*: the Women's Studies Program became a department after trustee approval on April 8, 1992.

In its early years in the 1980s, the program's goals were to make women's studies appear "intellectually respectable" at the college and to build faculty, student, and administrative support for its offerings as well as tenure for its key junior faculty members. The program always had a commitment to multicultural education and made this a requirement in its major in 1983, long before any other department in the college. The program has grown in a college that over the last ten years has had a liberal feminist ethic and the continued historical belief that its mission is the empowerment of women. If one phrase sums up what makes women's studies at Wellesley different from the rest of the college, it is our saying that "if Wellesley teaches our students that they can do anything, women's studies helps them to understand that if they cannot, it is not their fault."

TEACHING AT WELLESLEY COLLEGE

As a liberal arts undergraduate college, Wellesley traditionally has taken special pride in its teaching and small classes. Discussion, even in the lower-level courses, is an expected part of the classroom experience. By the time students are juniors and seniors, they participate in small seminars that constitute the core of their majors. Thus, as a women's college with small classes, Wellesley prides itself on giving "voice" to women. Speaking, discussion, and student participation in various forms are to be the hallmark of a Wellesley education.

While in recent years publications have become important to tenure and promotions, teaching remains, at least rhetorically, the heart of the college's mission. Students say they come to Wellesley over other Ivy League institutions because they will have more contact with faculty members who are expected to serve as exemplary teachers, role models, and citizens. Besides laboratory assistants, Wellesley has no graduate students serving as teaching assistants or graders.[5] Thus, much of the commitment to student learning—considered the core of women's studies elsewhere—is seen as central to both Wellesley's mission and its teaching practices. The institution publicizes and capitalizes on this seemingly unique commitment to quality teaching over "renting" the scholarly reputation of its faculty members to entice students to enroll.[6]

Despite the emphasis on teaching, what counts as "good teaching" at Wellesley is supposed to be normative but is often ill-defined. "Good teaching" is one of the things everyone knows when they see it but still can be elusive. Wellesley does make an effort to make its elements clear by requiring senior faculty members to visit classes of junior faculty members and by annual meetings that focus, in part, on a junior faculty member's teaching. Associate professors are again visited in the classroom when they are up for promotion to full professors. These visit reports serve diagnostic, but primarily evaluative, purposes. Teaching seminars and some support for innovative teaching is supported by the dean's office. In the last few years, a move to emphasize teaching has again grown. A Center for Learning and Teaching has now been proposed and an invigorated committee on educational research has been holding "shop talks" on pedagogy and providing "quick fix" grants for teaching purposes. Faculty members also are encouraged to meet students outside the classroom and to facilitate individual student interests through tutorials.

Students are required to fill out an evaluation of the teaching that is numerically quantified by the institution and used for tenure and promotion. The medians for departments, divisions, rank of the faculty, and the institution as a whole are distributed on a regular basis. However, unlike at Swarthmore and Bowdoin, for example, written letters about faculty members' performance are not solicited by promotion committees, which rely heavily on the statistical evaluations; students, however, are encouraged on their own to write about teaching.

The evaluation forms that Wellesley has used for most of the last decade (currently under review) involve three major questions: "Was the instructor in command of the subject taught in this course? Does the instructor convey his or her knowledge of the subject in ways that facilitate learning? Did your instructor demonstrate an ability to deal effectively with student work?"[7] As at many colleges, there has been continued concern at Wellesley about these questionnaires. Aside from the usual questions about how the numbers are tabulated and used, discussion has focused on how the questionnaires stifle pedagogical innovation. In thinking about the "in command" question in particular, one women's studies faculty member quipped: "The correct answer in women's studies' courses should be 'no.' But if the students say 'no,' I won't get tenure!"

Many of these questions were raised by a faculty Feminist Pedagogy Group, organized through women's studies as part of this FIPSE study. In response, the dean's office has reported that at least the "in command" question will be changed. Thus, our consideration of teaching and learning in women's studies had to be made in the context of the kind of evaluation that is ongoing at Wellesley.

KEY QUESTIONS

Given Wellesley's emphasis on teaching, women's "voice," and the respect accorded the intellectual content of women's studies in the institution, our overall query for the FIPSE project became: What makes women's studies at a women's liberal arts college different? We felt that Wellesley's Women's Studies Program would be no different than any other discipline at the college if we only "conveyed knowledge" or heard women's voices in the classroom. We wanted to know if women's studies was different: Did it change or affect students' personal lives, their intellectual lives, or their political beliefs? Did students feel pressure to give "politically correct" answers and to identify only with "feminist" ideas, as women's studies often is charged with in the media and by conservatives? Finally, we also wanted to know whether the pedagogy was different in women's studies classes and in what ways, given Wellesley's emphasis on student participation in particular. We were interested in the quality of debate among students and whether or not discussion and learning continued outside the classroom, and if so, with whom.[8]

METHODS AND SAMPLING

In the early spring of 1990, we wrote an open-ended questionnaire that tapped various aspects of these concerns (see pages 130–31). After a pilot test of the questionnaire in two classes, we administered the revised version to students by using a selected sample of courses taught in the spring of 1990. We waited until the last two weeks of the semester to administer the questionnaire, assuming that students would be in a better position to answer the questions at this late point. Since we were interested in examining whether women's studies courses differed from non-women's studies courses, we used a *matched* sample of courses offered in the social sciences.[9]

Courses were selected in the following way: Women's studies courses were defined as those courses listed through the Women's Studies Program. All courses (five) taught as part of the women's studies curriculum were included in the sample for a total of 135 questionnaires. Also included in this category were a sample of cross-listed women's studies courses (seven) in other disciplines for another 166 questionnaires. For the purposes of analysis, we

Rather than "closing" the American mind,
women's studies courses seem to have "opened
up" our students to critical and different ways
of thinking and valuing knowledge

---

will treat all the core and cross-listed courses as women's studies courses for a total of 301 women's studies' questionnaires (68 percent of the sample).[10]

Non-women's studies' courses were those courses that were not cross-listed, but were in the same discipline as the cross-listed courses. In order to pull a matched sample for each cross-listed course selected, we selected a course (at the same level of the curriculum, where possible) that was not cross-listed with women's studies. We surveyed five control courses for a total of 140 questionnaires (32 percent of the sample).

We telephoned faculty members who taught all the courses chosen for the survey and asked for their participation. All solicited faculty members were very cooperative (only one cross-listed women's studies faculty member did not participate). Faculty members were asked to distribute the survey during the last twenty minutes of class and to designate one student to collect the questionnaires and drop them off in a designated box.

This sampling strategy yielded a total of 441 questionnaires; 32 percent were control surveys and 68 percent were either core women's studies or cross-listed women's studies courses. Students in both groups were similar with regard to race and ethnicity, though students in women's studies were slightly older than those in non-women's studies classes. This may reflect the fact that students wait to take women's studies courses as electives when they are in their later years in the college. At the time of the survey, only 4 percent of the students in either women's studies or non-women's studies' classes were women's studies' majors. This is important because what students report to have learned in women's studies classes is not a reflection of their *a priori* choice of major.[11]

The responses to questions were coded. A student assistant tallied the responses of each question and provided in-depth quotes in order for us to understand what the percentages meant.

We also wrote a separate open-ended interview guide to use with the majors and alumnae of the program. A random stratified sample of alumnae was interviewed by telephone, and all graduating majors in 1990 were interviewed on site. In the latter case, interviews were tape recorded and then transcribed. Questions were similar to the course questionnaire with the addition of queries about how women's studies affected their career decisions and lives. While this data is very interesting, time constraints did not allow us to analyze this material quantitatively for this report. However, we have used some of the qualitative comments.

These questions were shaped by the two central investigators for the project: Rosanna Hertz in sociology and Susan Reverby in women's studies. These ideas were discussed in a Feminist Pedagogy Group that met for three semesters to discuss multicultural education, the institutional barriers to women's studies teaching, and problems with teaching evaluations. We also discussed the questionnaire with faculty members on the Women's Studies Advisory Board.

FINDINGS

☐ *Does women's studies affect students' lives?* There was little difference between women's studies and control courses on how students perceive the effects on their intellectual lives and political beliefs. Most students say that their courses affected them in positive ways. In the women's studies courses, however, students tend to see the change as making them more critical learners and participants in social change.

For instance, in the control group, in response to a question on how the course affected their intellectual lives, student responses included:

> *It helped me think in a more orderly manner and logically.*

> *This course has just inspired me to learn more about the world and to maybe even become part of the system that is now deciding what future outcomes will be.*

> *I am more knowledgeable and can contribute more to various conversations.*

In the women's studies courses, the student responses were more critical about thinking and about social change. It appears that the students in the women's studies courses felt they were active learners rather than passive recipients of received knowledge. Rather than "closing" the American mind, women's studies' courses seem to have "opened up" our students to critical and different ways of thinking and valuing knowledge. Sensitized to human diversity in her women's studies course, one student explained that it "will help me be more open-minded in dealing with people and situations in the future." Students in these courses answered the query on intellectual change by saying, for example:

> *It helped me to be more open-minded in terms of analyzing ethnic and racial issues. It also in some ways steered my point of perspective to-*

ward a more feminist—(Asian)—oriented stand.

It has given me a chance to write papers about things I care about, and it has given me "ammunition," for lack of a better word, against those who try and beat me down.

It has expanded my mind in every direction. I am more deeply affected by any form of racism or discrimination because I am so much more aware of it.

Powerful stimulant to exploring old territory in new ways, taking note and sharing with others what I have discovered about history—who and what is left out and included and why...it was great fun to try and sort things out.

Women's studies courses appear to make it possible for students to center what they are learning intellectually upon their own lives and experiences. But in this regard, self-emancipation through learning becomes something larger than self-aggrandizement or simply "empowerment." The self becomes rooted in an intellectual agenda. This is a far cry from the focus on "women's problems" that worried the Wellesley faculty two decades ago. While these comments are about "personal changes," they are clearly rooted in intellectual considerations, demonstrating William Blake's dictum, "for a tear is an intellectual thing." For instance, students wrote:

...it has brought into question many aspects of my life which I had never before questioned or viewed as political or philosophical—it has opened up awareness of questioning which has prompted me to actively pursue personal answers.

This course really has affected my personal life in the sense that I am more aware of the way gender/class has played a role in my life. Now if a male says something that I find offensive, I can verbalize...how I feel.

It's a liberating feeling to look at my world through a different/non-sexist perspective! I'm taking charge of my life more now because of this awareness.

In contrast, this answer in the control courses was much more narrow and instrumental. Students saw the courses as helping them read the newspaper better, make moral decisions about unemployment, renew their interest in a particular topic, or direct their job searches. It appears that in the women's studies classes, critical engagement is rooted in an internal or self-understanding of the world, while in our control courses this engagement is more external and pragmatic.[12] On many of the women's studies questionnaires, students spoke about making future commitments to social change in practice, such as doing work in communities or becoming politically active.[13] They saw their lives as connected to others in a globally linked way.

The effect of women's studies on our students' lives was most poignant in the comments from the majors and alumnae. By making the decision to major in women's studies, these students were acknowledging that their commitment to this field was different from those of students just taking a course or two. Many of the majors and alumnae saw the applicability of the women's studies courses both in their senses of self as well in their daily lives:

> *"It's hard to fight the enemy with outposts in [your] head," we were quoted in class. Women's studies is a friend in my head.*

> *I think it's given me a bit of more confidence that...books aren't always the key; that sometimes the answers are right inside of you.*

> *...it's learning that does more than fill your brain. It fills your body, it fills your heart, [and] it makes you grow....*

Other majors and alumnae spoke eloquently of the way women's studies had changed their awareness of the world. Phrases like "it changed the questions I asked myself," "it's made me sensitive to obstacles faced by other disadvantaged groups," or "my life will be devoted to women's issues...it's my life's mission" pepper their responses. Many of the alumnae discussed how it had shaped their career choices or guided their "intellectual and professional life." The effect seems clearest when one student, asked what she can do with the major, replies, "Oh, I can do anything, I just have a broad base of humanity, and I can just stem [off] from that." As one student concluded, "that's the big difference in women's studies [from other disciplines]: there's not only the opportunity to argue, but there's almost a challenge to do something about it."

☐ *Does women's studies teach divergent points of view?* Women's studies courses at Wellesley are not different in a statistical sense from the controls in encouraging multiple points of view. However, what "divergent points of view" means is clearly different once the qualitative data is read. When asked if different points of view were encouraged by the professor, almost three-quarters of the students in both groups said "yes." In both groups, students felt they were exposed to contrasting theories and differing ways to consider a topic and were encouraged to find their own answers. In the control group, however, students interpret different points of view to mean that faculty members teach divergent *theories* to explain similar phenomenon rather than differing political viewpoints. Students rarely understand that different theories in all disciplines are suffused with political viewpoints. In women's studies, where students come into the courses expecting the subject matter to be suffused with political viewpoints, they still see the professor as presenting contrasting *political views* but not different theories. This reflects the continued problem that to discuss gender, race, or class is perceived as "political"; by contrast, to ignore these categories entirely is not perceived as "political."

In discussions with the faculty, however, it is clear that many times faculty members see themselves as presenting "objective" analyses of differing theoretical positions. Because the students see the material itself as "loaded," however, the meaning of objectivity takes on a different cast in women's studies than in other fields. Faculty members often struggle in women's studies courses to help students see that there are not just differing "opinions" about particular issues but underlying theoretical differences that could have political consequences. As many of us have come to rethink what knowledge is and how it is constructed, different disciplines have begun to recognize the deeply subjective aspects of research. The view that the researcher is not dispassionate, objective, or simply a conduit to the intellectual community is becoming more commonly acknowledged.[14]

Similarly, this set of issues needs to be discussed about teaching. In the Feminist Pedagogy Group convened to consider such questions, Wellesley women's studies faculty members were particularly articulate about the problems of being seen as "non-objective"; these problems confront the women's studies professor and the professors of color (even more sharply), regardless of subject matter.

Women's studies teachers are struggling to find a new definition of "objective" and "good teacher" that clearly fits with the kinds of materials they are presenting and an understanding of the impact their course content has on students. If women's studies professors do not merely present "objective" facts nor arbitrate conflicting viewpoints as the "in-command" figure, they are searching to find a new way to describe their teaching. Perhaps this is best summed up in Barbara Hillyer Davis' analysis that the role is one of "simultaneous translator...hearing and giving back in other words what another person has just said, and at the same time presenting an explanation in another language which will illuminate for a second group without alienating the first."[15] One student used a different term for this when she labeled the classroom experience one of "mutual discovery":

> I think there is a lot of difference between teaching someone, like standing up in front of a classroom and spitting out information and expecting the students to absorb it and learn it, and learning through...mutual discovery, which is more possible in women's studies because it relates so personally to your life....

In our Feminist Pedagogy Group discussions, we found that not all of us functioned as "simultaneous translators" or were certain that this was always the best way to function. Disciplinary and personality differences were evident among women's studies faculty members. In sum, while we can say that the women's studies faculty members demonstrated a variety of pedagogical approaches, they all shared a willingness to try different teaching techniques and to focus on connecting the student to her learning.

☐ *Does women's studies pressure students to give "politically correct" answers?* When students were asked if they felt "pressure to give 'politically correct' answers" and to explain what they meant by this, the majority said that they did not feel this pressure.[16] In fact, women's studies students wrote rather extensive commentary in which they emphasized how many different viewpoints were overtly encouraged in the classroom, suggesting the "simultaneous translator" role was working. "She tried to present all points of view and/or always made it safe for differing views to be presented," explained one student, while another said of the professor, "She made it seem okay to have different points of view and that there is never only one 'right' point of view." In mediating what are sometimes necessarily intense emotional responses to subject matter, one professor was praised because "she taught us to try to connect with the person whose idea was at hand—rather than taking a separated, confrontational approach."

Our findings do suggest, however, that something different is going on in women's studies courses in terms of how students experience the discussions.

Despite the affirmation by 70 percent of the women's studies students that their classes did *not* pressure them to conform to a classroom "line," 30 percent of the women's studies group and only 14 percent of the control group felt silenced or at risk expressing unpopular opinions.[17] At first, we considered the hypothesis that there simply is more discussion in women's studies and that this would affect students' sense of more people saying the same things. However, our statistics on classroom format do not bear this out: 88 percent of the students in the control courses and 84 percent in the women's studies classes reported that the "learning environment" was structured as discussion and lecture. Only classroom observations might tell us if there is more talking from students in the actual discussion times in women's studies as opposed to other courses.

What may be at issue is less the time for talk in some quantitative sense than the *nature* of the talk itself. We suspect that the actual topics of women's studies courses allow for more discussion of deeply felt and controversial issues. The work of our colleague, David Pillemer, and his students in the Psychology Department on what Wellesley students actually remember about their classroom and college experiences supports this hypothesis. Pillemer found that Wellesley students overwhelmingly "remember" interpersonal and emotional encounters.[18]

If students are more connected to the issues under discussion in their women's studies classroom, we suspect their strong positions on these issues may be due to their connecting the discussion with the emotional concern they felt at the time. This explanation is supported by the student answers in a set of questionnaires from a women's studies history course. They reported more controversy over the interpretation of the ending of the one novel they read in the course than in the seemingly more "factual" historical materials. As one student commented, "maybe it is difficult to debate history."[19] The students' answers also make clear that the pressure they felt comes from the student culture, not the professors. As one student wrote candidly, "I don't feel the pressure. I may apply it." Another in a control class wrote, "The professor is very accepting of all ideas, even if the students generally aren't."

We note that this survey took place under the conditions of the hothouse atmosphere at Wellesley when the issue of Barbara Bush as Wellesley's commencement speaker was being debated both on the campus and throughout the country's media. (A petition from 150 Wellesley students questioned the appropriateness of Mrs. Bush as the graduate speaker, and this set off a firestorm of controversy concerning the unresolved issues about the changes in women's and family life.) The course surveys are peppered with comments about women's roles in American society and reflect the content of the Bush controversy. For instance, one student in a women's history course reported: "Students at Wellesley don't want to hear about women who choose more traditional roles such as wife and mother. To support such a choice is to be 'politically incorrect' in a women's studies class. The mind set is that this is what women did when they were oppressed—now that they are liberated, only the most meek would make such a choice."[20]

We feel it is disheartening to read the student comments from this question, but their honesty needs to be recorded. Thus, one student said, "People hesitate to state what they really feel because they *don't know* if it is right and will feel scorned by those who have 'political rightness' mastered." Another noted, "Sometimes when I disagree with what the majority of the class is saying, I don't speak up because I feel too uncomfortable." Or, in the words of another student, "There seems to be a party line on feminist issues that we had better not waver from. However, it is masked in a feeling of openness."

The problem is best summed up by a student who wrote, "The pressure is there all the time irrespective of being in this class or outside—the pressure to go with the sway of public opinion." At an elite women's college where there is a college culture of high achievement for women and a legacy of politeness as the norm for women's behavior, there may be pressure to make students feel they should not speak up and express a minority view. Long before "p.c." became a nationwide shibboleth, the problem of conformity and the failure to hotly contest ideas of any kind in the classroom were widely discussed by Wellesley faculty members. As one student wrote, "It's a combination of societal pressure not to rock the boat and Wellesley pressure to be nice." It also is possible that this conformity is a result of the primary late adolescent culture that pervades the college.[21] Not every student conforms. As one women's studies student declared, "I refuse to fall into one more form of politeness."

This "politeness" is further complicated in women's studies, where the subject matter is so linked to a sense of self. Students often write that they feel that to be critical of someone's ideas is to be critical of them as a person. As one student reported in a women's studies class before beginning her disagreement, "Don't jump all over me, but...."[22] Encouraging students to feel "safe" to voice criticism is one of the tasks discussed many times by women's studies faculty in the Feminist Pedagogy Group. However, if the theories that link women's development of self to connection with others are valid, then

The women's studies students reported discussing
the course materials outside the classroom
20 percent more than the controls

we may indeed be asking students to do something that forces them to be in tension with their developing sense of self.[23] The difficulty of helping students to understand differing points of view about deeply held identity beliefs, at a time when they are still working out who they are themselves, may be reflected in these responses as well. As one student wrote, "...sure there's a little pressure, but that's usually brought on by personal insecurity." How we work to promote "safe" debate without encouraging mere posturing, competition, and disconnection needs further thought. More research on peer pressure in the women's classroom should be done.

How much students' unwillingness to engage in debate is linked to their "shyness" also would have to be studied. Studies suggest that there is a slightly higher percentage of shy students at Wellesley than at coeducational universities. Research on shyness suggests that the metacognitive tendencies of shy people include "think[ing] about 'who does this situation want me to be?' rather than 'how can I be me in this situation'," which could be a factor in the classroom culture. Similarly, another faculty member who has read admissions files for Wellesley over the last two decades anecdotally reports that more of the letters of recommendation in the late 1980s as compared to the late 1960s describe the student as "quiet."[24]

Our students' answers also suggest that the words "politically correct" may not always mean what such a phrase has come to mean in the media in the last two years. Some students clearly thought this meant more of a classroom-based "party line" regardless of the topic. Thus, in one control class in answer to the "p.c." question, a student wrote she felt the pressure because "if you disagree with the professor he will squash you because he has more knowledge and therefore will give a more persuasive, irrefutable argument."

□ *What quality of debate occurs in women's studies?* While we have sought to investigate the reasons why some women's studies students, more than students in the control group, felt pressure from their peers to sign on to a common way of seeing the world, the vast majority of students in both groups did not experience such pressure. In fact, the statistical comparison between the two groups also suggests that women's studies students debate issues far more frequently both in and out of the classroom. Of all our questions, the numerical differences between the two groups was widest in the two questions about debate and discussion.

When we asked, "Do students debate or argue among one another?" 80 percent of the students in the women's studies classroom answered "yes," as opposed to only 55 percent in the controls. As noted, this difference is not one of format. As one student expressed eloquently, "Yes—debate, argue—no. Everyone respects everyone else's beliefs. I've never seen anyone jump down anyone's throat, but there are certainly a wide variety of opinions." Yet in the very same class another student reported, "There is usually a predominantly liberal or feminist general opinion in class (in most classes in general), and it is difficult to go against this attitude." These divergent reactions to what has happened in the same course suggest how little we really can learn from statistical generalizations and how different students actually are experiencing a course even when they are sitting in a shared classroom. Only 25 percent of the women's studies students answered "no" to the question of whether students argue among one another. By contrast, 48 percent of the students from the control group, or almost half, answered "no."

Talking and learning in women's studies takes place in many settings. We asked students how often they discussed course readings and lectures outside the classroom and with whom. The women's studies students reported discussing the course materials outside the classroom 20 percent more than the controls did (84 percent in women's studies said they had such discussions either constantly or occasionally as opposed to 63 percent of the controls). Even more striking, 17 percent of the women's studies students said such discussions were constant, as opposed to only 6 percent of the controls.

There is, however, very little difference between the groups on the question of with whom these discussions take place. The only difference is slightly more discussion (18 percent versus 13 percent) with male friends by the women's studies group. We believe this reflects the fact that the women's studies courses do raise issues about male/female relationships that the students then test in discussion with their male friends. The courses also may provide the students with a language and the "cover" of an intellectual dialogue to discuss more "personal" male/female issues. Many women's studies students also report increased dialogues with their mothers.

What our questionnaires did not tell us is whether there is more debate as well as discussion taking place outside the classroom than in it. With friends, roommates, or family, and away from any kind of real evaluative situation like a class (especially ones like women's studies where students know discussion *really* matters), students may feel freer to actually wrestle with the materials and ideas they are learning.[25] Despite students' memories that there is much discussion in women's studies classes, faculty members also report there is sometimes a good deal of silence, especially when the topics are particularly sensitive.

We suspect that the silence, or the sense of pressure, also may come from the topics and reflect the real limitations of the set classroom time and its evaluative nature. Often, students need more time to process a set of ideas, to reflect upon them, to speak to others before they really know what they think.[26] Faculty members thus have found that if complex ideas can be introduced a number of different ways and returned to later in the course, the discussions often are more fruitful. Research on women's studies learning therefore may have to take into account what happens outside the classroom as much as what actually happens inside during class time or studying.

In conclusion, our findings demonstrate the limitations of relying on quantitative evaluative data and the ways they "flatten" human experiences. Even when the quantitative answers were statistically similar between the women's studies and control courses, careful reading of the actual answers suggests that the *meanings* of the answers varied widely between the women's studies and control courses. Thus, the qualitative answers told us much more about what was really happening in the courses and gave us a deeper sense of how we might begin to "count" the meanings of our students' responses. These answers also demonstrated how much women's studies classes honed students' critical thinking and their own sense of themselves as not merely learners but active participants in linking intellectual endeavors and changing conceptions of the self to social change.

IMPACT OF THE PROJECT AND FUTURE PLANS

For the faculty members, the project enabled us to make self-conscious what is for many of us unconscious. In our discussions, we discovered joint problems of topics in the classrooms, expressed concern about both silences and pressures, and became particularly aware of the difficulties facing our colleagues of color. The project also led us to discuss with the relevant committees on campus and with the dean both evaluation problems and the need for more money for internal research on teaching. We became very aware of how the pressure of the student evaluation questionnaires kept faculty members, especially junior faculty members, fearful of innovation and controversy in their classrooms. This report also will be given as a lecture in the faculty's ongoing teaching seminars sponsored by the dean's office. Although some parts of this report gave us pause, we felt encouraged in the end by the comments of students in our classes and by the words of one who noted what women's studies had meant for her: "I will continue to question my beliefs and will continue to try to educate myself." This seems to us to sum up succinctly what we hope women's studies does for all its students.

We think our report raises the need for further studies on the following questions:

☐ What are the relationships between the late adolescent student's identity development and the kinds of issues raised in women's studies? How does peer pressure affect student learning?

☐ How are we to understand the meaning of "silences" in the women's studies classroom, and how are we to measure the "talk"?

☐ How can quantitative and qualitative research on classroom learning be used together to give a fuller picture of student learning?

☐ What kind of changes will have to be made in student evaluation questionnaires when the course content is perceived as "political"?

☐ What difference does widespread societal discussion of "political correctness" mean for the women's studies classroom and its mission as we face the twenty-first century?

☐ Can we follow women's studies students in a longitudinal manner to examine how much "social change" they actually become part of?

☐ How can we talk about "objectivity" in a way that helps students understand more fully what women's studies is attempting to do?

☐ How much does the very subject of women's studies—and its link to an emotional/affective style of learning—affect what students actually remember about their courses?

☐ Should we, or can we, attempt to help students disengage the personal from the content of the courses? How do we make them understand that while the "personal is political," it is not always true that the political is personal in the way they have come to understand it?

In sum, women's studies in a women's institution is ironically in a difficult situation: It must make gender matter and not matter in a context that struggles to make gender matter and not matter, too. The obvious demands on women's studies in coeducational institutions—to support women's centers, create role models, serve as focal points for women's issues, teach in different modes—take on subtler and different shadings in the setting of a small liberal arts college dedicated to women's empowerment and excellence in teaching.

In questionnaire responses from students and discussions among the faculty, we tried to determine what does make women's studies "different" at Wellesley. Our findings suggest that ultimately it is the subject matter of women's studies that shapes the parameters for teaching and learning. For many students, especially those coming directly from high school, women's studies is the first time that women and gender are legitimate subjects of study. In connecting the student through "mutual discovery" to herself and the wider world at the same time, women's studies creates a critical edge in its students and a critical stance in its teachers. This criticalness connects intellectual sharpness to the contemporary issues that the students face, or that they come to understand, that structure the lives of women whose life circumstances are or have been quite different from their own.

As our comparative data suggest, while there is as much discussion in women's studies as in other Wellesley classes, students perceive *both* more conformity and more debate in women's studies. We believe this reflects, in part, the pressure of "politeness" that still defines many women's cultures. Because the material is so important to the students and their lives, they both think differently about it and speak in "pregnant pauses" as well. Sometimes, however, the issues appear so overwhelming they do not know what they think. Often, only time and life experience will help them sort this out. We think, therefore, that the seeming contradiction—more conformity pressure and more debate—really is not contradictory.

Further, our data show they do speak about it much more outside the classroom. Thus, women's studies requires that we reconsider the learning boundaries of our courses. Innovative assignments, returning to similar topics in non-linear ways, use of the silences, and even the seeming conformity in a dialogic manner throughout the course may be required if we are to take advantage of the kind of learning that is already taking place.

Finally, we will have to use some of the new analyses of identity formation and community to come to terms with the pressures our students feel and the learning they are doing. Students in women's studies, as in other ethnic and black studies courses, are part of an effort to forge a new kind of learning and contestation over critical ideas. As historian Joan Wallach Scott has argued, "Contests about knowledge are now understood to be political, not only because they are contests, but because they are explicitly about the interests of groups." How we consider this and help women's studies students forge a sense of self that is both connected and open to difference remains our greatest challenge.

1. We gratefully acknowledge the participation of Wellesley College faculty members in the surveys and discussions that made this report possible. We also thank Holly Benton, Lisa Bergin, Laura Kossoff, Jennifer Schoenstadt, and Margaret Potter for their assistance in the data collection and coding. We thank Laurel Furumoto of the Psychology Department for her helpful suggestions on sampling technique. Tim Sieber and Caryn McTighe Musil made invaluable editorial suggestions. Both Suzanne Hyers and Margaret Centamore provided technical assistance, including "translating" from MAC to IBM and back.
2. *Wellesley College Bulletin* 81 (September 1991): 42, 48.
3. Susan Reverby, "Women's Studies at Wellesley Over the Decade," presentation given at A Celebration of Nan Keohane's Decade as Wellesley's President, October 18, 1991, Wellesley College.
4. It is interesting to note that this is the only academic unit in the college where all faculty members have initially been hired on a half-time basis. Even though the program has tenure-track positions, it has never been given a full-time, tenure-track line to begin with. This is unusual at Wellesley, although the college does have a history of providing "regular part-time" work with benefits and the possibility of tenure. This slow building of the program also reflects the cap on faculty increases in the 1980s.
5. When enrollment goes above eighty students in a semester, a faculty member can request a grader. This is rare and few faculty members teach this many students in a semester on what is now a two-courses-a-semester load.
6. The "renting" idea is Arthur Stinchcombe's; see Arthur Stinchcombe, *Information and Organizations* (Berkeley: University of California Press, 1990), chapter nine, "University Administration of Research Space and Teaching Loads: Managers Who Do Not Know What Their Workers Are Doing."
7. "Wellesley College Student Evaluation Questionnaires." The forms in fact leave room for the students to write comments, but these are only seen by the faculty member and are not used for evaluation. Therefore, the qualitative information on these forms is not being used to illuminate the quantitative scores. We will return to this point in our discussion of findings.
8. As a by-product of these questions, we learned a lot about the content of the courses without actually examining the syllabi or asking students about it directly. We had no hidden agenda in finding out what was taught in classes. Content was not conceived of as central to our research design.
9. We focused on social science courses because there are very few humanities and no science courses that are cross-listed in women's studies. At Wellesley, philosophy and history are considered part of the social sciences division.
10. Commitment to women's studies was measured by courses that were either part of the women's studies core curriculum or cross-listed. The reason for this is that cross-listed courses are at the option of the individual faculty member who chooses to see his or her courses as part of the women's studies curriculum. A screen by women's studies is done very informally, and faculty members are not required to submit syllabi for acceptance.
11. What we do not know, and would be interested to know in future surveys, is how many students even know that the courses they select are cross-listed with women's studies. This additional information would tell us whether or not students are conscious of a feminist style of teaching or presumed feminist content to the courses when they select their courses. Our hunch is that students are not aware of this and choose courses simply on the reputation of the faculty member.
 We suspect that even if students do not know about the bureaucratic cross-listing, they are

aware often of the faculty member's approach and can tell from the course title and description something about its content. At a small residential college, a good deal of informal information is known and shared about faculty members. In retrospect, it might have helped if in our survey we had asked students why they chose this course and if they knew it was cross-listed in women's studies.

12. This kind of instrumental view of education is, of course, fairly common; see Michael Moffatt, Coming of Age in New Jersey (New Brunswick, N.J.: Rutgers University Press, 1989).

13. If we had the time, it would be fascinating to do longitudinal studies and see what actually happens to these students in ten years' time.

14. These issues have been discussed for a number of years and are central to much women's studies thinking. For more recent discussion in other fields, see for examples James Clifford and George E. Marcus, eds.,Writing Culture: The Poetics and Politics of Ethnography (Berkeley: University of California Press, 1986) and Peter Novick, That Noble Dream: The "Objectivity Question" and the American Historical Profession (New York: Cambridge University Press, 1988).

15. Barbara Hillyer Davis, "Teaching the Feminist Minority," in Margo Culley and Catherine Portuges, eds., Gendered Subjects: The Dynamics of Feminist Teaching (New York: Routledge, 1985), 250.

16. We should note that this question was framed before the media circus around "political correctness" came to town.

17. These statistics are skewed by one course in the women's studies group where nineteen out of twenty-five students replied yes. However, if we throw out this course from the data, almost a fourth of the women's studies students still say yes.

18. David Pillemer, et al., "Memories of Life Transitions: The First Year in College," Human Learning 5 (1986): 109–23; Lynn Goldsmith and David Pillemer, "Memories of Statements Spoken in Everyday Contexts," Applied Cognitive Psychology 2 (1988): 273–86; David Pillemer, et al., "Very Long-Term Memories of the First Year in College," Journal of Experimental Psychology: Learning, Memory and Cognition 14 (1988): 709–15.

19. It is, of course, very easy to debate history. This was a large course taught by a visiting professor who may not have felt comfortable opening up the debate on a regular basis.

20. The debate around the selection of Barbara Bush and the Wellesley students' petition questioning her appropriateness will be the subject of a larger study, not related to this FIPSE report, that Hertz and Reverby are now completing. Two years later as we complete this report, this issue has clearly not gone away. Tellingly, this time the media concern is focused on a possible presidential wife, Hillary Clinton, Wellesley Class of 1969. Jerry Brown's jibe at Bill Clinton for sending state business to his wife's law firm led her to query if Brown expected her to be home with the kids serving milk and cookies. The subsequent media response to this was reminiscent of the Bush debate. Thus, the pressure students feel at Wellesley to achieve in the work world, and their sense of being silenced around traditionally "female" activities, are certainly not limited to the women's studies classroom.

21. We acknowledge that most classes at Wellesley also have returning women students who are older than "traditional-aged" students. But they do not shape the classroom culture as a whole. How much they can influence more traditional-aged students when they are still outnumbered in the classes remains to be studied. For a parallel analysis on tokenism, see Rosabeth Kanter, Men and Women in the Corporation (New York: Basic Books, 1977).

22. Reading of student entries to journals for "Introduction to Women's Studies" and comments in "Politics of Caring" course.

23. A number of researchers have written on this topic: Janet Lever, Carol Gilligan, Nancy Chodorow, etc. The idea of the "self in relations" is most theoretically developed by the Stone Center group at Wellesley College, see Judith Jordan, et al., eds., *Women's Growth in Connection* (New York: Guilford Press, 1991).

24. Jonathan Cheek, "Faculty 'Shop-talk': Teaching the Shy Student," Wellesley College, February 18, 1992; Personal communication, Maud Chaplin to Susan Reverby, March 24, 1992; see also Jonathan Cheek and L. A. Melchior, "Shyness, Self-esteem and Self-consciousness," in H. Leitenberg, ed., *Handbook of Social and Evaluation Anxiety* (New York: Plenum, 1990), 47–82.

25. As one of the authors of this report has observed, students' journals in the introductory courses demonstrate, for example, much more questioning and complex thinking than is usually articulated in the classroom.

26. The silences also may reflect student reaction to materials outside their own experiences or their life stage. For instance, abortion elicits a hotly contested debate, while infertility or reproductive technology is less likely to provoke such passionate discussion.

27. Joan Wallach Scott, "The Campaign Against Political Correctness," *Change* (November-December 1991), 37.

STUDENT QUESTIONNAIRE
WELLESLEY COLLEGE

This questionnaire is part of a study being done by Wellesley's Women's Studies Program as part of a national survey. To do the study, we are asking students in selected women's studies and non-women's studies courses to answer this brief questionnaire. Your answers should reflect your experience in the class where you received this survey. Your name is not requested and your professor will not see the survey. S/he will merely collect them and return them immediately to the women's studies office. We deeply appreciate your taking the time to do this.

Directions

If a question does not apply, please write "not applicable." If you do not have an answer or don't know, please write "don't know."

Course number and name: _____

Background Information

1. What year do you expect to graduate?

2. What is your age?

3. What is your race/ethnicity?

4. What is your major? What is your minor?

5. After graduation are you presently planning to attend graduate or professional school?

           Yes   No   Don't know   [circle one]

In what fields? [specify degrees and fields]

Questions About This Course

1. How has this course changed or affected your personal life?

2. How has this course affected your intellectual life?

3. Did it change your political beliefs? If so, how?

4. How was the learning environment structured in the classroom? (e.g., lecture only, lecture and discussion, student led, sat in a circle, etc.)

5. How does the learning environment in this class compare to any courses you have taken in women's studies? (Women's studies courses and courses cross-listed in women's studies can be used as comparisons.)

6. Is there much discussion in this class?

7. Do students debate or argue among one another? [provide examples]

8. How often did you discuss course readings and lectures outside the classroom?
      Constantly   Occasionally   Rarely   [circle one]
      Only when studying for an exam   Never
If so, with whom? [specify relationship: roommates, female friends, male friends, family]

9. Do you feel there is pressure to give "politically correct" answers?
      Yes   No   [circle one]
If yes, please explain your answer.

10. Were different points of view encouraged by the professor?
      Yes   No   Sometimes   [circle one]

11. In terms of course content, did you learn how to think about an issue or social problem from different political or theoretical points of view? [give examples]

12. Do you feel that you will apply what you learned in this class to your work and/or further education?
      Yes   No   Don't know   [circle one]
If yes, how?

■

CUNY–
HUNTER COLLEGE
FEMINIST EDUCATION

BY MICHELE PALUDI AND JOAN TRONTO[1]

Hunter College of the City University of New York, reflecting
both the political commitment of its women's studies program
and the richly diverse student population, assesses their goals and
accomplishments in three areas: multiculturalism, critical thinking, and integration of knowledge. Particular attention is paid to
the relationship of women's studies to the community and to the
program's advocacy component.

Founded by Thomas Hunter as a normal school to educate women whose career goals included teaching children and adolescents, City University of New
York–Hunter College has sustained its century-and-a-quarter commitment to
educating women. As one of the oldest branches of City University of New
York, Hunter College is now coeducational but 73 percent of its nineteen
thousand students are women, a percentage that has not varied since 1985.
Even among undergraduate non-degree students—the majority of whom are
participants in a Senior Citizen Program—two-thirds are women.

In graduate training programs at Hunter, women represent a larger percentage of students than is found in the student population as a whole. In
1990, for example, 76.6 percent of the graduate students were women. And
there are more women matriculating in graduate programs (78.7 percent)
than among non-matriculating students (71.1 percent).

Approximately 53 percent of Hunter's student population are minorities.
The largest minority representation is in the African American, non-
Hispanic category, with Hispanic Other and Asian or Pacific Islander second
and third. The ethnic classifications of Hunter's student body have remained
relatively stable over the past three years. Within the graduate programs,
black, non-Hispanic constitutes the largest minority group (14.9 percent in
1990); 67.3 percent are white, non-Hispanic.

The Women's Studies Program at Hunter College, officially begun in the
mid-1970s, has been central in women's studies since the inception of this
field of study. In 1983, the Hunter College Women's Studies Collective published *Women's Realities, Women's Choices*, the first comprehensive textbook

In order to learn about other cultures, students
need to draw connecting links between their
own experiences and the experiences of others

for introductory women's studies. Since then, Hunter's Women's Studies Program has continued to grow and evolve, adding new faculty members and striving to offer a curriculum that reflects the diversity of women on a global basis while remaining at the forefront of women's studies scholarship.

The Women's Studies Program at Hunter College has been one of three departments/programs (with Anthropology and Urban Affairs) that have shown the largest growth since 1985. Women's studies has gone from thirty-two FTEs in 1985 to fifty-eight in 1990, representing an 81 percent increase. An interdisciplinary academic program that seeks to preserve, expand, and share knowledge about women and gender, women's studies reexamines women's heritage and the role of women in contemporary society and in all cultures. It aims, through a focus on women's experiences, to open fresh perspectives throughout the entire curriculum. Women's studies at Hunter relies upon a broad community of affiliated faculty, staff, and students and is administered by a coordinator and a policy committee of elected student and faculty representatives.

Women's studies at Hunter College includes three components: curriculum, scholarship, and advocacy. Through participation in the FIPSE project, our program has sought to assess our goals and accomplishments in three areas: multiculturalism, critical thinking, and integration of knowledge. Throughout this project, we have tried to be as inclusive of our women's studies community as possible in the formulation of goals and in their assessment. As a result, we believe our assessment demonstrates that what we have hoped to develop as the strengths of our program are, in fact, strengths of our program. While work remains to be done, we believe that this assessment has helped us to recognize the crucial ways in which women's studies provides the students of Hunter College with "the courage to question."

MULTICULTURALISM

I remember in my "Women in the Third World" class, one of the first things my professor talked about was embracing similarity in the heart of difference. And it took me so long to understand what she meant, and maybe I...just took [it]...my own way, but I felt...it was about... getting yourself out of your context somehow, or recognizing that you are in your context, and everything that you see, and everything that you believe has so much to do with...where you come from.
WOMEN'S STUDIES STUDENT, 1991

The goal of multicultural learning involves a complex set of intellectual and personal traits. In order to learn about other cultures, students need to be able to draw connecting links between their own experiences and the experiences of others; to comprehend cultural differences; to deal with "culture shock"; to clear away subjective obstacles to multicultural learning such as racism and ethnocentrism.

New York City is a world city; the students at Hunter College reflect the extraordinary ethnic diversity of the globe. Nonetheless, a number of aspects of life in New York City and at Hunter College make the emergence of cosmopolitan citizens of the world problematic. First, though New York consists of people from all over the world, large parts of New York City are rigidly segregated by ethnic group and by class. Many New Yorkers live in extremely insulated communities. These structural problems are compounded by difficulties in establishing sufficient trust for multicultural understanding. As levels of incivility increase in the city as a whole, no single individual's or group's efforts for multicultural understanding will be automatically rewarded by the recognition, appreciation, or acknowledgment of others. Consequently, the high psychic costs of trying to understand others may seem too high a price to pay for uncertain results.

To assess how effectively the Women's Studies Program accomplished its complex goal of reflecting multiculturalism, we examined data in three different areas: curriculum, scholarship, and collective conversations with students.

CURRICULUM
An examination of Hunter's women's studies curriculum reveals a concerted effort to offer multicultural courses, hire faculty members from diverse backgrounds, and prepare existing faculty members to weave multicultural issues throughout their courses. The data suggest that the program's goal to infuse a multicultural perspective in the women's studies program is being met.

The proportion of the curriculum that focuses on explicitly multicultural themes is significant. During fall 1990, for example, the Women's Studies Program offered six out of twelve multicultural courses: "Women in the Third World"; "Women and Music in World Cultures"; "Autobiographies of Black Women Literary Artists"; "Working Class Women in the United States, 1865–1960"; "Changing Roles of Women in China/Japan"; and "The Politics of AIDS: Seminar in Political Behavior." During spring 1991, the Women's Studies Program offered seven out of sixteen courses on explicitly multicultural themes: "Women and Development"; "Race, Gender, and the

Movies"; "Black Women Literary Artists"; "Lesbian Voices in the Twentieth
Century"; "Women in the Middle East"; "Women, Art, and Culture"; and
"Decolonizing Desire: Fiction By Third World Women."

Students also can choose from among several additional women's studies
courses regularly offered in the program that have explicitly multicultural
subjects: "Black Women in the Americas," "Puerto Rican and Latina
Women," and "Immigrant Women in New York City." Two other cross-listed
courses regularly offered are "Gender, Ethnicity, and Disease" and "Black
Women Writers: Cross Cultural Connections."

To expand such course offerings, the Women's Studies Program has
hired new faculty members and worked with existing faculty. Over the past
several years, the program has hired additional faculty members who bring an
international and multicultural perspective to women's studies and has hired
adjuncts to offer additional courses in subjects such as "Black Women in the
Americas," "Immigrant Women in New York City," and "Lesbian Voices."

In order to prepare faculty members in multicultural women's studies
scholarship, the college has continued to support faculty development seminars on a university-wide basis. During summer 1990, a Ford Foundation-
sponsored project to integrate material on women of color into the curriculum
received support from Hunter College and included faculty members from
women's studies. The college supported for the third year the City University-
wide Faculty Development Seminar on Balancing the Curriculum for Gender,
Race, Class, and Ethnicity, in which women's studies faculty members played
a central role. The newly renovated Women's Studies Library/Resource Center also contains books, articles, and audio/visual materials rich in multicultural resources to assist faculty with their curriculum integration projects.

Additionally, faculty members teaching "Women's Studies 100" and other cross-listed courses made concerted efforts to balance their class materials
for ethnicity, sexual orientation, age, race, and class. Almost every section,
for instance, in the "Women's Studies 100" course included either Audre
Lorde's *Sister/Outsider* or Johnnetta Cole's *All American Women*. A review of
the syllabi in general revealed that numerous articles on the experiences of
lesbians, older women, African American women, Afro-Caribbean women,
Puerto Rican women, Latinas, Asian American women, Native American
women, and others also were typical.

Funds from the Hunter College Pluralism and Diversity Grant were used
for integrating global materials into the introductory course in women's studies. Funds from this grant also are being used to help faculty members work
on race and gender balancing curricula in a variety of disciplines. The

Women's Studies Program in conjunction with the Psychology Department, for example, has designed a program that will encourage students and faculty members to consider culture, ethnicity, sex, gender, class, and race as important psychological variables and to note the bias in traditional psychological theories and research paradigms. Designed by the current women's studies coordinator, Michele Paludi, the course includes four components: (1) acquisition of educational materials dealing with curriculum integration, (2) development of a resource manual on curriculum integration, (3) faculty development seminars to address curricular and pedagogical issues, and (4) development of a new course in the Department of Psychology called "Psychology of Gender, Ethnicity, and Race," which was taught in spring 1992.

Like several other institutions nationally, Hunter College has begun to explore adding a pluralism and diversity requirement to its distribution requirements. Not surprisingly, faculty members in women's studies have been actively involved in the discussion. Among the tenets of the proposal is the requirement that all students take a course focusing on women and women's contributions to the disciplines.

Expanding the multicultural emphasis in the curriculum beyond the classroom walls, Hunter also received grants from the Ford Foundation and the Aaron Diamond Foundation to support women's studies student internships in women's reproductive health care in New York City and to sponsor a three-day conference on balancing the curriculum for reproductive rights issues in a global perspective. Currently the project is focusing on developing a training program to enhance the reproductive health awareness of Latinas in New York City.

The success of such efforts in attracting diverse students to women's studies can be seen in the number of women of color, lesbians, and older women who are women's studies majors. In 1991, twelve women graduated with majors in women's studies. Among them, one older lesbian is attending Harvard Law School, one older African American woman is attending graduate school in creative writing at Michigan State University, and an African American woman is studying genetics at MIT. Suggesting both their training in multiculturalism through women's studies and the encouragement to do multicultural research, recipients of the 1991 Women's Studies Prizes wrote papers and poems reflecting multicultural issues such as "Race and the Press: Newspaper Coverage of the Central Park Jogger Case." Likewise, the Community Service Awards, presented to the *Returning Women* Magazine collective and to Satoko Yagiura and Adelaide Sakeflyo, demonstrate a similar affirmation of multicultural work.

SCHOLARSHIP
Further evidence of the multicultural focus of our Women's Studies Program is illustrated by our monthly colloquium series. For fall 1991, the program devoted one month to the following themes, all of which included material about diverse women: "Women's Studies in the Academy: Scholarship, Pedagogy, and Advocacy," "Current Issues in Women's Health: Research and Social Policy Applications," and "Women's Mental Health and Well Being." For spring 1992, the following themes were featured: "Literary and Media Images of Women," "Violence Against Women," and "Women and Disabilities." The 1991 Bella Abzug Lectureship was given by Loretta Ross and Adetoun Ilumoka and devoted to "Reproductive Rights: An African/African-American Dialogue." In 1992, the lectureship will be devoted to sex and race discrimination in the academy and workplace and will be presented by Catharine Stimpson.

In addition, Hunter is one of twenty-six Rockefeller Foundation Humanist-in-Residence sites in the country. This grant-funded program has offered two fellowships each year, beginning in 1990–91, enabling feminist scholars to work on a research project related to gender and feminism in Third World contexts and to participate with women's studies students and faculty in a monthly seminar on this topic. Annual themes for the humanist-in-residence program have been Social Constructions and Representations of Gender in Third World Societies, Women's Cultures of Resistance and Organized Feminist Movements, and 'Third World' Women/'Western' Women: Differences, Commonalities, and Cross-Currents of Experience. To date, Hunter has hosted four scholars: Vivien Ng (a historian at the University of Oklahoma), Sylvia Marcos (a psychotherapist in Mexico), Jacqueline Alexander (a sociologist at Brandeis University), and Sitralega Maunaguru (a poet, peace activist, and lecturer in literature at the University of Jaffna in Sri Lanka).

Faculty members also collaborate with students on a variety of research projects, publish papers, and present work at conferences. Examples of research currently being conducted at Hunter that have a multicultural theme include: the interface of racism and sexism in academic and workplace sexual harassment; Greek-American women; immigrant women in the United States, 1840–2000; Italian women authors, Medieval–Renaissance; minority women in academia; women and international migration; women in Central America; women in Latin America; and cross-race mentoring in the academy.

COLLECTIVE CONVERSATIONS

Donna Murdock, a women's studies student, organized a series of collective conversations with students to evaluate whether, in their experience, the Women's Studies Program fostered multicultural awareness. In a series of small-group discussions with alumnae and current students, most of whom were women's studies majors, students recognized that progress has been made in recentering the Women's Studies Program to reflect the wide diversity that typifies women's lives. As one student put it:

> ...the Women's Studies Program has really evolved, evolved into something that's really helpful to women.... [T]hey've put in more courses and they're always bringing in...speakers...it's not only about white women. And for me, that's important, being a black woman.... I couldn't identify with something where I never see myself!

Confirming the sense that women's studies courses had made serious progress toward being multiracial in content, another student revealed how different women's studies classes were than she had imagined:

> ...my mother's always told me, "there's certain things you don't say around white people!"...so me coming with this kind of prejudice, I really felt that they had to prove themselves to me. You know, it was..."So what is this women's studies about, if it's all about white women?" But I found that it really wasn't like that.

Echoing this student's sentiments, a white student commented on the transformative effect of her classes on her own consciousness:

> I have learned a lot about...how other women feel...how black women feel in society...with...racism and sexism. I wasn't aware of how they felt until they spoke up and told me. How Indian women feel and...Asian women feel, and I think I have less now of an ethnocentric view...where I think our culture is the best. I no longer feel that way at all.

Overall, students also felt women's studies
addressed multicultural issues far more directly
and productively than other departments

Other students commented on how the atmosphere established in the
classroom helped students as they negotiated their multicultural differences.
One student commented, "The class was made up of very diverse ethnic
groups, and the respect and interaction and sharing that went on was emotionally and intellectually supportive." Another expressed it this way:

> I think that women's studies has…helped me learn not to stomp on
> other people's opinions and other people's feelings, and how to get
> across "this is why I don't agree with you and this is what I believe in
> and this is why." And…that has helped me in my political science
> courses and my political life and in my life.

In addition to the overall praise of the program, students offered suggestions for meeting their need for more dialogue in courses about racism and
other "isms." "I would also like to see some more stuff implemented on
racism in our…classes and dealing with white people's racism," suggested one
student. A few women felt that inclusion of women of color sometimes only
came in special sections or at the end of courses. The insistence on continuing to improve the multicultural aspects of the Women's Studies Program is
represented by a student who praises the program highly even as she demands it strive to do more: "I think we have a very good multicultural, multiracial program, and I think…it's just admirable…seeing…the program
[change] to where it's more multicultural, multiracial. And I…still think we
have a ways to go with it, you know, I…really do." Overall, students also felt
women's studies addressed multicultural issues far more directly and productively than other departments. As one student put it, the "women's studies
community is more sensitive than other communities in Hunter College.
And I have many friends who…are really sensitive to my differences, and I
can talk about that. And that's really great."

CRITICAL THINKING

> …women's studies opens up with questions, and so…that clicked for
> me…. That's really the biggest difference in women's studies and any
> other courses I've taken…. [Y]ou question all the time, all the time.
> WOMEN'S STUDIES STUDENT, 1991

Perhaps no single goal is more often repeated as a central tenet of liberal arts education than the goal of helping students learn to think critically. Although the goal of critical thinking may seem to be an issue of "learning skills" rather than a broader goal, we conceive of critical thinking as a more complex activity. In order to engage in critical thinking, a learner must be able to see herself as capable of critical analysis, to use tools of analysis, to possess sufficient knowledge and perspective to engage in fruitful and substantive critical analysis. Thus, the goal of critical thinking involves several components: it requires "empowerment," in both a structural and a subjective sense; it requires knowledge of tools of analysis; and it requires a reservoir of situated, comprehended knowledge.

Hunter College as an urban public institution primarily consists of working-class and first-generation college students. Students at Hunter frequently come from backgrounds that either are educationally deficient (where low demands have been placed on them to write or to comprehend large bodies of material, theoretical perspectives, abstract ideas and thinking), or they perceive themselves to come from deficient backgrounds. Sixty percent of students entering Hunter require remedial work in reading, writing, or mathematics in order to do college-level work. In addition, many students are older and returning women who are unsure of their skills even when they are adequate. Consequently, it is important that we not take for granted the students' temperamental preparation for critical thinking. Thus, in order to speak of the goal of critical thinking at Hunter College we must speak about the development of a base of knowledge, tools of analysis, and a way to instill in our students the confidence and sense of self that are necessary for critical thinking.

Three assessment instruments were used in analyzing our progress in helping students in critical thinking skills: course syllabi, exams and paper assignments, and informal classroom writings. Evidence derived from this assessment supports the conclusion that students in women's studies courses are encouraged to think critically in their classes but that we might be more self-conscious about the importance of this goal.

COURSE SYLLABI

Syllabi of women's studies courses stress the need for students to develop skills of critical thinking. Although not all of the ten introductory women's studies syllabi reviewed used the language of "critical thinking," at least one did, defining it as "an ability to direct informed questions at everything you read, see, and hear." Another syllabus included, as a course goal, "to develop our intellectual ability of analysis."

One instructor, for example, teaches the introductory course in women's studies in a way that helps students learn foundations for a feminist restructuring of the academic disciplines. She focuses on methodologies and theories in a variety of disciplines, including psychology, economics, political science, and history, and offers feminist correctives to the portrayal of women in these disciplines. Her goal is to have students question the treatment of women in subsequent courses they take. Other faculty members teaching the introductory course revolve their lectures/presentations and discussions around themes, such as gender as socially constructed, the distinction between sex and gender, women's health concerns, and women's career development.

EXAMS AND PAPER ASSIGNMENTS

Course assignments can be a vehicle through which students can develop skills in critical thinking. To foster critical thinking, women's studies courses at Hunter stress paper writing and essay exams—unlike many other courses in the college, especially at the introductory level.

Often, assignments require students to engage in research, assess the adequacy of that material, and reflect on the importance of the research. For example, the first assignment in one introductory women's studies course required students to browse through professional journals in women's studies and think about the importance of one essay in contemporary scholarship. Rosalind Petchesky's "work" assignment required students to interview two women whose work experiences were likely to have been different and to compare them. Joan Tronto's "caring" assignment required students to track the kinds of caring work done in their households and reflect upon these results to investigate gender roles in their households.

Exam essay questions frequently require integration of material from several sources that necessitates a critical reflection of ideas. Marnia Lazreg's "Women in the Middle East" course, for example, required students to compare Edward Said's "orientalist" practice with an essay on *Arab Women in the Field*. Joan Tronto asked students in the introductory course to discuss some implications of claims such as, "Patriarchy oppresses all women." This provided an opportunity for students to reflect a broad range of knowledge and the need to define, to qualify, and to dispute commonly heard overgeneralizations.

Additional evidence that students do learn analytical skills are apparent from the Women's Studies Prizes. While several awards went to collections of poems, others have been awarded to students who have written analytical essays, such as "Fetal Protection Policies: A Discriminatory Policy or a Business Necessity?" "Race and the Press: Newspaper Coverage of the Central Park Jogger Case," and "Dangerous Appetites: Eating as Metaphor in Christine Rosetti's 'Goblin Market'."

INFORMAL CLASSROOM WRITINGS
Students in the introductory women's studies classes were asked to informally provide information about whether the course fits with their educational goals. As one woman stated:

> This women's studies course has helped me to see things in a different light. I've realized that I've believed many things that are not true, so in general, my overall awareness has expanded. I am more critical of what I hear [and] read.

In the course survey conducted of introductory women's studies classes during fall 1990 and spring 1991 (see pages 154–55), many students commented on aspects of critical thinking as an outcome of the course. A typical range of remarks included statements such as: "an empowering experience"; "This course definitely made me think for myself"; and "It introduced me to a whole new world of ideas and concepts." Another woman wrote:

> This class was much more in-depth and required much more work on the part of the student. Most intro courses consist of at least 100 students, 2 multiple choice tests and a text that is opened twice.

In the collective conversations, Donna Murdock noted that students felt the program had become more self-conscious over the years in its goal of fostering critical thinking. The consensus among students was that it was important to make critical thinking an expressed goal. In comment after comment, the students felt challenged to think in their women's studies courses.

For some it was overwhelming, but they suggest that the kind of thinking demanded of them was distinctive and worth the extra work:

> ...a lot of people take women's studies courses because they think they're going to be easy, and then they flip when they get in there and they find out these are probably the hardest courses! Because, first of all, you have to think.... It's not like math, it's not like just about any

Some students experience a new tension between
exercising their critical faculties in women's
studies and repressing them elsewhere

---

other discipline in the school where you don't have to think.

Another student found she could transfer to other courses what she
learned in women's studies about critical thinking:

> *...in terms of looking at things...in more of an analytic type
> way...and using critical skills,...I really owe that to women's studies
> and it also helped me in my other courses...because it's not as much
> what you see, it's how you see it.... I've always thought the more
> ways you can see something, the more of it you'll see.*

Another woman stated:

> *Women's studies is a very participatory kind of education.... [I]t offers
> us a way to empower ourselves and to obtain a voice, and when you
> have that voice, you're going to start using it.... You turn around and
> you say, "now wait a minute!"*

Students in the collective conversations valued learning to speak their
minds:

> *...part of the difference about being in women's studies is you have...
> input into the course and you say..."I didn't see such and such includ-
> ed in this...[or] this experience is limited." And that's one of the things
> you can do in a women's studies course that you can't do when you're
> taking [another] course.*

The quotations underscore the importance of how students conceive
of critical learning. It requires an opportunity to talk in the first instance.
Second, it requires a willingness by the instructor to surrender the role of
sole expert. Third, it requires a willingness by the instructor to show how
scholars ask and formulate questions or do their work. Fourth, it requires
practice at these skills. And, fifth, it requires support and patience on the
part of faculty members who ask students to critically analyze academic disciplines. For some students, their newly acquired critical thinking skills are not
always invited in other courses. As represented by the following quotation,
some students experience a new tension between exercising their critical faculties in women's studies courses and repressing them elsewhere:

...taking women's studies courses has a good effect and a bad effect for me,...[the good effect is] bringing this awareness of diversity to you.... [T]he bad effect [is] the resultant critique that you bring to your other classes.... [Y]ou're almost forced to put these blinders on, you know, when you start looking at other materials...where you're expected to look at it in a traditional way, so...I find myself having two personalities here you know, the kind of analysis and freedom I have in a women's studies course and then the more narrow view I'm expected to take and I'm graded on in other courses.

INTEGRATION OF KNOWLEDGE

When I got into...women's studies...the professor encouraged [me to] "Speak up, talk louder" and I was like "wow, this is different from...how the world is." And...I felt good being in a place where I could express myself the way...of my choosing.... I didn't have to stifle my voice....

WOMEN'S STUDIES STUDENT, 1991

Although Hunter College is a liberal arts college and does not view the task of education in narrowly vocational terms, we do expect that the kinds of critical learning in a multicultural environment that we offer will deeply affect our students' lives. We expect that students will change their perspectives; we also expect that students will act to integrate their new perspectives into their lives. They may change their course of study, for example, to avoid courses that do not consider women's studies perspectives as valid. They may change their majors. They may change their career plans or how they think about key issues that affect their lives. We expect that the decisions students make during and after their women's studies courses will reflect their new learning and knowledge. Additionally, women's studies students are likely to experience dissonance and conflict as they juxtapose new material and perspectives from their women's studies classes with their values and lives in a predominantly sexist, racist, ethnocentric society. The integration of the women's studies perspective into their lives is likely to prove difficult; these difficulties will be reflected in our classes. We need somehow to convey to students, though, that it is possible (to use Elizabeth Minnich's phrase) to be "tough-minded and tender-hearted."

Such a goal is of special importance at Hunter College because many students view education in terms that are too narrowly vocational or instrumental. Furthermore, a criticism often heard of American higher education is that it lacks integration. In assessing the integration of knowledge gained in women's studies courses into students' academic plans and lives, we also can assess the contribution that women's studies makes to the broader goal of liberal arts education.

In women's studies classes, students are given opportunities to analyze their experiences outside the classroom for underlying sexist and feminist principles. The juxtaposition of theoretical and personal, experiential knowledge contributes to students' anger and guilt at the same time it fosters their awareness of feminist frameworks.

In order to assess students' integration of knowledge, the Women's Studies Curriculum Committee devised a survey for participants in the introductory women's studies courses during the fall 1990 and spring 1991 semesters. Students were asked to comment on the following issues: the value of the course to them as a whole, whether a sense of community was built in the class, whether the course met their expectations, and comparisons between this course and other introductory courses. Responses from these open-ended questions include:

☐ On the overall value of the class:

> I feel that it has had a large impact on how I view the world. I find more and more that I notice behaviors, situations, and find them disturbing for reasons that had never occurred to me before.

> I hit apathy and despair a few times because the anger just got to be too much to bear. I think that there needs to be some kind of weekly discussion group or something to vent feelings of frustration.

> This course had a big impact on my way of thinking. It enabled me to view my way of life and the world around me.

> It forced me to become aware of a lot of realities that perhaps I didn't want to face. I'm much more aware of the discriminatory attitudes against women that are around me everywhere.

☐ On community:

> The class was made up of very diverse ethnic groups and the respect
> and interaction and sharing that went on was emotionally and intellec-
> tually supportive.

> I feel that our class has become a community. When I had to speak in
> front of the class, I never felt nervous. All of my classmates gave me
> encouragement and a feeling of belonging.

In the discussion from the collective conversations, women generally
noted that they made connections between their women's studies courses
and their daily lives. However, these connections often were problematic.
Students suggested the need for support groups, ongoing contacts, and more
dialogue among students to foster further connections between their cognitive and emotional learning. Sample responses include:

> ...the women's studies courses that I take go beyond this classroom,
> this paper that I'm writing, it goes out and just...touches everything
> else that I'm involved in...because it gives me a way to see, a way to
> think, a way to question everything, so it's applicable everywhere for
> me.

> Women's studies has for me merged my education with my own life
> process, my own personal development and brought them together so
> it's much more enriching and much more real, where...in other classes
> you memorize, you read and...you put it away in compartments.

That Hunter's Women's Studies Program does not want students to put away
their new knowledge into compartments is emphasized overtly by one of the
women's studies awards established, by its internship programs, and by its
Women's Studies Club. Through these vehicles, students are encouraged, rewarded, and given college credit for integrating knowledge in such a way
that it affects one's behavior.

Significantly, it was an alumna, Sylvia Faulkner, who established a fund
in her name that is used each year to award a $500 prize to a women's studies
major who has written an essay that integrates her experiences in the Women's Studies Program at Hunter College. To date, five Sylvia Faulkner

Awards have been presented.

Through internships, women's studies students are challenged to move knowledge out of compartments and into the world. Transforming their own thinking and actions, integrated knowledge becomes for many students a way of applying that knowledge to transform society itself. During 1990–91, student interns participated in a variety of projects, especially those sponsored by a Reproductive Rights Grant. Students were placed at Students Organizing Students; the Reproductive Rights Task Force, Policy Development Unit, Manhattan Borough President's Office; Childbearing Center, Morris Heights, the Bronx; HELP/AYUDA (an AIDS education organization in East Harlem); STD Education Project, New York City Health Department; New York Community Trust;. Latina Roundtable on Health and Reproductive Rights; Boehm Foundation; ASTRAEA Foundation; NOW-NYC; National Congress of Neighborhood Women's You Can Community School; *Returning Women* Magazine; Women's Health Education Project; and the American Civil Liberties Union-Reproductive Freedom Project.

Many interns expressed in their reports that they were able to connect the theory and scholarship from women's studies courses into their work. Many students also were offered jobs as a result of their internships; others discovered new career goals and options.

Similarly, students who are members of the Women's Studies Club have transferred what they have learned about integrated knowledge into the activities they organize. During the 1990–91 academic year the Women's Studies Club facilitated several workshops and discussion groups to deal with the integration of scholarship and action. Sample topics included academic and workplace sexual harassment, relationships, and racism.

WHAT WE HAVE LEARNED,
WHAT WE NEED TO DO

Participating in the FIPSE assessment project definitely has affected our program. Most importantly, our participation has created a tone and an opportunity for self-conscious thought and action about what we are doing as a program. It has confirmed in many cases our intuitive judgments about how well we are succeeding with our program goals, but it also has given us areas to focus on for improvement as well as entirely new areas to investigate as we continue to incorporate assessment into our regular routine of evaluating what we are doing educationally.

The FIPSE project has provided us with a focus around which we have organized our annual retreats for the past three years. One of our serendipitous findings, then, is how valuable it is for the program—majors, new students, regular faculty members, adjuncts, staff—to set aside a day for discussion and consideration of our goals, pedagogy, and direction.

For example, since our program has been striving for some years to increase the amount and kind of multicultural offerings in women's studies and on the campus at large, it has been extremely important for us to assess both our accomplishments and our needs for the future. One of the most difficult aspects of making education more multicultural is creating an atmosphere of trust and mutual respect. The assessment techniques we have used this year show that we are moving toward accomplishing this end, even though no one yet believes that we have dealt entirely satisfactorily with this issue.

Faculty retreats that focused on the assessment project have helped us sort out where we want to do additional work. One concern, for instance, raised repeatedly in retreat discussions, has been the way new knowledge, especially new knowledge that causes one to reevaluate old ways of seeing the world and other people, often results in emotionally charged class sessions. Many of the students who participate in the introductory course in women's studies never have encountered feminist philosophies in prior courses. They may have no one at home with whom to discuss the class content; they may be seen as "rocking the boat," questioning their family's religion and values, and/or called derogatory names because of their association with feminism and women's studies. At Hunter, we believe that the classroom needs to become a place where women can feel good about themselves and others without the fear of being laughed at or considered "unfeminine." Pedagogical techniques including journal writing, experiential exercises, introspective autobiographies, and cooperative learning structures have had the power to replace self-doubt with certainty, low self-esteem with respect and caring.

Expressions of anger in the classroom sometimes stem from students realizing they may not be living their lives according to feminist principles; they also may feel that their voices as women of color are not being heard. Students may, as a result, fail to attend class regularly, play devil's advocate in each session, and/or attempt to take leadership in the classroom. Very commonly, manifestations of anger in the classroom become fixed on the instructor because of her expressions of feminism and multiculturalism as she interprets them. One way that some of our faculty members deal with this anger is to acknowledge it, claim its transformative powers, and direct it toward individual and social change. In order to meet this goal, for example, Michele

Paludi devotes class time to interpersonal communication skills, especially the use of "I" statements—for example, "I feel _____ when you _____ because of _____." This technique has helped participants give constructive feedback in a supportive atmosphere, producing a more honest classroom. Occasionally, students' anger becomes fixed on other students. This has manifested itself in directing homophobic and racist remarks toward other women in the classroom. Some faculty members have translated these comments into a discussion about a "continuum of feminism"—that there is not one kind of feminist. In addition, devoting class time to how to argue with ideas rather than people has been helpful.

Faculty members have discovered from such conversations how helpful and reassuring it is to discuss pedagogy with committed colleagues. We discovered that we need to hold more discussion of women's studies pedagogy within the women's studies faculty and with faculty members in the disciplines. The FIPSE project also has provided additional opportunities to pull together and share ongoing work on pedagogy, especially research in that area done by our own women's studies faculty.

Given how beneficial the faculty members felt their participation was in the project, it is no surprise that students felt similarly. The students and alumnae were quick to point out to the program coordinators how much they valued being consulted in the assessment project. It became a concrete way of enacting the empowerment and critical thinking that the project itself hoped to investigate. Several students hoped that the program would continue such collective discussions and figure out a way to build them into the program's regular activities, both for the eager students and for those who were more reluctant to participate initially.

For a group of faculty members, assessment has lost its negative overtones of coercion from outside forces. Especially for faculty members most involved in this project, learning about assessment as a tool for curriculum improvement, and not as a means of disciplining the faculty and student workforce, has been extremely valuable. At Hunter College, women's studies faculty members are important constituents of the college community, often serving on major committees elsewhere. Another consequence of this grant, then, is that we have created a core advocacy group for assessment. Such a core has an impact university-wide in terms of Freshman Year Initiative, work done on the Undergraduate Course of Study Committee, the Committee on Remediation, the Provost's Advisory Committee on Remedial and Developmental Programs, and within the Faculty Delegate Assembly and

University Faculty Senate.

Materials collected for the FIPSE project also are useful in explaining the nature and extent of gender harassment and will be used by members of the Sexual Harassment Panel to train the President's Hunter College Cabinet. Certain assessment instruments developed for the FIPSE project, such as the surveys in "Women's Studies 100," are going to become an ongoing source of assessment in the future. The surveys turned out to be an invaluable way to monitor from one semester to the next how a particular course fared. The curriculum committee in women's studies plans to continue its use and perhaps extend it to other women's studies classes as well. Similarly, we discovered how useful our newsletter and annual report are as assessment documents because they reveal much about the program, its history, concerns, and areas of focus.

The FIPSE project also has caused us to consider some new areas of investigation and collaboration. The project, for example, has focused our attention in a new way on the relationship between women's studies and the liberal arts curriculum. This focus is particularly valuable at Hunter College at the moment since there is an ongoing debate about whether to include a pluralism and diversity requirement in the basic distribution requirement.

Another area we hope to explore further, both in more precise focus groups and with more help from Hunter's Office of Institutional Research, is the question of the relationship of women's studies to retention. We might hypothesize that, since retention seems to be strongly linked with a sense of attachment, the kind of community formed in women's studies classes (which was clearly demonstrated by our work on the FIPSE project) might prove useful in retaining students.

The Women's Studies Program also is thinking in new ways about its relationship to remedial and developmental programs. Thinking about basic pedagogical questions such as reading and writing skills in "Women's Studies 100" has raised within the curriculum committee in women's studies the question of whether women's studies courses might not be linked effectively with sections of remedial and developmental courses at Hunter. One of the most serious problems for students in developmental courses here is their lack of access to regular courses in Hunter's curriculum so that they may begin to do college-level work. "Women's Studies 100" seems a most appropriate bridge course. The program has contacted members of the developmental programs to discuss this future collaboration.

Finally, the FIPSE assessment has influenced directly the activities and

programs in women's studies. As a result of the project, the program has created for itself for the first time a list of alumnae and majors. Now that these
lists have been prepared, it will be much easier to keep them up-to-date and
accurate. As such, they will become a rich source of new data for questions
we will continue to raise about what happens to students who take women's
studies courses.

The project's focus on fostering multicultural awareness has contributed
to two of the faculty development workshops for the 1991–92 academic year.
One concerned applying for funding for research on women and ethnic minority women in particular, and one concerned publishing textbooks in the
areas of race and gender. We also have prepared a list of faculty research interests in the interface of race, class, and gender, making such copies available at a variety of places on campus.

The project's work on integrating knowledge into our lives has been
partly responsible for several other program activities this year. The first was
a "Women's Fair," something the program hopes to offer each semester, at
which organizations from Hunter College as well as throughout New York
City display materials and discuss their work in a variety of areas students requested. Among those subjects are AIDS, cancer, gynecological care, and
mental health practice.

That same semester, a resource manual was prepared and distributed
with referrals and resources for women's studies students that contains information about physical and psychological care in New York City. A second
manual dealing with multicultural issues was prepared in spring 1992.

Hunter's Women's Studies Program also is in the process of establishing
a mentoring program for women's studies students. Mentors will be Hunter
alumnae who are doing feminist advocacy in New York City, providing students with concrete examples of how to implement knowledge to transform
people's lives.

Emphasizing the importance of applying new knowledge to the society
in which we live, the Women's Studies Program also plans to collaborate
more closely with the National Council for Research on Women, a ten-year-
old coalition of sixty-nine research and policy centers around the country.
NCRW's centers have a special mission to create opportunities for connecting
research to policy issues and practitioners' needs. Hunter's Women's Studies
Program already has helped the council prepare a resource manual on academic sexual harassment.

The FIPSE project, then, has been effective in helping us assess where we have been, what we have done well, and what directions we need to go in as the program moves into a new phase of development with the recent appointment of a new coordinator. Hunter women's studies faculty members share a continuing commitment to create a climate where a variety of students' cultural experiences are valued, where students are taught to think critically, and where students are encouraged to integrate knowledge with life. The FIPSE project has extended the collaborative model of working together with students and faculty members, all of us learning cooperatively in the process. This, we believe, is the major goal of feminist education.

1.We wish to extend our appreciation to Donna Murdock and Ruth Weisgal for providing us with demographic information and summarizing the material from Hunter College's participation in the NWSA grant on "The Courage to Question." Donna Murdock deserves special recognition for her role in conducting interviews with women's studies students and alumnae. We also wish to thank Provost Laura Strumingher and Associate Provost Shirely Hune for their support of this project. Our colleagues Marnia Lazreg, Rosalind Petchesky, and Barbara Winslow deserve recognition for administering surveys to students in their classes during the 1990–91 academic year. And we thank the women's studies students and alumnae who were gracious in participating in our projects. Finally, we would like to recognize the coordinators of Hunter's Women's Studies Program since its inception in the mid-1970s: Sarah Pomeroy, Dorothy Helly, Rosalind Petchesky, and Michele Paludi.

SURVEY OF PARTICIPANTS
IN INTRODUCTION TO WOMEN'S STUDIES
CUNY–HUNTER COLLEGE

PART I:

1. Your year at Hunter:
___ first-year student
___ sophomore
___ junior
___ senior

2. Your sex: ___ Female ___ Male

3. How do you identify yourself in terms of your ethnic identity?

4. Your age:
___ 15–20
___ 21–30
___ 31–40
___ 41–50
___ 51–60
___ 61–70
___ 71+

5. Your major: _____
Your Co-Major or minor: _____

6. Why did you take "Introduction to Women's Studies"? (check all that apply)
___ A friend recommended it
___ It was one of the few open at the time I wanted
___ I wanted to take a/another women's studies course
___ I am a women's studies collateral major
___ I am thinking about becoming a women's studies collateral major
___ The subject matter intrigued me
___ I wanted to take a course with this professor
___ Other (please list)

7. Additional information about yourself you would like to share with us:

PART II:

We would like to know the ways the introductory course has had an impact on you. The following questions deal with this issue.

1. Comment on the value of this course to you as a whole.

2. If you had to describe this course to a friend, what three adjectives would you use? Why?

3. Did this course meet your expectations? Why or why not?

4. If the instructor of this course could have done something differently, what would that have been?

5. If you could have done something differently in this course, what would that have been?

6. Please suggest three topics you believe need to be discussed in the introductory course?

7. Compared to other introductory courses you have taken (e.g., introductory sociology, introductory psychology), how has "Introduction to Women's Studies" been similar?

8. Was there a balance between the survey-scope of the course and some more in-depth investigation? Please explain.

9. Please identify three major themes from the introductory course in women's studies.

10. Do you think that a sense of community was built in your introductory course? Why or why not?

11. What readings did you find particularly useful in this course? Why?

12. This is your space! We welcome your comments about any of the items in the survey and additional information about the introductory course you would like to share with us. Thank you again.

■

OBERLIN COLLEGE

SELF-EMPOWERMENT AND DIFFERENCE

BY LINDA R. SILVER[1]

Oberlin College examines some of the distinctions and tensions,
as well as the commonalities, among students and faculty members of diverse identities, rather than embracing a single, singular
conception of women's studies teaching and learning. Focusing
their assessment on both students and faculty, then, Oberlin College examines student learning and self-empowerment; collaborative learning; and relational understandings of race, ethnicity,
class, gender, and sexuality.

Oberlin College, founded in 1835, is an independent, coeducational institution located thirty-five miles southwest of Cleveland, Ohio. In 1841, it was
the first American college to grant undergraduate degrees to women. Oberlin
also was a leader in the education of people of color; by 1900, one-third of all
black graduates of predominantly white institutions in America had graduated from Oberlin. In keeping with its own origins in nineteenth-century social change movements, the college today has a national reputation as an institution that encourages intense engagement with intellectual and social
issues and challenges students to combine scholarship with activism and social responsibility. Currently, Oberlin's student enrollment is 2,750, with
2,250 students in the College of Arts and Sciences and 500 in the Conservatory of Music (Oberlin course catalogue, 1991–92).

Efforts to initiate a women's studies program at the college began in the
early 1970s and culminated in 1982, when a formal program officially was established. It is run by a committee of faculty members and students, directed
by a faculty member, and administered by a part-time coordinator.

With one full-time faculty member, the program offers five core courses,
including an introduction to women's studies and a senior seminar. In addition, the program offers core courses focusing primarily on women or gender
cross-listed with fifteen departments and programs including Anthropology,
Black Studies, Philosophy, Russian, and Theatre and Dance. Students also
may choose additional work from among almost one hundred related courses
offered by sixteen departments or programs, all of which treat a topic or

In a survey of majors and minors...three quarters named [their women's studies courses] as the most intellectually stimulating courses they had taken at Oberlin

theme involving gender as part of the course material. By the midpoint in the 1991–92 academic year, there were sixty women's studies majors and fifteen minors. The Women's Studies Program is one of Oberlin College's fastest growing academic areas.

Student demand for women's studies courses far exceeds the ability of the program to meet that demand. With only one full-time professor responsible for the introductory course, the practicum, and the senior seminar as well as several other offerings, wait-lists for courses sometimes run as high as two hundred students. Requests to the administration from students and from the Women's Studies Program Committee have met with very limited success, running up against not only competing requests from other units of the college but also against a period of economic uncertainty and financial retrenchment. Recognized needs of the program, such as an intermediate-level feminist methodology course and modifications to strengthen the practicum, will remain unmet until at least one additional full-time faculty member is hired.

The steady growth of the program and the ever-increasing popularity of its courses can be explained in part by the students' awareness of the interrelationships between race, gender, class, and sexuality. The program prides itself on its attempts to take these issues seriously and to provide a conceptual framework that integrates the multiple categories. As one student puts it:

> Women's studies is not just about gender at Oberlin.... What's so important to me about women's studies here—and if it hadn't been this way I don't think I would have continued with the major—is that it's about a lot of different systemic oppressions, and central to these are race and class and gender. Nor is it just about women.... I'm not saying...that WOST students are always concerned with race, class, nationality, and sexuality issues. But we have a base we can build on....

In a survey of majors and minors conducted several years ago as part of a class project, all of the respondents said they found their women's studies courses to be intellectually challenging, and three quarters named them as the most intellectually stimulating courses they had taken at Oberlin. The students conducting the survey assert that "such an exceptionally high number of academically satisfied students within a single department is quite unusual. While there were complaints about the program, there was no disagreement that these students felt very challenged." Even students who

arrive at Oberlin as self-proclaimed feminists praise the program for its power
to transform and challenge. As a 1982 women's studies graduate explained:

> *The college (or specific teachers and groups there) took that feminism*
> *seriously—educated, expanded, challenged, layered, enriched that*
> *stance, truly enlarging my knowledge and experience.*

PROGRAM GOALS

During the first year of participation in NWSA's FIPSE national assessment
project, the Women's Studies Program Committee devoted substantial time
to discussing its goals, its future, its faculty and curricular needs, and its student audience. The basis for our discussion of the goals of our Women's
Studies Program was the catalogue copy that currently describes us as:

> *a multidisciplinary program exploring topics concerning women, gen-*
> *der, and difference, in the humanities, social sciences, and natural sci-*
> *ences. Course work includes scholarship by and/or about women of*
> *varying racial, ethnic and class backgrounds and sexual identities in*
> *literature, the arts, history and theory; it also analyzes the experiences*
> *of men and women with respect to social, psychological, cultural and*
> *biological factors influencing the construction and representation of*
> *gender. Women's studies courses often involve the investigation of ma-*
> *terials previously neglected by scholars and new methodological and*
> *critical approaches to materials customarily treated in other ways.*
> *Such courses may as a result propose revisions in the content, meth-*
> *ods, and assumptions of particular disciplines in light of recent feminist*
> *scholarship.*

Going beyond the catalogue description, we stressed that our aims are
multicultural and interdisciplinary; we see the program striving on the one
hand to achieve analytic clarity and rigor and, on the other, to facilitate personal growth and student voice. We see important interconnections between
what appear as separate categories in the NWSA/FIPSE proposal: knowledge
base and learning skills. We see ourselves as trying to foster tolerant, critical
habits of mind in which students learn to question their own assumptions, in
order to explore the ideological underpinnings of knowledge to see the connections between structures of knowledge and structures of society. We want

We want to communicate how differential
access to power and authority—with respect to
gender, race, class, and sexuality—shapes our
understandings

---

to foster a self-reflexive criticism that identifies and, beyond that, locates epistemological formulations within social structures. We want to communicate how differential access to power and authority—with respect to gender, race, class, and sexuality—shapes our understandings. Our discussion stressed that the knowledge we seek to communicate in women's studies is not a simple body of information but rather a question of approach and conceptualization. In this way, we see logical connections between women's studies and other programs dealing with ethnic and minority peoples and people of color.

We are currently trying to make our women's studies program more truly interdisciplinary, and we believe our own core program courses have contributed to making connections between disciplines. At the same time, we think it is important to encourage the growth of more courses in a variety of disciplines across the curriculum. At present, our disciplinary strengths are centered in the humanities, with some representation in the social sciences and real weaknesses in the area of the natural sciences. Unfortunately, such curricular lopsidedness hinders our programmatic goals.

We also are consciously working to continue our progress toward a program where multicultural issues inform every aspect of our program, including our curriculum, our faculty, and our student audience. We seek to involve people of different ethnic and racial backgrounds and sexual orientations at all levels. In other ways, too, we are continuing our efforts to reach out to a variety of student constituencies, including women and men, and students from a variety of fields from the natural sciences, social sciences, and humanities, irrespective of majors.

For many, the issue of learning skills includes assisting students in developing a personal voice and expression, as well as basic confidence in learning. We are concerned that our students learn to "authorize" their own ideas and identities; this issue is especially important for traditionally marginalized groups such as women in general and especially women of color and lesbian and bisexual women. For faculty, our goals for ourselves include learning to encourage different modes of expression and reevaluating why certain skills are deemed important.

In terms of feminist pedagogy, we seek to foster critical, tolerant, investigative thinking, and we encourage students not to reproduce knowledge but actually to produce it as well. To do this, we think feminist pedagogy must demonstrate a sensitivity to questions of social differentiation in the classroom and in the learning process. Again, feminist pedagogy must strive to give voice. In working on the NWSA/FIPSE project, we on the faculty articulated once more our goal of experimenting further in methods of presentation and evaluation, of undertaking cooperative learning projects, and new orientations in our off-campus practicum projects.

Finally, we all concurred that personal growth has a special place in women's studies and that encouraging creative, critical thinking and fostering voice would empower students and heighten their awareness. We like to think that what we do in women's studies classrooms will have a positive impact on how our students see themselves and what they are doing in the "outside world" beyond our academic context. We hope that students are learning how to create new knowledge and new group relations.

ASSESSMENT PLAN

Our Women's Studies Program is grounded in the recognition of differences: differences between courses, in the courses of study followed by our diverse majors and minors, among our students, and among our faculty. Rather than embrace a single, singular conception of women's studies teaching and learning, then, our objectives in conducting our self-assessment entail getting at some of the distinctions and tensions, as well as the commonalities, among students and faculty members of diverse racial, ethnic, class, gender and sexual identities. Thus, we recognize and hope to highlight the positionalities from which learning and teaching occur in our program. To this end, moreover, we focused our assessment on both students and faculty members. The questions we posed were:

☐ *Does student learning entail self-empowerment?* We understand self-empowerment as a matter of agency and social responsibility and self-understanding as inseparable from an articulated sense of social responsibility. Thus the self-empowerment we hope to teach involves students' coming to an understanding of the identity and history of their own group(s) within the context of understanding the identities and histories of members of other groups, all such understanding being situated within substantive knowledge of socio-cultural structures. Self-empowerment also entails gaining an understanding of the tools of disciplinary and social analysis and of modes for effecting social change.

☐ *To what extent does collaborative learning occur, and how effective is it?* We defined pedagogy as a matter of shared responsibility and shared work and recognize that the weight of responsibility differs from class to class. We do not want to prescribe what the collective nature of learning is for the entire program; rather, we want to assess whether the pedagogical structures of a given class are appropriate to the objectives—and the composition—of the class. Moreover, given our understanding that knowledge is produced and not simply acquired, we want to learn the extent to which our students are engaging in genuinely collective work and how that work is being done. Since collaborative learning means working with and learning from people who are different from oneself, we specifically want to learn whether/how our students are negotiating and mediating differences, how they are putting themselves on the line, and what the outcomes are.

☐ *Does a particular course foster a relational understanding of race, ethnicity, class, gender, and sexuality?* Specifically, does it help students understand the significance of these categories? Does it identify how they operate individually? Does it identify how they operate in conjunction?

METHODS OF ASSESSMENT

Students in women's studies courses, senior women's studies majors, alumnae, and faculty members were the four groups upon whom the assessment focused. Written self-statements (see page 176) were administered three times during a semester to students in seventeen courses. These students were not necessarily women's studies majors or minors, and their degree of engagement with women's studies varied from fairly intensive to virtually none at all. Senior majors taking the women's studies senior seminar interviewed one another as part of a class project. A questionnaire was mailed to college faculty members and another was inserted into an issue of the program's newsletter, *WomaNews*, and mailed to alumnae. Supplementing these methods of gathering data was a set of student interviews conducted by a senior major who served for one semester as the project's research assistant.

The shape of the assessment plan as it developed tends to reflect the growing national debate about multiculturalism and the questions asked about women's studies programs in terms of this debate: What fosters student learning and self-empowerment? How can courses encourage a relational understanding of gender, race, class, and sexuality? Does feminist pedagogy differ from other types? How do women's studies courses affect students' lives and life choices?

STUDENT LEARNING AND SELF-EMPOWERMENT

Self-empowerment stands out as the program goal most important to students. The results of the assessment suggest that students' understanding of the meaning of the concept develops over the course of their college experience and is influenced by the intensity of their engagement with women's studies. By senior year, a women's studies student, for instance, revealed in an interview that her agenda in women's studies started with issues she could apply specifically to herself and her position and spread out into "looking at systems of domination: ...it's about power and how society is structured."

In the self-statements, no question directly relating to or mentioning the term "self-empowerment" was asked. However, answers to questions about "the most significant thing you have learned" in terms of either process or content elicited responses that connote self-empowerment: "I've learned how to think.... I have a whole bunch of alternatives open to me that I want to take. I am engaged" (junior, art major). In student responses, self-empowerment occurred almost twice as often as the next cited category—collaborative learning.

> The most important thing...was not just getting my hands on information but also on a method...of knowing what to look out for and what to do when I see it.
>
> JUNIOR, WOMEN'S STUDIES MAJOR

> I have gained a sense of feminist literary criticism with which I may not only approach all other literature but also which I may apply to my personal life.
>
> SENIOR, ENGLISH MAJOR

> I have learned something about coalitions and the difficulties of trying. I have learned to distinguish between guilt and power. I learned about silence and what it means. I have learned to encompass a global context into my thinking and, hopefully, acting.
>
> SENIOR, SOCIOLOGY MAJOR

Self-empowerment was also central to the comments of the senior students who were interviewed. As one senior put it, "Self-empowerment is of the utmost importance because without it, you are immobilized." In the interviews, however, the link with social responsibility was more apparent. When asked to describe the changes in their expectations of their women's studies education between their first and last college years, the majority commented on how their interest had shifted from personal to social issues. One student told the interviewer that she had experienced a "growth that is a natural progression in women's studies," that her "first exposure to feminist coursework centered around issues of self" and that as she developed better and more numerous skills she "desired to politicize and problematize the personal." When included in a list of Oberlin's Women's Studies Program goals, self-empowerment and the linking of personal with social responsibility were rated together as most important.

> *What's important to me is having a language not only to represent myself but to talk about political change.... It's more about feminist thinking and method as opposed to "feminine" or "women's issues." It's about learning how to address marginalization and difference.*

Another student stated that women's studies helped her see where she has "work to do in this world" and how to do that work; she did not see women's studies as a "personal tool for me to learn how to feel good about myself as a woman."

While students commented on the primacy of empowerment as both an educational goal and as an outcome of the feminist education they receive at Oberlin, neither alumnae nor faculty members ranked it first among the stated program goals of student self-empowerment, recognition of differences, collaborative learning, and understanding the relationships among race, class, gender, and sexuality. Alumnae were reluctant to give a ranking. Comments like "All are important" or "It's impossible to rank hierarchically things that are so interrelated" were common. However, when asked if and how the women's studies courses they had taken at Oberlin had influenced their lives, many alumnae singled out the self-empowering nature of the critical thinking in which they had been encouraged to engage. Classroom teaching practices and relationships with peers and faculty were characterized as providing the freedom and courage to question, a means toward empowerment, a catalyst toward political action, and a model for sorting through social issues.

We were interested in finding out if women's studies alumnae continue to be involved in feminist activities after they graduate. In other words, were they empowered toward social action? The broad categories of feminist activities identified by Linton were used as a basis for this inquiry.[2] Conceptualizations of feminism represented by these activities included reproductive rights clinics, battered women's shelters, marches, networks, political action, women's crafts, filmmaking, voter education, and research.

All of the alumnae who responded had participated in most of the sixteen activities specified. The involvement of many had, in fact, begun at Oberlin and had been carried on after graduation, often in the professions they now practice, such as teaching or law. This seems fitting for graduates of a college whose motto is "Learning and Labor" and whose women's studies program currently is considering how to strengthen students' ability to relate theory to practice. One graduate articulated the importance of developing in students "the ability to see how theory shapes practice and how practice— the real, changing world—keeps pressing at the boundaries of theory."

The most critical comments about the Women's Studies Program at Oberlin came not from students but from faculty members who were not teaching in the Women's Studies Program. The survey sent to Oberlin's general faculty revealed that there was striking variation in how the program is perceived and accepted (see pages 174–75). In contrast to the evaluations by students who had taken women's studies courses, a minority of faculty respondents, both female and male, construed the program's goals as being ideological, political, or indicative of "one big counseling session." In reply to a question about the impact of the program on the college, one female humanities professor, who is not part of the Women's Studies Program, wrote:

> *[It has had a] terrible impact—the program has politicized and ideologized students instead of promoting objectivity in education.... I must withdraw my support for this program until it becomes less ideological and more in line with the spirit of true academic excellence at Oberlin....*

A long-time professor of mathematics, who also is not part of the program, stated that the goals of the program "make [it] sound more like a political party than an academic department. I have been supportive of women's studies in the past, but I am not willing to support a political party in disguise."

Notwithstanding these views, the vast majority of faculty members support the program and its stated goals. As one faculty member argued, "Its continued existence is of core importance to the mission of the institution," and another echoed these sentiments: "...the role of the program as an institutional basis for dissent is absolutely vital to the educational mission of the college." Still others praised women's studies because it "...gives legitimacy to the college's progressive and tolerant reputation." Recognizing that some faculty members "see in women's studies radical lunacy writ large," a respondent nonetheless valued the program because it "promotes attention to multiculturalism and politics." Finally, another faculty member explained why students were so attracted to the Women's Studies Program: "[It] has the most interesting faculty and the most interesting ideas." When asked what goals, if any, they would add to those stated, the goal of critical thinking was added most often. This coincides with the alumnae's recognition that they had, in fact, been taught to think critically, which they valued even more after graduation. According to one faculty comment, critical thinking was cultivated in women's studies courses:

> In the past couple of years, I've noticed that students who have taken at least the introductory course in women's studies are better trained in critical thinking than many other students. So I gather that critical thinking is more consistently encouraged by women's studies pedagogy than can be assumed across the curriculum.

COLLABORATIVE LEARNING

In the self-statements, collaborative learning was ranked by students as second in importance only after self-empowerment. In commenting on collaborative learning, one student, for example, explained, "I've not learned as much in any other class at Oberlin in the past three and one half years" (senior, art major). Another commented: "I think collaborative learning is effective in any class.... I appreciate this method in my sociology and psychology class and wish it were more common in my economics classes" (junior, economics major). That students come to realize through collaborative learning that their peers can be sources of new knowledge is apparent in the following self-statement: "I am constantly learning from classmates.... In this class, with the issues we discuss because they're personal, and public/political, cooperative learning is really effective and eye-opening" (sophomore, women's studies major).

As a pedagogical method, collaborative learning more readily challenges students to mediate differences which emerge as students work closely with one another. The process is not an easy one, according to one senior:

> We are in the process of negotiation [of difference]; ...we are (supposedly) committing ourselves to frank discourse with faith in one another's central worth, but it's hard. We are so untrusting and quick to judge or reluctant to judge at all.

SENIOR, LATIN AMERICAN STUDIES MAJOR

Most students, nonetheless, have developed strategies for negotiating differences that include "recognizing and dealing with them," "respectful listening," and "allowing for conflict." While the strategies do not always work, students felt that the challenge to interact across differences was educationally productive:

> *I've tried (and occasionally failed) not to assume things about people from different backgrounds...and I've been curious about what they think. It's worked pretty well...a lot of communication is going on.*
> SENIOR, HISTORY MAJOR

An alumna concurred with students about the value of collaborative learning, especially in terms of its application after graduation:

> *Collaborative learning is particularly important because it requires a recognition of one's own strengths and also a recognition of difference. It's an important life skill to be able to work with others, engaged in our differences. Politically, this is significant.*
> 1991 OBERLIN COLLEGE GRADUATE

Senior seminar interviews reiterated what other students had said about both the importance and the challenge of collaborative learning. As one senior described it, "collaborative learning was valuable and...it was certainly attempted but at times was difficult." Another captured the dynamic classroom interaction that can flow from collaborative learning: "The classroom becomes a setting for exchange and question and a form of activism. And I haven't had it in every classroom in Oberlin...maybe two or three."

Some seniors, however, were more skeptical about how uniformly collaborative learning actually was integrated into every women's studies course. While one senior felt it "is one area that...has been very successfully met at times," she also felt it "has simply been given lip service at other times." Another senior, who had taken only women's studies courses for two consecutive semesters, stated she was weary of the collaborative learning approach, adding, "I wish there was more lecturing."

RELATIONAL UNDERSTANDING
OF RACE, CLASS, GENDER, AND SEXUALITY

While students ranked self-empowerment and collaborative learning as the two program goals that they considered most important, both women's studies alumnae and faculty members placed greatest importance on teaching students to understand the relationships among race, class, gender, and sexuality. Comments from graduates and faculty members, moreover, suggested that this understanding was integrally related to the recognition and analysis of difference. For example, one alumna wrote:

> *Although I was aware of sexual and racial oppression and my opposition to them when I arrived, Oberlin opened my eyes to a multitude of issues in which...difference-based oppressions play a part and in the ways that they all interact. It added to my ability to analyze power....*
> 1985 OBERLIN COLLEGE GRADUATE

For many graduates, Oberlin was their first opportunity to be reflective about the relationships among class, gender, and sexuality. It often was other students within women's studies and beyond it who triggered intellectual and personal growth:

> *Before I came to Oberlin I had had neither the freedom nor the opportunity to question or even develop any ideas about these issues. The students I met were the main way this questioning and development took place.*
> 1985 OBERLIN COLLEGE GRADUATE

Another alumna had a similar experience: "At Oberlin, I...discovered I was a feminist. It was also the first place I ever met openly gay and lesbian people" (1982 graduate). What women's studies seemed to provide for many students was the conceptual framework for understanding complex relationships between systems of oppressions. As one women's studies graduate explained:

> *I was exposed to critical thought on these issues and provided with the means to make links between them. [Oberlin] taught me to ask questions—not just attempt to give answers. I became more equipped to examine my own racism and classism at Oberlin.*
> 1988 OBERLIN COLLEGE GRADUATE

Alumnae surveyed—all of whom had taken women's studies courses—strongly believed that Oberlin had influenced them regarding these issues; through Oberlin's tradition of tolerance, its respect for diversity and difference, its strong feminist and humanist tradition, and its inclusiveness of a variety of life-styles, values, ideas, and backgrounds. Blending the experience as a women's studies graduate with that of the institutional culture of Oberlin College itself, one student commented:

> *Oberlin provided an inclusive environment in which I was free to test and expand my creative and intellectual potential without feeling limited. I learned the meaning of egalitarianism and have applied that approach to life after Oberlin.*
> 1984 OBERLIN COLLEGE GRADUATE

Oberlin's faculty has given questions of difference and issues of multiculturalism primacy among its concerns for several years. After much debate college-wide, a multicultural diversity requirement was added last year to the general college requirements as well as to the requirements for the women's studies major. Two women's studies faculty members, Chandra Mohanty and Gloria Watkins, organized and convened a year-long faculty working colloquium entitled "Pedagogies of Gender, Race, and Empire," which included a panel discussion of cultural diversity at Oberlin and several speakers on "oppositional" and non-Eurocentric pedagogy.

Even among critics of the Women's Studies Program, its leadership in these areas is acknowledged. One professor noted the impact of the program on the college as "profound" and remarked that "the program has [had] important spillover impact on many disciplines and majors." Another commented that the "rigorous analysis" of these issues in women's studies courses raises students' awareness of the linkage between the local and the global. Still another praised women's studies for the way its multicultural feminist theory enlightened and empowered students:

> *Students learn more about the interrelations of gender, race, class, and sexuality in the social and ideological construction of power and knowledge than in any other program.... They gain empowerment by being taught to query and challenge the status quo of accepted knowledge forms.*

Student responses on the self-statements indicate that this kind of understanding is considered integral to women's studies. All of the students answering questions at the beginning of the semester about race, gender, sexuality, and class said they expected these issues to be covered in class. Most of them expected all four categories to be covered, while the rest specified which they thought would not be. Although this varied by course, class and sexuality were the two categories most students assumed would be excluded.

At mid-semester, students were asked if gender, race, class, and sexuality were, in fact, being addressed. Over half of the students stated that all four were woven into the course. A smaller proportion of students stated that not all categories had been incorporated into the course. Although this varied by course, students cited race, rather than class or sexuality, as the category most frequently excluded.

Self-statement number three asked *how* questions of gender, race, class, and sexuality were being addressed. Comments included: "Through readings, discussions, theorizing..."; "In terms of how [race] shapes people's identities and how much it is tied to other factors like gender.... How to re-analyze and re-address these conceptions"; "[The class] tried to address all of these together. It's difficult to assess how well it ultimately managed to do so"; "This class addresses [these issues] as integral and inseparable from WOST"; and "Before taking this class I had no idea how much race, class, gender, and sexuality were involved in forming feminist thinking...."

Senior seminar students recognized the multiple layers of meaning involved in issues of differences. In every interview, students commented about difference which was often cited as one of the most valuable learning experiences. As one student explained, "There's such a consciousness with [women's studies] of the importance of interdisciplinary study, of discussing difference and of having a language for discussing difference." For another senior, the most valuable part of her learning in women's studies was her newfound ability to see the "layered-ness and interconnectedness of the different systems that center around gender, race, class, and sexuality." In explaining to those who ask her what women's studies is, a senior answers by saying:

> ...we study how gender, race, class, and sexuality fit into systems of government and knowledge.... So it's not necessarily "woman." It's how men and women interact...and what affects their behavior or their position or their experience.

Perhaps the clearest statement of how successfully women's studies courses provided students with the intellectual framework for understanding relationships of power is captured by the senior who said:

> The first,...most important lesson I learned was the notion of center and...who is placed at the center.... That this system creates a situation where people of color, and women, and working class people are marginalized and targeted [has] sort of become central to how I think about the world.

WHAT NOW?
THE ROLE OF THE ASSESSMENT IN PLANNING

Since Oberlin's participation in the national assessment project began almost three years ago, much in our program has changed, yet much has stayed the same. High turnover among women's studies faculty and among those who run the program has meant that relatively few people who helped to develop the original assessment plan are still around to witness its completion. Only two of the current members of Oberlin's Assessment Task Force have been on it for more than the current year, none since its beginning. That the final assessment resembles fairly closely the one envisioned three years ago attests to the strength of the initial planning. That it mirrors some of the perennial problems of the program—namely, shortages in the time and human energy needed to provide continuity and planning for the future—suggests that the program has arrived at a critical moment in its history.

The FIPSE/NWSA assessment at Oberlin has become part of an intensive internal examination of the program organized in the fall of 1991 to develop a five-year plan that will provide for increased coherence, stability, and growth. So far, the examination has focused on staffing, curriculum, and pedagogy. Our assessment dovetails with each of these concerns.

It did not require a formal program assessment to tell us that women's studies courses, particularly those few that are offered as the core program, are in great demand. For several years, that story has been told by the number of names on computer-generated wait lists and, far more compellingly, by the disappointment and frustration voiced by students who sometimes cannot get into the introductory course until their senior year—and then only if they have a major or minor in the program.

The assessment does show quite clearly, however, that current students, graduates, and faculty members find the core courses in particular to differ qualitatively from other courses in the college. Far from being "rap sessions," as one of the few negative comments described them, they offer not merely a *sense* of empowerment, as might be concluded from data on students, but *actual* empowerment, expressed as social action, and shown by alumnae data. Moreover, the way that students experience and conceptualize "empowerment" appears quite clearly to develop from the personal to the social at least in part in relation to the intensity of the engagement with women's studies.

The assessment also shows that women's studies classrooms—again, particularly in the core program courses—involve students as active collaborators in a multidimensional, interdisciplinary learning experience that is rarely found to the same extent in more traditional non-women's studies courses. Some do not always find this comfortable but still choose to grapple with the discomfort rather than to reject it. They find, by and large, "the courage to question," or to develop what many among the alumnae and faculty members called "critical thinking."

We also have learned from the assessment that women's studies courses seem to offer a space—although not necessarily a "safe space"—for many different social, racial, and sexual identities. The terms "multicultural diversity" and "recognition of difference" are pallid in light of the intense encounters, confrontations, discoveries, and revelations—individual and collective, emotional and intellectual—that occur within that space. The very creation of that space by instructors and students often is searing.

The nature of Oberlin's women's studies program, as indicated by the assessment, requires close attention to methodological and critical approaches and to continuous conversation among students, faculty members who teach core courses, and those who teach cross-listed courses. It also requires a degree of mediation within the college community that is not required of those disciplines whose scholarly norms are customarily considered to be unconcerned with ideology or politics. We recognize the fact that program development and faculty development are intertwined and that the future of women's studies at Oberlin depends on both.

The need for greater curricular coherence is an outgrowth of the evolving disciplinary uniqueness of women's studies. The development of feminist theory has been concomitant with cross- or supra-disciplinary work in such areas as the international division of female labor, the "first world's" construction of racialized sexualities during and after colonialism, and reconstitutions of gender in new and re-emerging nations. Growth in the field of women's studies may well account for the increase in the number of majors in Oberlin's program; students now are choosing to go beyond supplementing their college education with a few women's studies courses and are turning instead to a fully realized major.

As we continue our discussions regarding long-range planning and the future of the Women's Studies Program at Oberlin, we will build our future based on insights generated by NWSA's FIPSE grant. In our original assessment design, we claimed that we intended to investigate "some of the distinctions and tensions, as well as the commonalities, among students and faculty members of diverse racial, ethnic, class, gender and sexual identities." Three years later, this statement continues to challenge and engage.

---

1. Thanks go to the members of the Women's Studies Program Committee over the last several years for their participation in and support of the assessment project and to the authors and compilers of the various documents upon which the report draws: Carol Lasser, Gloria White, Chandra Mohanty, Sandy Zagarell and Claudia MacDonald. Thanks to Mary Andes, student assistant on the assessment project; and special thanks to women's studies minor and computing center consultant Sue Patterson, for recovering what seemed for a while to be permanently lost text.

2. A. Jaggar and S. Bordo, eds., *Gender/Body/Knowledge* (New Brunswick, N.J.: Rutgers University Press, 1989).

FACULTY QUESTIONNAIRE
OBERLIN COLLEGE

1. Some of the goals of Oberlin's Women's Studies Program are:
☐ student self-empowerment
☐ recognition of differences
☐ collaborative learning
☐ understanding the relationship between race, class, gender, and sexuality.
Which of these goals do you consider most important? Are there others you would add?

2. Which of the following activities in your opinion are the most important to the future of the Women's Studies Program? Please rank from 1=least important to 7=most important.
___ change program status to department
___ raise funds from alumni to create an endowed chair in women's studies
___ lobby administration and trustees for more support, financial and otherwise, for the program
___ improve the representation of women of color on the faculty and staff and among students
___ increase the visibility of the program
___ address questions of difference and diversity within the women's studies curriculum
___ increase number of full-time faculty (currently one person)

3. What impact do you think the Women's Studies Program has on Oberlin College?

4. What significant learning experiences do you think women's studies courses offer students?

5. Do you believe that women's studies courses differ in pedagogy
—in how students learn—from non-women's studies courses?
    Yes   No   If yes, how?

6. Have you ever taught a course that was cross-listed with women's studies? Yes   No

7. Have you ever taught a women's studies-related course?   Yes   No

8. Do you include any of the following perspectives in the courses you teach, whether or not they are women's studies courses? Perspectives on:
☐ Gender
☐ Class
☐ Race
☐ Sexuality
     (most of the time, some of the time, rarely, never)

9. Do you ever approach your subject with an integrative analysis of gender, race, class, and sexuality?
Yes   No   (Please explain)

10. Which of the following teaching techniques do you use?
☐ lectures by teacher
☐ presentations by individual students
☐ discussions led by teacher
☐ discussions led by individual students
☐ discussions led by groups of students
☐ other:

11. Are you faculty or administration?

12. How many years have you taught at Oberlin?

13. Do you teach in the conservatory or the college?

14. In what division of the college do you teach?

15. Are you female or male?

16. What is your race/ethnicity?

17. We welcome your comments about the Women's Studies Program as we plan for the future.

STUDENT SELF-STATEMENTS

Student Self-Statement #1

1. Do you expect this class to address questions of race?
   Do you expect this class to address questions of gender?
   Do you expect this class to address questions of sexuality?
   Do you expect this class to address questions of social class?

2. Do you expect this class to take a feminist approach? What does this mean for you? For example, does it mean:
   a. inclusion of women authors, artists, scientists, etc., in the syllabus
   b. discussions of systems of race, gender, and class
   c. an analysis of power relations in terms of hierarchy, oppression, and exploitation
   d. other:

3. What kind of learning environment do you expect? For example, only lecture, only discussion, both lectures and discussion, student-led discussion, faculty led-discussion? other?

4. What kind of learning environment do you prefer or learn best in?

5. If you expect discussion, do you expect to be actively engaged in discussion or do you expect the teacher to lead most of the discussion?

6. What do you hope to learn in this class?

Student Self-Statement #2

1. Does this class address questions of race? How?
   Does this class address questions of gender? How?
   Does this class address questions of sexuality? How?
   Does this class address questions of social class? How?

2. Is this class taking a feminist approach? Please explain.

3. Collaborative learning is defined as a pedagogical style that emphasizes cooperative efforts among students and faculty members. It is rooted in the belief that learning is social in nature and stresses common inquiry as a basic learning process. Do

you think collaborative learning has taken place in your classroom? In what specific ways?

4. Since true collaborative learning means working with and learning from people who are different from oneself, how have you negotiated and mediated those differences?

5. What are some of the significant things you are learning in this class?

Student Self-Statement #3
1.   Has this class addressed questions of race?   How?
     Has this class addressed questions of gender? How?
     Has this class addressed questions of sexuality? How?
     Has this class addressed questions of social class? How?

2. How would you characterize the most important things you have learned in this class (in terms of content and process)?

∎

UNIVERSITY OF MISSOURI–COLUMBIA
FOR WOMEN'S SAKE

BY MARY JO NEITZ WITH MICHELLE GADBOIS[1]

> The University of Missouri–Columbia investigates three areas: personal transformation, pedagogy, and difference. The three principal questions of their assessment plan are: What kinds of personal transformations occur in students who take women's studies courses? Do students think women's studies courses are taught differently than other courses? And, do students in women's studies gain a new understanding about the connections among gender, race, class, and sexual preference?

The University of Missouri was established in Columbia in 1839 as the first public university in the Louisiana Purchase territory. In 1870, the university was approved as a land-grant university under the Morrill Act of 1862. It is the largest of the four campuses in the University of Missouri system, with a residential campus and statewide extension program. The University of Missouri–Columbia is located in the middle of the state, halfway between St. Louis and Kansas City. More than 85 percent of the undergraduates are Missouri residents. The majority of out-of-state students come from adjacent Illinois and Kansas. Each year, about 25 percent of the undergraduates are new students, freshmen, or transfers. The student body numbers twenty-three thousand and includes seventeen thousand undergraduates.

Data gathered in the Missouri Undergraduate Panel Study (MUPS) provides information about the student body and an important context for interpreting the responses of the women's studies graduates to our questionnaire. The MUPS study drew a representative sample constituting 30 percent of the students entering as freshmen in 1982 and 1985. The students are overwhelmingly white and midwestern: In 1982, 92 percent identified themselves as white/Caucasian, 5 percent as black, and one percent as Asian American.

Less than 10 percent of the 1985 sample came from a distance of more than five hundred miles. In the 1985 sample, about 20 percent of the freshmen had pledged a sorority or fraternity, and a quarter of the first-year students had full- or part-time employment (this percentage increases to more

"I am so pleased because women's studies has provided me with the strength to never settle for anything that deprives me of all I am worth"

than half for juniors and seniors). When asked about their political views, 57 percent of the students identified themselves as "middle of the road." Twenty-one percent identified themselves as conservatives compared to 15 percent liberals, and 1 percent identified themselves as being on either the "far left" or the "far right."

For such students, women's studies is a challenge. As one women's studies graduate said:

> I had never been so challenged. I have never worked so hard on any-thing in my life. Women's studies was an opening to myself. For the male-identified part of myself, this was the greatest challenge of my life. I am so pleased because women's studies provided me with the strength to never settle for anything that deprives me of all that I am worth.

Each of our graduates said that they would encourage other students to be-come involved in the Women's Studies Program, but one cautioned: "I'd tell them to do it. [But] it is not easy, and if you are not ready to deal [with is-sues], don't do it."

THE WOMEN'S STUDIES PROGRAM

The initial impetus for women's studies at UMC came from students. In 1969–70, the Academics Committee of the Association for Women Students contacted faculty members from a variety of departments requesting an inter-disciplinary course on women. That course was taught in 1971. Six years later, the university appointed a woman who was a graduate student in English to be the half-time coordinator. In 1980, women's studies achieved formal program status, and in 1981, the first student graduated with a wom-en's studies degree. After a national search that same year, the first full-time director with teaching responsibilities in women's studies was hired.

With the full-time director, the program moved from the "cafeteria" ap-proach of its early years to a more coherent program informed by feminist theory. The Women's Studies Committee developed a set of interdisciplinary core courses taught through women's studies and also established stringent cross-listing procedures that distinguished between women's studies courses (guided by feminist principles) and women-related courses (with significant content centered on women and gender). The attempt to build an integrated curriculum occurred in the face of opposition to feminism and disbelief in

women's studies as a scholarly endeavor.[2] In 1983, a course on the connections among gender, race, and class, which became central to the program,
was added to the core curriculum and taught by the director. In 1988, when
authorized to recruit a full-time faculty member in women's studies, the program hired a woman of color with expertise in this area to teach the course
and develop other offerings on race and gender.

Currently the program offers twenty-six courses taught by nineteen affiliated faculty members. Although faculty concentration is highest in arts and
sciences, cross-listed courses also are located in nursing, education, and jour-
nalism. In part because of this intercollege teaching program, women's studies has been located fiscally in the provost's office rather than in any one college of the university.

More than eight hundred students take women's studies courses each
year. The number of majors, however, always has been small, ranging from
one or two to ten graduating in a year. The majors pursue a dual degree combining women's studies with another discipline of their choice. At a university where most students consider themselves "middle of the road" politically,
and only 15 percent see themselves as "liberal" (and 1 percent as radical),
becoming a women's studies major is a deviant act. Yet because of their small
numbers, the majors form a group supportive of each other within this relatively hostile environment. They also work closely with the office staff and
faculty members, and most have served on the Women's Studies Committee.
These majors are a central focus of our assessment.

DESIGNING AN ASSESSMENT PLAN

In the first year of the FIPSE project, each program was asked to produce a
statement of the goals of the program and to think about ways of assessing
whether or not our goals for student learning were being met. This task
proved to be difficult for us for a number of reasons.

In the first place, faculty members had negative feelings about assessment. Our governor had been involved early in the push for state-mandated
assessment and, unfortunately, brought that to Missouri in a way that pitted
state-funded institutions of higher education against one another. The governor's model—one that has been endorsed by the board of curators—is a rigid,
quantitative, "value-added" approach. At this institution, then, assessment
was politicized in such a way that many faculty members saw assessment primarily as a weapon to be used against them.

Second, the project came during a transitional period within the program: We were discovering that goals and processes clearly articulated in the early 1980s no longer had consensus backing from members of the committee. The second half of the 1980s had been a period of consolidation and institutionalization for the program. Departments began hiring faculty members with expertise in women's studies, greatly expanding the course offerings as well as participation in the program. Yet these women had not been involved in the development of the program and did not necessarily share the perspectives of those who had. This became more apparent when the director, who had provided much of the vision for the program throughout the 1980s, took a leave of absence in 1988–89 and resigned from the program the following year.

Finally, even without the particularities of our institutional context, there are inherent difficulties in the process of formulating goals. The instrumental approach to assessment often fostered by institutional exigencies was rejected: No one wanted to repeat the "assessment process," wherein departments had tried to figure out what kind of information the administration wanted from them, and the most efficient way to get it, in order to place the department in the most favorable light. Yet consensus processing requires shared interests and a long time frame; it was not clear that we had either.[3] What we did have was a real passion for teaching and a long-term commitment to exploring feminist pedagogy.[4] Pedagogy became, then, the basis for two faculty development workshops held in the fall of 1990 and 1991, which ultimately gave focus to our campus assessment design.

In the fall of 1989, we also held a series of potluck dinners attended by faculty, staff, and student members of the Women's Studies Committee, to discuss key concerns we had about student learning. We reviewed some of our documents, including our mission statement and our cross-listing guidelines, and began to formulate program goals. Our discussions ultimately led us to how we could do the following:

☐ support our students as ambassadors of feminism
☐ continue to address the campuswide problems of sexism, racism, and other injustices
☐ create with our students a setting in which all voices may be heard
  ■ create a safe place for personal growth and for nurturing relationships
  ■ create discomfort and introduce risk by shaking core unexamined assumptions
☐ transform the self and challenge ideologies as a critical function, encouraging personal and intellectual transformation and moving from understanding one's own personal experiences to understanding others'

☐ maintain self-consciousness about methods, including the ways in which research strategies presume certain kinds of gender arrangements

☐ place our studies at the intersection of race, class, gender, sexual preference, and other categories of analysis, fostering the understanding that truth is partial

☐ incorporate multidisciplinary/interdisciplinary perspectives in the course

☐ realize the possibility of the course as a laboratory, open to risk for students and instructors alike

☐ facilitate the development of self-esteem through the successful engagement of difficult tasks

☐ increase the pool of literature known in our subject areas.

We did not translate these concerns directly into a set of "assessment questions" formulated in terms of "how can we measure to what extent are we doing these things," yet they informed faculty discussions, classroom assessment, and the questionnaire we eventually administered to graduates.

Rather than developing an assessment plan that would be imposed on the faculty members teaching in the program, we worked toward a model of assessment grounded in the activities faculty members already were carrying out in their classes. We talked in terms of "faculty development" instead of "assessment," believing that a good assessment project would, in fact, contribute to better teaching. Since many women's studies faculty members used journals, peer review, and papers as assignments in their classes, the first faculty development workshop examined how such assignments already embedded in courses could become a rich source of systematic feedback about what students learn. Pat Hutchings, from the FIPSE Project National Assessment Team, led the workshop session on portfolio assessment. As a result of the workshop, five faculty members undertook projects in their women's studies classes during 1990–91.

For our second faculty development workshops the following year, we invited another member of the National Assessment Team, Jill Mattuck Tarule, one of the authors of *Women's Ways of Knowing*. She focused our attention on students as knowers. Combining the insights and methodologies learned in the two faculty development workshops with a preliminary analysis of the student responses to the questionnaires, we began to formulate an assessment design for our campus. Ultimately we investigated three areas: personal transformation, pedagogy, and difference. Undergirding our assessment plan were three principal questions:

☐ What kinds of personal transformations occur in students who take women's studies courses?

☐ Do students think women's studies courses are taught differently than other courses and, if so, how?

☐ Do students in women's studies gain a new understanding about the connections among gender, race, class, and sexual preference?

In the process of working with outside assessment experts, we realized that we had a number of data sources about our students that we had never used fully. For example, our student evaluation forms, used in all women studies courses, provide a wealth of information about women's studies students, including demographic information as well as responses to courses and teaching. We envisioned using this data to provide a demographic profile of our students over the last ten years. The course evaluation form in use from 1983–1992 also asked extensive questions about classroom atmosphere. We hoped to analyze that data quantitatively, separating out responses of relevant subgroups of students, such as women studies majors from nonmajors. Unfortunately, time constraints prevented us from carrying out this part of the assessment project.

We were able, however, to compile limited demographic information about our students. In the ten-year period from 1981 to 1990, thirty students graduated with degrees in women's studies. Of these, six (or 20 percent) were African American. We also looked at those students who had taken three or more women's studies classes over the last five years.[5] Of these additional eighty-nine students, 13 percent were African American, with another 3 percent Hispanic. In a university where only 5 percent of the entering freshman class in 1985 were African American, the disproportionately higher percentage of minority students in women's studies is striking.

We also mailed an open-ended questionnaire to all of the women's studies majors who had graduated as well as to current majors and minors. The original questionnaire was based upon one that Wellesley College's Women's Studies Program developed.[6] Fifty-four questionnaires were mailed out to women who had graduated between 1981 and 1990 and to current majors and minors. Eighteen responses were returned. Although small in number, the responses offer notable interpretations of the experience of the Women's Studies Program from a core group of students over the first decade of the program's existence.

STUDENT LEARNING IN WOMEN'S STUDIES

Looking at the experiences of graduates gives two kinds of information not easily available in other ways. First, it is a way of evaluating the program, as opposed to individual classes. Second, it is one way to begin to assess education in women's studies over a longer time frame than a single semester. In the responses—from people who chose both to major in women's studies and to answer our questionnaire—students describe women's studies as unique. Yet it is hard to isolate what it is that makes it unique. Nonetheless, the sense of connected learning and personal transformation surfaces repeatedly in these women's accounts, as do references to women's studies pedagogy and course content.

PERSONAL TRANSFORMATION

Through the UMC women's studies experience, women students discovered self-empowerment and became more critical about how they think and evaluate the world. This critical mindfulness accompanied the women in many aspects of their lives. They developed new goals for learning and redefined what is intellectual as well as what is political. Most wrote about coming to understand the social construction of society. All students—from their very diverse backgrounds—wrote that they felt validated and transformed. Women's studies seems to have been particularly important for women who had a minority status—women of color and lesbians, for example. The women report that they became angry but also that they learned to articulate their anger. They came to see themselves as knowers, and they came to value the support of other women.

The change that accompanied this self-empowerment ranges from women reporting that they would no longer tolerate racist and sexist jokes to a reevaluation of the definition of self, knowledge, and politics. A typical comment was the following: "I watch TV, read magazines, look at advertisements, and assess movies differently than I did before taking women's studies courses. I am more aware of messages about women. I am certainly more critical than I used to be."

For some majors, recognition and acceptance of their lesbianism was a very large part of the validation and self-discovery found in women's studies. The women's studies environment often was the only place on campus where lesbians felt safe. Accompanying this sense of safety came empowerment as a woman and as a lesbian. One woman wrote, "I connected to my woman-self, black-self, and lesbian-self from taking women's studies courses." Those who spoke of their lesbianism told how the women's studies experience taught them to question the "givens" and to trust their own perceptions of the lives they had chosen for themselves. "One teacher showed me there was some place to go—that you could be smart, older, a dyke, and have a place in the world."

Two-thirds of the majors felt a great amount of anger as they became aware of systemic oppressions. Some learned to articulate this newly acquired anger and use it productively. One student explained how her anger gave her what she called "double vision." This "double vision" provided her with a multiplicity of ideas as opposed to one single patriarchal definition. For other students, their anger made them feel an urgency about changing the world. Still others were shocked to confront the kind of resistance to equality they encountered as they attended their other classes, interacted with friends and family, and saw society through new eyes. All reported that they were more likely to notice sexism in courses, texts, and in popular culture, but they also reported they were better able to verbalize their disapproval and anger.

In addition to discovering how to transform anger into insights and action, women students spoke of new goals for learning. The following was a typical comment: "Most positively, I learned to think and appreciate education for learning's sake." Learning became more than students wanting to receive good grades. Some students reported with satisfaction that they carried these changed expectations into their other classes. Some, however, expressed frustration as their changed selves encountered the status quo in other disciplines.

One-fourth of the students reported discovering a new sense of community with other women. One wrote: "I have put much more energy into the women in my life...." Another said, "I value my time more with my female friends." Maintaining friendships with women who share a feminist perspective was important to almost every major. "I now don't believe I am the only one fighting these battles," said one student, echoing another who said that women's studies gave her a sense of not being alone.

Women's studies courses radicalized what students perceived as intellectual beliefs and radicalized how they defined what is political to them. Their definitions of politics changed. Prior to taking women's studies, one woman described herself as young and fairly apolitical. Through women's studies she came to a different definition: "All is political, i.e., a reflection of social power relationships, open to political analysis, and changeable by political/collective action."

Another stated, "I stopped being a Democrat because that is what my folks were. I learned the difference between voting a ticket because people had a party affiliation and voting for ideas you cared for deeply." Another proclaimed, "Everything I do as a woman in a patriarchal world challenges the dominant culture. This kind of life is political. The courage to speak out in political ways comes and goes; however, the notion to deeply question… would not exist if it had not been for my women's studies courses."

The students also attributed changes in their conceptualizations of feminism to women's studies courses. They learned that feminism includes many different kinds of feminisms. When addressing these diverse feminisms, students reported that the wide variety of views were liberating to them. The kind of expansion of views reported by the following woman was common:

> I guess before I encountered women's studies I thought "feminism" was a small movement for "women's rights." Once I went through the door into women's studies, I realized "feminism" is shorthand for a transformative, broad, varied upheaval of female thought, activity, and power across the planet. Quite a change.

Another reported, "I have realized that feminism means a concern not only with issues relevant to white, middle-class, hetero-women but also with issues of race, class, nationality, physical condition, and sexual preference."

These students perceived that women's studies transformed their lives. They attributed the transformation to differences in how the courses were taught and what the course content was. Graduates' responses to both of these demonstrate the extent to which women's studies is indeed a risk-taking endeavor that generates questions rather than proclamations.

PEDAGOGY

We asked students if they felt that women's studies classes were taught in an alternative pedagogical style and, if so, to describe one course as an example. For many students, sitting in a circle symbolized the difference. One of the first graduates of the program said that most of her women's studies courses offered an alternative teaching style:

> For instance, in a "Women and Science Fiction" class-first off we would sit in a circle (vs. the teacher at the front and students behind) we read science fiction by women authors and discussed it not only for

"literary" value but the questions it raised (or failed to raise) about our lives. At the end of the class we were asked to come up with essay questions for our own exam—an exercise that honored our ability to spark thoughtful inquiry.

Another summarized the differences by saying, "The basic sense of sitting in a circle and including individual women's personal experiences as part of any theoretical discussions [typified] my women's studies experience."

The higher level the course, the more students felt comfortable sitting in these circles sharing their personal experiences. In the seminar atmosphere, students felt more at ease learning through exchanging experiences with classmates. Each student said that the involvement of personal experience in classroom discussion was a part of their women's studies encounter. "There is always a place for those who feel at ease to discuss their experience. The instructors used journals, personal writings, and diaries to facilitate the process. That's the difference women's studies makes." For this student and for half of the respondents, sharing their personal experiences was comfortable, and their women's studies classes were the only places on campus where they felt able to do so.

A few, however, felt discomfort sharing their experiences. One student said that any situation ruled by academia cannot always be safe for students. Although another woman explained she generally profited from sharing experiences, she also said she sometimes felt pressured to share when she did not want to. Self-disclosure also was referred to in some of the responses as "show-and-tell" sessions, perhaps implicitly referring both to pressures to perform and risks of public disclosure. One student offered the following reflections:

People started telling stories and trusting that it was the right kind of atmosphere to do this. I thought it was good to finally hear people talking about their experiences and sharing their ideas about them, but I believe that some of the topics that were assigned were treated too flippantly by the students...because it was obvious that most students took it very seriously and what they revealed was very intimate and private, but the way people reacted was more like gawking than understanding.

Discussion, rather than lectures, was the main vehicle for learning in women's studies classes. Sometimes the topics were particularly conflictual. One graduate said, "Students got into it about correct classroom participation versus the freedom to say what you wanted and how you wanted." One student remembered times when no one in the room knew how to stop one student from silencing another. Although the instructors were reported as trying to prevent this kind of behavior, they were not always able to do so.

Even though the discussions sometimes appeared to be intense debates, one woman explained:

> ...it didn't really feel conflictual, but more like we were trying to figure out the truth together. I think that trying to figure out the connections among gender, race, and class was difficult in all my women's studies courses.

The presence of conflict in the classroom generated a wide spectrum of responses from students. One woman wrote, "It sometimes seemed to be the pretense that there were no conflicts when they clearly were [there]." By contrast, another was distressed by the lack of debate in the classroom: "In order to get to the center of what is going on we need to learn to feel that conflict is okay when communicating with one another."

When asked explicitly if the instructor encouraged different points of view, every respondent answered "yes." According to students, instructors themselves often brought up different points of view, which encouraged students to model the professor's behavior. Over half said that different political and theoretical points of view within feminism were introduced, which proved beneficial in subsequent classes. Beginning with the introductory course, "Feminism: The Basic Questions," students reported that they were introduced to traditional thought as well as to liberal, socialist, radical, cultural, global, and womanist theories within feminism. One student remarked, "I think women's studies was an *excellent* introduction to the broad spectrum of thought because it taught me to look for the underlying assumptions of writers on various issues, and I learned how one's conclusions on issues or social problems are shaped by the vehicles used to arrive at them. This has been invaluable." Another said that women's studies provided a place for her political perspectives whereas political science, her major, did not.

Women's studies professors also encouraged an exploration of different points of view in part through the great diversity of the assigned readings. There was, according to students, such a spectrum of experiences, values, and perspectives that students gained a new appreciation of the difference in each women's individual experience. One said, "We heard voices from other

A surprising finding was that the students
felt that race was an easier topic to address
than class

---

students and read books that were non-patriarchal that helped encourage us
to think about issues from other points of view." Many of the students even
responded in the questionnaire with quotations from a women's studies text
that had changed their perspective on difference, such as Paule Marshall's
Praisesong for the Widow, Alice Walker's *The Color Purple*, or Audre Lorde's
Sister/Outsider.

Respondents reported that women's studies teachers honored difference
as long as a student's comment did not degrade other people. While tolerance for difference was high in the women's studies classroom, at the same
time students claimed that instructors pointed out weaknesses in opposing
points of view. One student said, "If one argued for pinko commie liberalism,
it was as valid as conservatism if the *arguments* were valid." Another described what she labeled as a radical approach: "One instructor definitely
wanted to hear from everyone. She genuinely found all of her students interesting, rather than getting something out of imparting secret knowledge to
the masses." That same student also thought it was radical at UMC to construct a course in which women were the subjects of the course, not merely
tacked onto the class, as if women's exclusion from textbooks were the only
sexism. If the instructor chose to teach from what students defined as a radical feminist perspective, she also was said to introduce more notions of difference into the classroom. According to a student taking "Women, Race, and
Class," breaking down difference begins with the kind of individual story-
telling that typically takes place in women's studies courses. At such a junc-
ture, a distinctive women's studies pedagogy overlaps with its distinctive
content.

EXPLORING DIFFERENCE: RACE, CLASS, AND SEXUAL PREFERENCE

For the past decade, feminist theorizing has been informed by an emphasis
on difference. Our program has sought to move the connections among gender, race, class and sexual preference to the center of the curriculum. When
asked about their learning in this area, not surprisingly, all the students wrote
about the course "Women, Race, and Class." One student remembers it as
very distinctive:

> *The first few weeks were used to introduce students to the "basics" of
> a women's studies course...such as patriarchy, sexism, racism, class-
> ism, homophobia, physicalism, ageism, and feminism. The class met*

twice a week. The first meeting was a lecture by one of the two in-
structors. I enjoyed the balance between the instructors. One was a
woman of color and the other was a white woman. The second was a
meeting of five or six students and a former student of the course (the
group facilitator)...this is where we discussed the course material.

Another said, "The experience in 'Women, Race, and Class' was more intense because the [small discussion] groups met every week. We answered
questions about our reading material and confronted one another on our
feeling of race and class."

There were varied responses when students were asked if race, class, and
sexual preference were talked about in their women's studies courses. All but
one student said that race was addressed more than any other subject. One
student said, "We spoke about it almost every day in class." Others reported
that race was in all women's studies course material. "We read many different
perspectives from Afro-American, Hispanic, North American, lower-class
women, upper-class women, etc." Another confided, " 'Women, Race, and
Class' was the greatest attempt by any instructor(s) to pull theory into experience. Those two women [co-teachers] will be in my heart forever."

Many courses include race, class, and sexual preference as they fit into the
discipline being taught. "Racism was addressed more in some classes than others. This did not necessarily reflect some bias on the teacher's part. For instance, race was not a topic in 'French Women Writers' but was the central
topic in 'Black Women: Catalysts for Change'." One student said, "In
'Chinese Women's History,' race was the main topic. We focused on trying to
learn from their perspective rather than our own. Race was a minor issue, but
an issue in other classes."

It is possible that part of what the students sense is a difference between
talking about race and talking about racism. In this area, we also find some
criticism of what students refer to as "liberal instructors" who are not "really
dealing with issues of race." In the way that many of the students used the
phrase, "really dealing with an issue" means connecting it to one's own experience as oppressed and oppressor. By this standard, an instructor who incorporated descriptions of experiences of people of different races might still be
accused of "not dealing with race." The issues of how learning occurs are
thus intertwined with the issues of what is learned.

A surprising finding was that the students felt that race was an easier
topic to address than class. This is not to say that race was easy, but race is

clearly defined in American culture (perhaps too clearly, given that race often is conceptualized in terms of two opposing groups—blacks and whites), whereas class is conceptually muddled. One student wrote the following reflections:

> *Everyone could handle race rather than the question of class. Black, white, or otherwise, not too many people wanted to question the reasons why they were at the university. For all, the university is a ladder upward or at least a barrier away from what is perceived to be a part of what is the lower class. My realization of this grew after reading* Praisesong for the Widow *written by Paule Marshall. The main character was a black woman who had lost part of her being as she involved herself in what Tracy Chapman calls "black upward mobility."*

The students reported that many of their courses examined various issues involving the impact of class on women's lives. Some instructors addressed the subject by listing class in their syllabi and the impact of "labor" and "women and work." Other courses addressed classism and how it intersects with other oppressions. Despite such efforts, students reported that class was not addressed as frequently as race. One woman summed up her remarks by saying, "class got short shrift. One classmate of mine with a very blue-collar background thought it was because at college, it's too scary to question the class structure because everyone's striving to move upward. It would threaten our reasons for being there, particularly for black women."

Just as a gap was reported in the coverage of race and class, students believed that while sexual preference was included it was discussed even less than class issues. Most students remembered the extent to which it was discussed and what happened in the classroom as a result:

> *'85 it was scary and cutting-edge: touched on in larger classes, sometimes to the disgust of some students, a larger issue in smaller classes where students trusted each other more. Sexual identity and desire, I remember, were difficult to theorize about then. Some effort [was made] in French Feminisms class—but [it was] bewildering.*

Students reported that lack of attention to sexual preference was sometimes a result of the instructor's reluctance and sometimes to the students' inability to accept the diversity of sexual preferences that existed among the women in the classroom. Several students noted that often, in history and English classes, "sexual preference was tacked on like most women's studies courses are tacked on to mainstream courses."

The women's studies students who responded to our questionnaire wanted the program to provide an arena in which students of all colors and cultural backgrounds could understand issues that were not raised or discussed in depth in non-women's studies courses. It also was important to them that women's studies provide an appreciation of each level of a woman's life, culture, and tradition. Several mentioned that women's studies should provide a place of "safety" for students who do not feel accepted in other departments at the university. As we think about the students' remarks, it is critical to remember that all of these women are, in fact, *double majors*. By majoring in women's studies they do not avoid whatever is offered/required by other departments. Despite the fact that one of our program goals is "to support students as ambassadors of feminism," in reading student responses one is struck by how difficult that task is and the degree to which they find the university to be a hostile place.

CONCLUSIONS

Engagement in this project reflects and enhances an ongoing concern with pedagogy in our program. The interviews and development workshops with faculty members demonstrate this commitment in many ways. The responses of the majors show the fruits of efforts to promote collaborative learning in women's studies. Yet these varied pieces of the assessment project also raise some issues for the program.

It is clear there is no single way of teaching a women's studies class and that different students respond differently to various classroom situations. It also seems clear that, in the words of one participant in our faculty workshop, "We do not learn about justice in the same way that we learn about the capitals of the states." Students and faculty members in the program need to continue to experiment with how to create optimal learning environments.

Yet the data also show some important differences in the experiences of the graduates of the program and the faculty members who teach in the program. One way to frame it is in terms of a contrast between interdisciplinary women's studies and multidisciplinary women's studies. The data from the majors and graduates reveal that the program for them consists of the interdisciplinary core courses. The data from faculty members reveal a model that is closer to that of a multidisciplinary women studies program. Faculty goal

statements suggest they are most concerned about doing feminist work in
their own disciplines.

In the student questionnaires, by contrast, the majors and graduates
overwhelmingly defined women's studies as the three interdisciplinary core
courses. They described these courses as "feminist" and "radical." They also
associated a distinctive pedagogy—more discussion and more collaborative
learning—where they learned that they had voices and felt validated.
According to students, the core courses integrated life experience with theory and made the intersection of race, class, gender, and sexual preference a
central concern.

Instructors in the cross-listed courses (which go through an extensive
course approval process and are taught from a "feminist perspective") are as
likely to be concerned about "feminist theory" as they are about "feminism."
The teachers' goal statements include a more central emphasis on teaching/
learning discipline-based knowledge. Many of these faculty members are doing women's studies within their disciplines.

The faculty members teaching cross-listed courses see themselves as
modifying their teaching styles to incorporate feminist pedagogy. A number
of them said that teaching women's studies classes allows them to take risks,
but these cross-listed courses are not identified by the majors as having the
distinctive style that characterizes the core courses. This in part may be because some of the key factors are out of a teacher's control. Instructors in
cross-listed courses complain of the difficulty teaching when the women's
studies students may not be grounded in the discipline, and the students from
the discipline are not grounded in feminism.[7] They also may have little control over the size of the class; the majors noted that the cross-listed classes
were often too large for the instructor to do much more than lecture. It is
possible, of course, that what we are seeing are the positive evaluations of
particular instructors who happened to teach the core courses.

We were not very successful in executing the quantitative part of our
project, and we want to note here the sheer difficulty we had getting information from "already existing sources." Quantitative data, such as the kind
the registrar has about all students, would have been very useful, but we
found it virtually inaccessible. Assessment projects like this one, which try to
make use of data already on hand, might do well to think about their own
record keeping. We found, for example, that we did not have addresses for
our graduates or even class lists for the students who took cross-listed courses
under the departmental numbers. There was a real sense that we did not

know who our students were.

We also underestimated the difficulty of analyzing data that could be obtained. Both qualitative and quantitative data is time-consuming to analyze. When we tried to hire a graduate assistant, we found that the ones with methodological skills already had research associateships (or did not know anything about women's studies), and the ones with a background in women studies had no methodologies training.

After the second faculty development workshop, the women's studies faculty members decided that they would like to begin a regularly scheduled faculty discussion group about pedagogy. One issue we plan to work on is greater inclusion of issues of race, class, and sexual preference across our curriculum. Another issue is the place of disclosure—for faculty members as well as students—in the women's studies classroom.

The differences that the majors describe between the core courses and the cross-listed courses also raise a question about the perceptions of those who are not majors. We know now that we have a significant body of students who take three or more courses but do not end up majoring in women's studies. We do not know—although we could find out—whether they are any more likely to take cross-listed courses rather than core courses. Neither do we know why they are not becoming majors.

The women's studies committee also was struck by the way students find validation through a "mirroring process" in women's studies. It underscores for us the importance of having diversity reflected in the program faculty. In the fall of 1991 we created a development fund for a speaker's series that will bring in one speaker each semester to bring us research and creative works in lesbian studies, named in honor of our former director who showed many students that they, too, "could find a place in the world."

1. We are grateful for the help of all the participants in the Women's Studies Program who took time out in one way or another to participate in the work of this project. Special thanks go to a number of them: In the first year of the project Carole Myscofski, as co-chair of the Women's Studies Committee, participated in planning the project and wrote the first statement of program goals. Elaine Lawless helped plan the faculty development workshop in September of 1990, and Kay Foley tracked down information about the institutional context. Barbara Bank contributed data from the Missouri University Panel Study. Magdalena Garcia-Pinto and Jan Colbert read and commented on a draft of the report. We also appreciate the support of Jeff Chinn, Vice Provost for Instruction, who helped fund the Women's Studies Assessment Workshop and paid the salary of Graduate Assistant Michelle Gadbois. Michelle's analysis of the student questionnaire was the heart of this project.

2. For example, proposals for core courses were turned back by university curriculum committees for "more documentation" to prove that such courses were intellectually respectable.

3. See Jane Mansbridge, *Beyond Adversary Democracy* (Chicago: University of Chicago Press, 1983), for an analysis of consensus decision making.

4. In the spring of 1990, as acting director I interviewed all the faculty members teaching in the program during that first year of the project. The collective passion for teaching is what kept me involved in this project.

5. For cross-listed courses we included students as having taken a women's studies course whether they registered through women's studies or through the faculty member's home department. This list was difficult to construct because women's studies only gets information on those students who register under the women's studies course number.

6. We did this with the intention of comparing responses with Wellesley, but Wellesley's project report analyzed a different questionnaire distributed to current students rather than to majors and graduates.

7. A few faculty members and students expressed dissatisfaction with a lack of cumulative structures throughout women's studies courses. The mix of students in all the courses meant that some time was always spent retracing basic grounding knowledge. One faculty member suggested that this problem might occur with regard to pedagogy as well as course content. In her classroom assessment project using journals in an upper-level course, she found that students who had not used them before engaged the task with enthusiasm, but others who had frequently kept journals in their women's studies courses responded in more perfunctory ways.

∎

CONCLUSION

*What I found in women's studies was a body of knowledge that taught
me to question not only the answers, but also the questions as well.*
ABBY MARKOWITZ, WOMEN'S STUDIES GRADUATE,
TOWSON STATE UNIVERSITY

When Abby Markowitz addressed a plenary of nearly two thousand participants at the 1989 national conference of the National Women's Studies
Association, those of us who had taught women's studies felt especially
proud: proud of her, proud of the tough questions she posed to women's studies, and proud of women's studies for the part it played in her education.
With four other women, Abby was on a riveting student plenary panel,
"Learning Feminisms: Journeys in our Lives." Just a week earlier, FIPSE had
recommended funding "The Courage to Question." Between then and now,
we have amassed an important body of new information about student learning. Just as Abby discovered, we have generated almost as many new questions as answers.

Our research, on the one hand, substantiates many ways in which wom-
en's studies has succeeded in engaging students intellectually and personally
in its subject matter and in their education. On the other hand, the research
also has pointed to numerous areas for further investigation. While we expect our findings to stimulate self-reviews within women's studies, we also
hope this report initiates ongoing conversations with colleagues across disciplinary boundaries. To meet the complex challenges on campuses, in our
classes, and in our communities, we in higher education must be practical vi-
sionaries collectively committed to the well-being of students. We hope *The
Courage to Question* moves us closer to creating that kind of educational
community.

In 1991, the American Association for Higher Education called its national conference "Difficult Dialogues" in recognition that the task before us
as educators is not an easy one. The emphasis was on the noun, *dialogues.*
Even if difficult, the imperative was to establish a conversation—a mutual
exchange of ideas—as we think through together what many say must be a

fundamental restructuring of the academy. In the American Council on
Education's *Educating the Majority: Women Challenge Tradition in Higher
Education*, authors Carol S. Pearson, Donna L. Shavlik, and Judy G.
Touchton argue that the age of simple adjustments to accommodate women
is over. What we need now, they propose, is "a major paradigm shift that allows for greater equity and quality in education, a shift that...also will enable
us to more effectively address the compelling societal issues of our time, from
competitiveness to hunger and illiteracy to world peace."[1]

Robert Hughes' lead article, "The Fraying of America," in the February
3, 1992, issue of *Time* magazine describes with some concern the paradigm
shifts he has observed. The shifts are occurring as our country undergoes
what some have called an identity crisis, spurred by a reappraisal of our national cultural heritage and a rapidly changing global citizenry. "The future
of American [self-interests]," he argues, "will rest with people who can think
and act with informed grace across ethnic, cultural, linguistic lines." He ends
with this warning: "In the world that is coming, if you can't navigate differences, you've had it."

Despite the small but highly visible minority of people who have piled
sandbags around what they perceive as their embattled beachhead threatened by the tides of change, the vast majority of students, faculty members,
and administrators in academia are seeking ways to move forward together in
response to national calls for dialogue, paradigm shifts, and institutional
transformations. At the center of the call for all three is women's studies.
Women's studies—established against the grain of the academy in the 1970s;
insisting that excluding half of humanity distorts truth and makes the claim
of excellence a mockery; and calling for a student-centered, socially conscious, and experientially informed pedagogy—is eager to be part of a national discussion about how to move forward with "informed grace."

The Courage to Question documents for the first time in a systematic way
some of what women's studies has discovered about student learning. From
our three-year research project on seven campuses, we have assessed not only
what is working in women's studies but, even more importantly, what *about*
women's studies seems, according to undergraduate students, to make that
experience so educationally distinctive—and according to alumnae/i, its impact a lifelong one.

☐ Is there understanding we now have about how students learn that might
apply in non-women's studies classes?

☐ Are there structures of knowledge, organizational strategies in courses, or pedagogical approaches in the classroom that others can adapt?

☐ As students in women's studies confront highly charged emotional issues and experience the intellectual and personal implications of diversity, are we gaining any insights about how to maneuver through that rough terrain?

We offer our report with the hope it will initiate a dialogue among colleagues so that together we may work to improve the educational experiences for all our students.

PERSONALIZED LEARNING

Whether the subject under discussion was the knowledge base, feminist pedagogy, diversity, critical thinking, or empowerment, students repeatedly linked the intellectual and experiential when they attempted to articulate what was distinctive about their learning in women's studies classes. A neat and clean separation of abstract ideas from personal experience, which is so characteristic of most traditional courses was missing in students' comments. Instead they wove back and forth, consistently connecting intellectual insights with their immediate lives. Such an integration surfaces, for example, in the CUNY–Hunter College student who explained, "women's studies...[goes] beyond this classroom, this paper...and just...touches everything else I'm involved in...because it gives me a way to see, a way to think, a way to question everything, so it's applicable everywhere for me." Rather than distancing themselves from the subject matter, students in women's studies typically became deeply engaged both intellectually and personally.

The University of Colorado has given a name to this phenomenon: *personalized learning*. They distinguish it from active learning, although active learning is a component. Personalized learning allows the student to use the intellectual to explain the personal—a "compelling connection." What emerged repeatedly in student comments was the powerful intellectual dimension of this personalized knowing. Though critics may portray women's studies as academically "soft," students tell a very different story. According to them, women's studies is more difficult precisely *because* its subject matter challenges not simply what you think but how you feel about what you think and what you do because of what you know. Students note how intellectually rigorous women's studies is and how much it challenges them to rethink all they have learned elsewhere. "I felt like I had a completely new brain," said a student at Old Dominion University.

Professors who fail to understand the role of personalized learning in women's studies fail when they attempt to teach a women's studies course.

Although hostile to women's studies and untrained in the discipline, a former colleague chose to teach a women and history course, saying it was going to be a "real" history course with none of "that sensitivity stuff." Two consequences occurred. Students abandoned the course in droves, and my colleague never understood why. The student response was baffling because the professor underestimated profoundly the intellectual power of feminist scholarship when it is coupled with students' personal responses.

By contrast, a feminist teacher weaves the experiential and personal, sometimes validating and sometimes contradicting—but always informing—students' intellectual response to material. As the chapter about the University of Colorado emphasizes, such connections are all the more compelling because of the larger context in which women's history and culture have been devalued and women's status subordinated. If a teacher does not understand such gender dynamics, he or she misreads students' responses. To include the personal as part of a course's subject matter is to move to the surface what previously has been dismissed or forced underground.

It comes as no surprise, then, that three schools—the University of Colorado, Wellesley, and Old Dominion—found the course content of women's studies, and not the pedagogy, the most decisive factor in determining the kind of student engagement that occurred. When each campus compared women's studies and non-women's studies classes with similar teaching styles and class sizes, what emerged as distinctive was course content: the intellectual grounding of women's studies that illuminated students' understanding of gender and, therefore, their own lives. In her essay, "Taking Women Studies Seriously," Adrienne Rich reiterates: "Without such knowledge women live and have lived without context, vulnerable to the projections of male fantasy, male prescriptions...estranged from our own experiences because our education has not reflected it or echoed it. I would suggest that not biology, but ignorance of our selves, has been the key to our powerlessness."[2]

When content links with lives, the transformation in students is palpable and lasting. Wellesley's report expands on our understanding of this process, investigating the differences in the ways students contrast women's studies and non-women's studies classes. In the latter, students spoke with much greater attention about the instrumentality of the knowledge they gained or its practical ability that helped them "do" certain things better. In women's studies courses, students spoke more about how to "be" in the world; their comments reflected more profound kinds of changes that altered their identities, their values, and their views.

Colorado's study found a similar contrast between student learning in women's studies and in non-women's studies courses. Students in non-women's studies classes described what they learned rather than how they learned to think differently about their own lives. In women's studies classes, students expressed ethical concerns paralleling and infusing their intellectual engagement. Students also said women's studies challenged them to judge, connect, and explore implications. Old Dominion echoed the same findings in examining connected learning. Through an emphasis on empathy, students more easily moved toward connecting with other people's experiences and blending that with new intellectual paradigms; students moved, in other words, toward something very akin to Colorado's personalized learning. Personalized learning promises to open gateways toward that world of informed grace we will need so desperately in our highly contested, pluralistic world. It also fosters what AAC's national report on the major, *The Challenge of Connecting Learning*, urges: "It is …important for [students] to care about subject matter and see its implications for the ways they live their lives. At issue is whether students can connect a field's subject matter and approaches with a variety of pursuits important to them, and whether their curiosity and concerns beyond the classroom can be deepened or shaped by the insights the field brings forth."[3]

The assessment studies in *The Courage to Question* reinforce the findings of an earlier unpublished AAC student questionnaire, which provided national data for AAC's three-year investigation of "Liberal Learning and the Arts and Sciences Major." As described in AAC's *Reports From the Fields*, when the results of the eleven different majors were compiled, women's studies was rated the highest of the majors in ten of fourteen questions and was in the top four in the remaining four categories. Students gave women's studies the highest marks for connecting different kinds of knowledge (89.2 percent); connecting course materials and assignments to personally significant questions (86.5 percent); identifying and exploring problems in the field in relation to significant questions of society (97.3 percent); exploring values and ethics important to the major (81.1 percent); and helping students develop an overview of the field's intellectual history (83.1 percent). Personalized learning explains why women's studies percentages were ranked so much higher than any other majors surveyed.

VOICE AND EMPOWERMENT

Perhaps no single refrain was heard more clearly in the reports than that women's studies courses gave students a voice and empowered them. As bell hooks explains: "The feminist focus on coming to voice—on moving from

Women's studies, our report suggests, contributed
to the students' gradual progression from voice to
self-empowerment to social engagement

silence into speech [is] a revolutionary gesture [and] for women within oppressed groups...coming to voice is an act of resistance. Speaking becomes both
a way to engage in active self-transformation and a rite of passage where one
moves from being object to being subject. Only as subjects can we speak. As ob-
jects, we remain voiceless—our beings defined and interpreted by others."[4]

At more elite colleges, where there were on the whole more privileged
students, students commented more on self-empowerment than voice. While
finding their voice and having it heard was ranked by ODU students, for example, as the most important aspect of their learning, self-empowerment was
most important to Oberlin students. At some campuses, like Wellesley, giving voice to women already is part of a wider overall mission permeating the
larger institutional culture. Such a context constantly reinforces the learning
goals in the women's studies program and permits the program to focus more
on how to translate that voice into action.

A participatory classroom environment with an emphasis on discussion
and a course structured with student-led assignments contribute to developing voice. The greatest contributor, however, is the content of women's studies. "I had not been exposed even to the idea that gender was a subject in
and of itself," wrote one Lewis and Clark graduate, while another said,
"Many of the ideas moved me, making me aware of unfulfilled desires in my
personal life and in the world as whole." Note again: movement occurs both
within an individual student and between that student and society.

Since the voices of many students, especially women, have not always
been welcomed, either in a class or in the dominant male culture as a whole,
simply using their voice at all is sometimes a great victory. Some ODU students expressed a reluctance to challenge that voice even when they dis-
agreed with it. Students feared driving a classmate back into silence, which
suggests the complicated dynamics in the women's studies classroom. Although in women's studies achieving voice is highly valued, so is critiquing
ideas. For students who have come to believe, through studying feminist theory, that ideas are inseparable from the person, there is a tension, then, between encouraging students to speak and expecting them to question what is
spoken. Creating a classroom that can negotiate this tangle demands a new
kind of communication for feminist teachers and for students alike.

In AAC/NWSA's *Liberal Learning and the Women's Studies Major*, a national task force described the developmental process as a student moves
from "moments of recognition," at which students understand in a personally
illuminating way how gender systems work in a given instance, to "moments

of empowerment," at which students learn how to negotiate with unequal power. The time between these two developmental stages typically is fraught with much emotion—disillusionment, anger, bewilderment, confusion, and distrust—before it becomes exhilaration, clarity, trust, courage, and agency. Such a journey is a delicate, uneven one, but it leads to students saying again and again how women's studies gave voice to their unuttered and unutterable ideas.

Unlike the consumer-driven Madison Avenue presentation of empowerment that presents the modern woman using her new power to purchase fancy cars, expensive suits, and exotic vacations, women's studies students talk of empowerment in relation to social responsibility. Students felt they gained their voices and then felt compelled, by virtue of the content of women's studies, to use that voice to improve the world for everyone. "What's important," said an Oberlin student, "is having a language not only to represent myself but to talk about political change." Such a notion is rooted in the belief that the self is not an autonomous unit detached from the rest of humanity but emerges in a context of relationships that are paradoxically an inescapable part of self-definition.

Women's studies programs at both Wellesley and Oberlin defined empowerment not as singular self-aggrandizement but as the power to be socially responsible to a larger community. Wellesley found that in distinguishing how women's studies courses specifically affected students' lives, respondents chose words like "commitment," "obligation," and "responsibility," which were absent from their descriptions of non-women's studies courses. As Wellesley's report clarifies, students in non-women's studies courses usually felt their courses would help them function better in the world; in women's studies courses, they felt their courses would help them change the world.

Oberlin also found evidence in undergraduates of both a sense of empowerment and actual empowerment in the form of social action. They extended their investigation to graduates, curious about whether students participated in citizen action after graduation. In every response, alumnae described specific ways they used their options in a democracy to affect the shape of their society. Women's studies, our report suggests, contributed to students' gradual progression from voice to self-empowerment to social engagement.

DEVELOPING CRITICAL PERSPECTIVES

AAC's *The Challenge of Connecting Learning* argues the necessity of fostering critical perspective in students. AAC calls for "an ethos of communication and contestation that ensures that no proposal stands without alternatives or arrogates to itself the claim of possessing the sole truth." A repetitive chorus in the assessment studies underscored how women's studies formulated an analysis that gave students the courage and skills to question norms, generalizations, and unexamined assumptions. For most students, a course in women's studies is the first time they understand that knowledge as well as gender is socially constructed: Available information is not a given; it is as carefully orchestrated as definitions of masculine and feminine. Confronted by their discovery of how much knowledge has been withheld from them, students learn how to seek out the ideological underpinnings of knowledge that is presented as complete, universal, and neutral. From that beginning, their capacities to bring critical perspectives to all kinds of knowledge are nurtured.

While critics claim that women's studies narrows students' intellectual options and turns teaching into mere propagandizing, the results of the project present a radically different portrait. The University of Missouri team has coined the phrase "critical mindfulness" to describe the increased attentiveness students reveal as they more readily articulate their judgments about society. Oberlin refers to "tolerant, critical habits of mind." For many students, developing a critical perspective is no mere academic exercise: it is a means of survival. In a gendered world of unequal power, students link critical thinking to empowerment. As Hunter College's team argues persuasively, many students whose opinions and lives are commonly disregarded often silently surrender their authority. Women's studies teaches them to reclaim it. As a Missouri student so eloquently states, "Women's studies provided me with the strength to never settle for anything that deprives me of all I am worth." The content of women's studies shows detailed pictures where once was a blank canvas, a critical framework where once was feigned neutrality, and a language to describe what had been nameless and invisible.

FEMINIST TEACHING AND CLASSROOM DYNAMICS

Feminist pedagogy has been central to the development of women's studies. Each of the seven women's studies programs included pedagogy among their initial learning goals, and pedagogy has surfaced as a particular area of focus on several campuses as a follow-up to the assessment study. Not surprisingly to those familiar with the field, the data from all seven assessment studies indicates that women's studies classes usually were more participatory, inclusive, and experiential than non-women's studies courses and typically involved more collaborative projects, class discussion, and practical applications of what students were learning.

For students at the University of Missouri, sitting in a circle summed up what was distinctive about a women's studies class. More than a simple arrangement of chairs, the circle suggests something about the learning environment most women's studies classes cultivate: exchange, collaboration, and community. Given the intense emotions some women's studies classes generate, the circle—whether actual or metaphorical—suggests the importance of containing and supporting the difficult work of integrating feeling and thinking. Since so many women's studies classes also explore the potentially divisive fact of difference and diversity, the circle is a reminder of where we connect in our common humanity whatever our differences.

At times pedagogy, like many other issues, could not be neatly confined within its boundary. As the University of Missouri's report put it, frequently "distinctive pedagogy overlaps with distinctive content." In Missouri's case, the overlap occurred when notions of difference were introduced in the classroom. For these women's studies majors, good teaching meant classes that interspliced such diversity into the normal class routine. Oberlin similarly relied on collaborative learning as a means of exposing students in a very immediate, practical way to opportunities for mediating difference.

In a few cases at Wellesley, student culture sometimes stifled student voices. While the data from Wellesley demonstrates that nearly three-quarters of the students in women's studies felt their voices were heard and divergent views were welcome, more students in women's studies courses than in non-women's studies courses reported that they felt silenced. The students—not the professor—silenced them, they explained. Both ODU and Missouri also have data that distinguishes between the behavior of the professor and that of the students. In all three cases, professors are rated exceptionally high for encouraging divergent points of view and for stimulating debate and discussion. Professors also are recognized for their efforts to protect students from being silenced by other students, although they apparently are not always successful. At Wellesley, it was not clear if students' opinions would not have been heard had they actually expressed them; some students *felt* their opinions would have been unfavorably received by some of the students in the class. The Wellesley report suggests that women's studies faculty members need to be especially attentive to such dynamics and that interventionist strategies may be necessary.

Student interaction also must be considered in the larger context of a classroom that typically engages students far more than the traditional class. The Wellesley data, for example, show 80 percent of students in a women's studies course say students debate or argue; only 55 percent say they do in non-women's studies classes. As both Wellesley's and Missouri's teams point out, student responses also vary regarding conflict in a classroom. In the same class, students may say there is too much debate and not enough. More research can help us understand more about debate, especially debate that generates powerful feelings.

These data also highlight the seemingly contradictory dynamics of comfort and risk in a women's studies class. Women's studies programs want to create a safe place that will nurture students' intellectual and personal growth. As Missouri, Colorado, and Oberlin demonstrate well, however, they also want simultaneously to challenge students to question and be self-critical, which often creates discomfort.

Far more revealing about Wellesley's data were startling statistics on how much women's studies students continue their discussion outside the classroom in contrast to the amount of out-of-class discussion generated in non-women's studies classes. Nearly 84 percent of women's studies students versus 63 percent of non-women's studies students reported talking "constantly" or "usually" about the content of their courses. Since the overwhelming part of an undergraduate student's life is spent outside the classroom rather than inside it, the Wellesley report has broad implications for women's studies and for education as a whole.

Such intellectual and personal engagement in the subject matter explains why women's studies students talk with such enthusiasm about the learning that occurs in women's studies courses. Content matters to students. It generates deeply felt emotions; its issues are unresolved and often highly contested in the world; and students are challenged, if not to resolve the issues, to find a way to live with the contradictions and uncertainties.

The student pattern also suggests that women's studies enhances students' voices even "off stage." In its discussion of personalized learning, the University of Colorado team reminds us that "students may be actively involved without verbalizing their responses in class." Wellesley's data certainly suggest that as well. If some students feel hesitant to speak in the public forum of a classroom, at Wellesley they appear to feel no such hesitation in private conversation. This may be part of a developmental process that permits hesitant students to be stimulated to voice opinions privately before gaining courage to voice them publicly. The out-of-class conversations also suggest that women's studies is helping to define a campus culture in which a community of people arrive at new understandings through dialogue.

Conversations at Wellesley occur with friends as well as family, and women's studies students discuss their courses more with male friends than non-women's studies students do. Similarly, the ODU team discovered that women's studies courses enhanced close student friendships more than non-women's studies classes did. ODU's data reveal that male students showed a greater increase in number of female friends than female students did. Contrary to male-bashing myths, our data suggest that women's studies triggers new kinds of communication and relationships between male and female students.

The Gender Studies Symposium at Lewis and Clark—which in 1991 ran five days and included more than one hundred students, twenty-five faculty members, and sixteen community participants—is an innovative model for fostering a student culture outside the classroom. With more than fifty events and eighty students presenting papers, the symposium has become for students a major intellectual event of the year; it stimulates an enormous amount of debate and discussion and puts disparate people in conversation with one another. Whether or not students had taken a gender studies course, they singled out the symposium as a major learning experience; for many, it was the catalyst for further social activism or student-initiated cocurricular activities. Appropriately, the section on feminist teaching and classroom dynamics in this report ends by focusing on what happens outside the classroom walls. *The Courage to Question* challenges us to consider how to generate even more cocurricular forums that give students opportunities to discuss, sort out, argue, clarify, and expand their learning.

DIFFERENCE AND DIVERSITY

Because the intellectual roots of feminist scholarship initially were formulated in its difference from the dominant male culture, women's studies created early in its history a language to talk about difference. Having devoted more than a decade to articulating distinctions among women—especially in terms of race, class, sexual orientation, ethnicity, age, and ability—women's studies has developed an increasingly subtle and comprehensive language and theory about diversity. Women's studies, therefore, promises to offer some useful insights about participating fruitfully in those "difficult dialogues" that are absolutely essential in our pluralistic society and world.

United States immigration patterns in the last decade have altered ethnic and racial demographics more than at any other period since the turn of the century.[5] New research has caused many to question the wisdom of repeating the assimilation pattern once so widely adopted because that pattern stripped new and diverse populations of their native culture and clothed them—often literally—in the garb of the dominant culture of the period. Education was one of the primary mechanisms for executing this assimilation, forcing many cultures underground in an attempt to create a homogenous, seemingly unified America. Many people, including those involved in women's studies, now are looking for ways to retain and even understand anew the heritages that mark each of us. One consequence of such an approach is that we may not have a common language, common culture, and, by extension, common nation.

The challenge to women's studies and others in education is to create a new dynamic in *e pluribus unum*, one that acknowledges differences while simultaneously building connections. Feminist scholarship has taught us to suspect assimilation models that erase our distinct identities. One of the most famous examples of the total absorption of a woman's identity into a man's in the name of civil orderliness is contained in the nineteenth-century legal principle "feme covert": A woman lost all legal standing by having her identity fully merged with her husband's. The concept functioned operationally as, "My husband and I are one, and I am he."[6] Intellectually repudiating the validity of structuring the world in such terms, women's studies argues that we must establish alternative models. The value of exploring a genuinely more pluralistic model emerges repeatedly from our assessment studies. Clearly, it is one of the most significant contributions women's studies can offer in the larger national debate about multiculturalism.

Fundamental to feminist theory is the assumption that as women we have differential and complex relationships among ourselves, carrying with us not only our gender but gender that is defined by our class, race, sexuality, and other markers. Fundamental to feminist pedagogy is recognizing the authority of experience as a source of knowledge. Unlike other courses, then, women's studies becomes—among other things—a collective autobiography of students, both male and female. Differences no longer remain abstract but are embodied in people who talk about those differences and sit next to you in class or work with you on a project.

The program learning goals of all seven participating women's studies programs articulated in a deliberate, self-conscious way the conceptual and personal importance of diversity. The translation of that goal varied according to the specific character of each institution. The imperative to create a multiracial, multiethnic program at Hunter College was driven partially by its diverse student population. On the other hand, first-generation students at the University of Missouri found race easier to discuss than class, while homophobia was a particularly difficult concept to talk about at ODU. But women's students verified everywhere that they came to expect a discussion of difference in women's studies classes.

How successfully those stated expectations were met was uneven, and whether enough was done was debatable among the students. Its integration as a conceptual goal, however, was recognized uniformly by students and verified by the data. Some programs were trying to put difference at the center of their program, and none were satisfied that they had done enough. Women's studies seems to be light years ahead of most other academic disciplines—except ethnic studies—in such efforts. Diversity is incorporated into women's studies courses in terms of both individual identities and people with different histories, cultures, and values. It is incorporated through an analysis of larger systems in which differences become embedded, reinforced, and defined and from which unequal power is allocated and perpetuated. It also is incorporated in the curriculum through readings, discussions, theories, internships, faculty members, and projects. Finally, it is incorporated through cocurricular events.

The two programs that investigated the knowledge base in women's studies, Lewis and Clark and ODU, each listed "diversity" as a fundamental learning goal and found students grappling with its implications very early in the curriculum. In querying how effectively their program promotes multiculturalism, Hunter College recorded an impressive variety of ways its women's studies program had sought to recenter itself. Among students, both white women and women of color attested to the impact the program had on their thinking, participation, and relations with other people. Many Wellesley students also credited women's studies with opening them up to understanding difference and giving them the courage to explore it rather than retreating to polite and uninformed silence. Deliberately encouraging differences to surface in a classroom and become part of the subject matter of a course can be as unsettling as it is illuminating. Emotions often are heightened, confrontations sometimes ensue, and the terrain is unfamiliar to many. Hunter College's report warns that the "high psychic costs of trying to understand others may seem too high" to some, which makes it imperative to do

By listening to the students themselves, we
correct myths and misinformation about what
kind of education takes place in women's
studies courses

---

all that is possible to lower the cost and increase the benefits of such exchanges. With a pedagogy that aims to create a climate of trust and affirmation and a theory that provides an analytical framework for understanding
differences, women's studies offers some promising models as well as evidence
of success in engaging students in multicultural learning.

THE WOMEN'S STUDIES KNOWLEDGE BASE

Because women have been excluded from the canon for centuries and because
women's studies is such a fluid and expansive field, programs are wary of creating a canon. Not surprisingly, then, when Lewis and Clark and ODU investigated the knowledge base in women's studies, each deliberately focused not
on particular pieces of information but on overarching concepts or, as the
Lewis and Clark team calls them, "knowledge plots." These two institutions
avoided the "Trivial Pursuit/Vital Facts for Your Daily Calendar" approach.
They were less attentive, therefore, to measuring whether students knew
when Mary Wollstonecraft lived than they were to learning whether students understood Wollstonecraft's critique of eighteenth-century female socialization. They cared more that students understood how white men ma-
nipulated white womanhood to justify lynching black men than whether
students could name the newspaper of Ida B. Wells Barnett. As *Liberal
Learning and the Women's Studies Major* argues, "More than simply a body of
information, however, women's studies is also an approach, a critical framework through which to view all knowledge."[7]

The Lewis and Clark report argues convincingly that despite an impression that infinite variety prevents gender studies from having curricular coherence, it does in fact have a shape. That institution's enumeration
of gender studies' eight knowledge plots and six learning skills should
prove useful to women's studies programs that are reevaluating their curriculum. ODU's report lists five key concepts, all of which overlap either
with Lewis and Clark's knowledge plots or learning skills. Such overlays
suggest that there are major conceptual links among diverse women's studies programs.

Students also seem to grasp more readily concepts that their own experiences validate. At Lewis and Clark, for instance, students understood diversity and the politics of sex/gender as well as cultural images of sex/gender and
the nature/nurture debate. At ODU, they understood most readily the social
construction of both gender and knowledge and grasped something of the
systematic interlocking oppressions of women and women's varied relation to

patriarchy. These results give credence to Lewis and Clark's assertion that knowledge plots are developmental. Gender studies students, they argue, first need to be grounded in the ramifications of gender inequalities and the political issues that created gender studies in the first place.

Because gender balancing at Lewis and Clark has been a serious and ongoing undertaking, key ideas such as the politics of sex/gender, diversity, or cultural images of sex/gender have been integrated into an impressive number of non-gender studies courses. Students therefore get some knowledge plots from sources other than gender studies. Women's studies and gender studies professors applaud such developments. Like writing across the curriculum, women's studies encourages the reinforcement of its ideas throughout the curriculum. But such efforts do not lead necessarily to the elimination of gender studies programs any more than writing across the curriculum has led to a national call for the abolition of English departments. What Lewis and Clark has discovered, however, is that certain concepts are more likely to be treated in gender studies classes than elsewhere. These include examination of women's creation of knowledge; communication; the body; and interpersonal relationships. Such discoveries have important implications for women's studies curricular development as a whole. Unfortunately, few campuses can boast as many gender-balanced courses as Lewis and Clark. More commonly, women's studies and gender studies programs carry the burden of conveying concepts rarely found elsewhere in the curriculum.

IMPLICATIONS OF THE ASSESSMENT STUDY

Our national assessment report represents three years of research on student learning in women's studies and gathers in one place data that help explain why women's studies students are so engaged intellectually and personally. We expect *The Courage to Question*, therefore, to be a catalyst for continuing to study how students learn. Each of our seven case studies reveals specific directions campuses will pursue as a result of discoveries made in the course of this research. By listening to the students themselves, we correct myths and misinformation about what kind of education takes place in women's studies courses. We want to emphasize how uninformative it can be to construct a universal student stripped of particularity and context. Arguing that we need "sensitivity to the multiple realities that coexist within our institutions" and crediting women's studies and ethnic studies for expanding our understanding of those realities, Ralph Wolff reminds us:

> *To capture these multiple realities, to learn anything meaningful about*
> *a campus, we have to start with the assumption that a single answer to*
> *anything just isn't adequate. We need multiple answers, and beyond*
> *that, multiple methods.*[8]

Our national report avoids single answers and single methods. We need not
only multiple answers but multiple questions as well.

In an academic hierarchy that too often ignores the value of research on
student learning and teaching, external and internal support for research
such as this—with its curricular, programmatic, and institutional implications—is extremely important. The Fund for the Improvement of Postsecondary Education in the Department of Education once again has been
the leader in supporting projects that promote educational reform and help
us assess what improves student learning. In the course of doing this research, we also saw clearly how much more effective learning is when the
larger institutional culture reinforces specific values. The broader institutional commitment to women's voice and empowerment at Wellesley College,
for example, enhanced the promotion of voice and empowerment in their
women's studies program. Similarly, the wider institutional promotion of tolerance, inclusiveness, and social responsibility at Oberlin College reinforces
similar educational goals embedded in its women's studies program, as did
the collegewide commitment to multiculturalism at Hunter College. While
educational reform may begin in an individual classroom, it need not end
there. Although a vibrant program like women's studies might offer a dynamic model of engaged learning, that is not enough. Students deserve more.
Institutions can set a tone, establish a standard, articulate values, and become powerful allies with faculty members in creating a context of inquiry
and affirmation.

The Courage to Question presents clear evidence that women's studies has
much to contribute to the national discussion of excellence, engagement,
and social responsibility. It also can help us remember how easy it is to ex-
clude and silence others instead of arranging a way for everyone to sit together and talk. By drawing from the insights gleaned in such a richly diverse dialogue, we can learn how to achieve the kind of education Mary Caroline
Richards describes:

Education…is the process of waking up to life…it requires…certain capacities for taking the world into our consciousness…That's why knowledge and consciousness are two quite different things. Knowledge is like a product we consume and store. All we need are good closets….When knowledge is transformed into consciousness and into will, ah then…knowledge…turns into capacity for life-serving human deeds.[9]

Richards is describing the kind of critical consciousness and energized engagement women's studies students display again and again as learners. She also is reflecting the kind of commitment to the world beyond our own boundaries that is stirred by women's studies—a commitment at the heart of liberal education. As an Oberlin student said, fully confident she could make a difference, women's studies helped her see where "she has work to do in this world." We hope *The Courage to Question* helps educators know where and how to begin "with informed grace."

1. Carol S. Pearson, Judith G. Touchton, and Donna L. Shavlik, *Educating the Majority: Women Challenge Tradition in Higher Education* (New York: ACE/Macmillan Series on Higher Education, 1989), 2.

2. Adrienne Rich, *On Lies, Secrets, and Silences* (New York: W. W. Norton and Company, 1979), 240.

3. *The Challenge of Connected Learning* (Washington, D.C.: Association of American Colleges, 1991), 16.

4. bell hooks, *Talking Back* (Boston: South End Press, 1989), 12.

5. For a fuller discussion of education's historical and contemporary role, see the special issue of *Education and Urban Society*, "Cultural Diversity and American Education: Visions of the Future," Vol. 22, No. 4 (August 1990), edited by Thomas G. Carroll and Jean J. Schensul.

6. Duncan Crow, *The Victorian Woman* (London: George Allen & Unwin Ltd., 1971), 147.

7. *Liberal Learning and the Women's Studies Major* (College Park, Md.: National Women's Studies Association, 1991), 8.

8. Ralph A. Wolff, "Assessment and Accreditation: A Shotgun Marriage?" in *Assessment 1990: Accreditation and Renewal* (Washington, D.C.: American Association for Higher Education, 1990), 13–14.

9. Mary Caroline Richards, *Centering in Pottery, Poetry, and the Person* (Middletown, Ct.: Wesleyan University Press, 1989), 15–16.

AAC and NWSA
present three publications from
"The Courage to Question"

The Courage to Question: Women's Studies and Student Learning features the results from seven women's studies programs participating in the three-year, women's studies assessment project "The Courage to Question," which was funded by the U.S. Department of Education's Fund for the Improvement of Postsecondary Education (FIPSE). The case studies include new research on multicultural learning, critical thinking, student voice, classroom dynamics, and integrating knowledge into life choices.

The Executive Summary to *The Courage to Question* provides an overview of the project. It is designed to make the core research findings from *The Courage to Question: Women's Studies and Student Learning* easily accessible to a wide audience. The Executive Summary is published and distributed by the Association of American Colleges.

Students at the Center: Feminist Assessment is designed to facilitate program assessment. This volume sets feminist principles of assessment in the context of the larger assessment movement. It features innovative assessment designs, a variety of methodological approaches, and practical advice about how to do a productive assessment project on a campus. *Students at the Center* contains questionnaires, scoring sheets, and interview questions; a directory of consultants; and a selected bibliography on assessment.

All three publications generated by "The Courage to Question" are available from AAC. For ordering information, contact the Publications Desk, AAC, 1818 R Street, NW; Washington, D.C. 20009; 202/387-3760. Bulk rates are available.

The Courage to Question and *Students at the Center* are available from NWSA. For further information, contact NWSA; University of Maryland–College Park; College Park, Md. 20742-1325; 301/493-4571.

THE NATIONAL WOMEN'S STUDIES ASSOCIATION is a national member-
ship organization committed to promoting women's studies and feminist education. It develops, promotes, and sustains women's studies programs through
curricular resources, publications, and conferences. By valuing the diversity of
cultures within our communities and the larger world, NWSA seeks to enhance
understanding of all women's lives through education and by integrating
knowledge and action. The association's network of women's centers provide
services to students and the larger community, while its network of pre-K–12
teachers promotes feminist education.

THE ASSOCIATION OF AMERICAN COLLEGES is the only institutional mem-
bership higher education association whose primary mission is improving undergraduate liberal education. AAC's goals—promoting lifelong humane and
liberal learning, strengthening institutions of higher education as settings for
liberal learning, and extending the benefits of liberal learning to all—are carried out through research, projects, publications, and workshops.

AAC's programs reflect its commitment to enhancing public understanding of
liberal learning, strengthening general and specialized curricula, improving
teaching and learning, increasing opportunities for access and achievement, and
developing institutional and academic leadership. Founded in 1915, AAC com-
prises more than 640 public and private colleges and universities.